The Company We Keep

◆IEEE

IEEE Φ computer society

Φ CSPress

Press Operating Committee

Chair

James W. Cortada
IBM Institute for Business Value

Board Members

Mark J. Christensen, Independent Consultant

Richard E. (Dick) Fairley, Founder and Principal Associate, Software Engineering Management Associates (SEMA)

Cecilia Metra, Associate Professor of Electronics, University of Bologna

Linda Shafer, former Director, Software Quality Institute, The University of Texas at Austin

Evan Butterfield, Director of Products and Services

Kate Guillemette, Product Development Editor, CS Press

The Company We Keep

by David Alan Grier

IEEE computer society

CS Press

Page design by Monette Velasco.

ISBN-10: 0-7695-4764-8
ISBN-13: 978-0-7695-4764-0
Computer Society Order Number: P4764

Dedication

For Doug, whose stories enriched these pages

And for Chery, who enriched his life

And of course, for Jean,

who has enriched mine.

Contents

Preface
Of Our Time

The present is no more than a temporary condition.

All My Sons (1947)
Arthur Miller

I found the advice deeply unsettling.

"You should make predictions in your book," an editor advised me. "People love to buy books that tell them what the future will be like."

Of course, I am not uninterested in the future. It arrives at our doorstep with a certainty that defies novel metaphors and presents us with ideas that demand our attention, whether we like them or not. Still, the future is not the same thing as our predictions about the future. Predictions tend to fall into two categories:

the uninteresting and the untrue. Both kinds of predictions tell us more about our present lives than the future.

Uninteresting predictions try to assess the current state of society or technology or politics or economy and then gently extrapolate into the future using our common understanding of social operations. While such predictions have at least a passing chance of being accurate, they actually tell us more about how we think society presently works than how we believe the future will be. As one might expect, uninteresting predictions tend to carry the dry odor of consensus and organization. They are found in the regular reports of the Federal Reserve Bank, the findings of blue ribbon panels, the International Technology Roadmap, most of the presentations at business roundtables, and almost any conclusion by a group of guys about sports.

The untrue predictions are mere reflections of our aspirations and nothing else. We pluck some ideal from consciousness and determine that we will achieve this ideal at some distant date in a manner uncertain. That ideal might be a nobler, healthier, and more just society that cares for the poor and unfortunate while standing as an example to the world. It might also be a galaxy in which we fight against the forces of injustice using nothing more than our sense of honor, the power of our mind, and one or two incredibly powerful forms of technology. This last prediction also tends to include many members of the both sexes who are wearing incredibly revealing but highly flattering clothes.

The genre of untrue predictions includes the cartoon series *The Jetsons*, the entire *Star Wars* oeuvre, the reports on tax rates and social policy from Washington think tanks, and the classic 1888 novel of Edward Bellamy (1850–1898), *Looking Backward*. Bellamy tried to give his predictions an air of authority by portraying them as a memoir written 112 years in the future, which would have been December 2000. However, his opening sentence places his ideas firmly in the center of untrue predictions. "Living as we do in the closing year of the twentieth century, enjoying the blessings of a social order at once so simple and logical that it seems but the triumph of common sense."

The triumph of common sense is, in reality, the ultimate purpose of prediction. Though we often think of common sense as simple, practical wisdom, it is actually common sensibility, the basic operational principles that are accepted in common by society. When anyone makes a prediction, they are affirming that society is run by rules, that these rules can be understood, and that they tend towards an expected end.

In common with predictions, both interesting and uninteresting, these essays accept the notion that society is shaped by rules and forces. It further accepts that these rules and forces are providing motion to our lives, as if we were being pushed across the ocean by some combination of currents and eddies. Some of these forces have distant origins. Some have developed from the nature of recent events. Both have shaped the channel in which we travel. Both need to be understood. We understand them best not by projecting our lives into the future but by pulling ourselves out of the flow and trying to assess our current position and activities.

Of course, we cannot entirely detach ourselves from our current time and place. To do so would require us to pull away from our daily tasks, the activities that we understand best, and attempt to get a vague apprehension of the context in which we work. We are offered little reward for such endeavor. Those "individuals most effectually promote the general progress," noted the pioneering geologist Charles Lyell (1797–1875), "who concentrate their thoughts on a limited portion of the field of inquiry." Yet somehow, we suspect that we find meaning in our contributions only if we can place our work in a larger context and believe that it will have some kind of place in the future.

Rather than settle for a prediction, untrue or uninteresting, these essays attempt to establish a dialogue with the future. Admittedly, the direct response will be limited, as the future takes its time to reply to any message. Nonetheless, it will respond, age by age, and offer its judgment based upon its own future state and wisdom. Rather than offer predictions to the future, which can be dismissed as trivially shortsighted, these essays attempt to capture a portrait of the technological character and explain, to that distant future, the nature of our community, the values that we hold, and the forces that have shaped our lives. Such writings may not provide the emotional thrill that editors seek, but they will, perhaps, offer a few hints of what the future will think of us.

Chapter I:
The Land Around Us

This morning at nine I was in the laboratory
watching a demonstration of the new electronic brain.
And on the way here, I stopped
and bought a few things at Bonwit's

Desk Set (1955)
William Marchant

Introduction
The Forces of Localization

I live in an activist neighborhood, one of those areas where individuals take up causes in the name of doing good for the broader community. Ellie, who lives three blocks to the west, organized a neighborhood patrol to walk the streets at night and discourage crime. Yousef has been worrying about a different kind of crime, a gang of rogue possums that took up residence in one of the alleys and demonstrated remarkable skill at ransacking garbage cans. When they lived on our block, Jeff and Marissa raised funds to build a playground in a nearby park.

Tim and Caroline, long before they were divorced, spent untold hours trying to encourage homeowners to celebrate Halloween by decorating their homes in purple and orange lights.

All these actions, and many more, were taken with the honest and sincere intent of making our neighborhood a better place to live. Although all the projects achieved their goal, each had unintended consequences. After it cleared the area of lurking burglars, Ellie's patrol proved to be a highly successful social event in which the participants eventually spent more time in a local diner than on the streets. Yousef expelled the possums only to find that a family of raccoons had taken their place. It appears that, in addition to being good at overturning garbage cans, raccoons are also skilled at picking kitchen locks and emptying refrigerators.

Jeff and Marissa easily collected the money they needed to build the playground, as our neighborhood was in the midst of a baby boomlet, but they found their plans thwarted when they discovered that the playground's proposed location was a historic site. For a weekend in 1812, the park had been a camp for invading British Forces. Jeff and Marissa needed the equivalent of an act of Congress to put a children's slide and jungle gym on the land.

The Halloween festival, of course, went far beyond Tim and Caroline's intent. It is now a major civic attraction and draws visitors from other parts of the city. Families bring their children to parade down the streets. Cars of teenagers come to party. Costumed revelers dance and preen. The local residents look at the mobs of people and wonder what has happened to the event that was once a little neighborhood party. Last fall, Yousef watched the crowds and shook his head. "This is what happens," he said, "from thinking locally but acting globally."

OF COURSE, THE COMPUTER INDUSTRY can provide multiple examples of unintended consequences, of actions that were designed to meet a local need but ultimately influenced a much larger community. In 1943, John Mauchly (1907–1980) described an electronic machine to compute ballistics tables, and the offspring of his idea created a multitrillion-dollar industry. The US Department of Defense asked for a communications network that would make it easy to share computing resources, and this idea evolved into the Internet with all of its services. A Cornell graduate student created a small program that could travel across that network, and suddenly no computer in the world was safe.

In my neighborhood, the intersection of the local and global is seen in the proliferation of broadband routers. On most nights, I can sit in my bedroom and find a dozen routers with enough strength to reach my house. They range from the Jeff's Boccinet (named for his dog) to Xshdict381, which is either the router's serial number or the name of a Klingon starship—I'm not sure which. A few are secured, but most are open to the world.

Lauren, a resident of a nearby basement apartment, once told me how she would borrow bandwidth from the house next door in much the same way that neighbors used to borrow cups of sugar from each other. She would scan the offerings and pick one that appealed to her. She was quite pleased that she knew how to connect to other networks, but she was also concerned about the effect of her action. "Won't the signals get mixed up?" she asked.

Little did Lauren know that all the bits pass through a common router that is bolted to a pole in the alley in same way that the sewage from our homes passes through a common pipe under the street. If you follow the swirls of data as they mass move through the city, you will find a path to the office of an energetic young man named Eli. Eli works at the Society for the Promotion of Goodness, one of those think tanks that mark the local landscape. He wants to eliminate all of our individual networks and replace them with a single regional or community network that will somehow change the world.

"They are the real thing," Eli explained when I expressed skepticism of his idea. "Community networks will give people access to hundreds of new services and new activities." To Eli, a community network is a civic organization, usually run by a government or a cooperative, that delivers high-speed wireless data connections for free or for very low prices. As he sees it, we need these networks to address five serious problems facing our world. First, they will allow city governments to make their services more efficient. "We can't have digital services until everyone is on line," he noted.

Second, they will bridge the digital divide that separates rich and poor householders by reaching those homeowners who can't afford broadband access. "Not everyone can pay for a high-speed cable connection," he added.

Third, these networks will improve education. "Think what will happen when every high school teacher can be available 24 hours a day," he pontificated, forgetting that many high school teachers might resist being available to their students every moment of the day and that students might not want to see their teachers outside of a structured setting.

Finally, Eli claimed that these networks will spur local economic development and promote regional tourism.

"Tourism?" I queried, not certain that I had heard him correctly.

"Yes, tourism," he replied. "Every neighborhood can promote its cultural and historic sites."

I started pondering how we might present our neighborhood. "Hoover Park: the neighborhood of community activists, five raccoons, and a historically significant jungle gym" didn't seem like the kind of slogan that would attract many visitors during the non-Halloween season.

ELI'S VISION OF COMMUNITY NETWORKS was grounded in a certain perception of time and place that was at odds with the American landscape. He was enamored with the story of Wireless Leiden, a narrative that embraced the social activism of 1968, identified with the social poverty that was prevalent in 1938, and somehow seemed relevant to the first decades of the 21st century.

Wireless Leiden was a project that supplied broadband services to 400,000 people in the western Netherlands. It had been started by three idealistic friends who wanted to build a citywide wireless network for internal and Internet communication with free access for everybody. The three friends had solicited donations from business and used common commercial hardware. They had ultimately recruited 70 volunteers to help with the project and still had only a minimal budget even though the network covered 150 square miles.

In the United States, Eli had hoped that a community network in Philadelphia would illustrate the value of his ideas and start the process of building such networks across the country. However, the project demonstrated the challenge of large-scale community projects. The problems began after the city had demonstrated a small community network in a park near city hall. Although the network was described as a way of providing universal Internet access, it was criticized as principally benefiting the rich and well-educated. "We're just taking money from hardworking families and giving it to people who can afford [smart phones] and laptops," wrote one critic. "If you don't have a job where you can use your laptop to do your work in a city park, it's not going to benefit you."

Each step of the way, the landscape that surrounded the Philadelphia project became more and more complicated. First the city faced a legal ban that prevented it from building or operating a community network. Next, they concluded that they could not allow volunteers to help deploy the infrastructure of the network. Furthermore, they recognized that residents would not allow the city to finance the project with civic bonds. Finally, they acknowledged that the technical plan for the network, a plan that had provided a simple network for Leiden, would not work in the more densely populated City of Brotherly Love.

The party that marked the completion of the first segment of the Philadelphia community network was Belshazzar's feast, though no hand descended through the Internet to write its message on the wall. The participants ate, drank, and were merry.

The criticisms ultimately led to a new legal restriction that prevented the city from operating a civic network. Looking for other ways to support broadband services, the project moved towards more conventional solutions that involved private corporations working with the city. "This is a major step toward achieving our vision of The Entire City Connected," boasted the project manager. Yet, in less than a month, he learned that he had been weighed in the balance and found wanting. The project was out of money. Tellingly, even the manufacturers of telecommunications equipment refused to advance the group any funds.

Eli continued as an advocate for community networks for another 8 or 9 months before he also ran out of funds, or perhaps the world ran out of interest. He packed his office, which consisted of little more than a laptop and a collection of photographs that showed him in the presence of the great and famous, and moved on to a new job. I saw his name a few weeks ago. He was advocating some new cause, one that had no real connection to computing technology. Deficit reduction, perhaps. Or the commercialization of outer space. He had taken his lesson and moved to a new problem.

The landscape of computing technology can appear deceptively simple, at least in the short run. It is filled with projects, all of them good, all of them worthy of our funds, all of them the vision of at least one sincere individual. That simplicity allows us to put our own neighborhood at the center of the world and erases the remnants of our work once a project is done. It is a global power, but it acts most vividly on the local stage.

01
Welcome to the Family

They don't listen to you. You know this for certain. It's hard enough to teach technical points, but it's impossible to impart even a little professional discipline to your charges. You try to cram some basic procedures into their heads, but with a sneeze these ideas escape through their nostrils and make a dash for the window like flies trying to escape on a spring day. At best, you hope that they buzz against the glass and remind the group of the points you were trying to instill: The assignment is due on Friday. The task is more confusing than you think. You had better start working on it before Thursday night.

But arrive five minutes early to class and you'll see something different. You'll discover that they watch you and learn lessons that you wish they didn't. They know the inflection of your speech. The slump of your posture. The quirks of your teaching style. Sharper than a serpent's tooth is the mockery of a student who does not know that you are present.

Yet mockery may be the only way they learn, the only way they can understand the weight of the responsibility they may someday assume. How else can you impart what it's like to make a decision, to risk your company, to take a chance with an untried technology?

FOR SEVERAL YEARS MY UNIVERSITY'S pre-professional student group entirely ignored the problems of career education because they really didn't know how to approach it, and also because they were having trouble simply recruiting enough members. Someone had advised them to "make computing fun," so they accepted that desperate goal. They tried to attract attention by offering prizes of expensive gaming computers for technological accomplishments or bribing business students into joining by arranging dinners of unhealthy foods and illicit drinks. None of this did much good.

For a time, Jorge took charge of the group and tried to recruit a few individuals with the long outmoded use of posters. He had some graphic design talent and knew how to borrow images in ways that elevated the activities of a small student group to a bigger stage. He created a poster based on a well-known sporting event, another using a photo from an inexplicably popular television show, and a third that compared the organization to a threatening yet tone-deaf hip-hop group.

Each of these brought a little notoriety to Jorge and may actually have increased membership a bit. None captured the nature of a professional organization except for the last one, which appeared shortly before he graduated. I caught my first glimpse of it in a back hallway as I hurried to some meeting of great importance.

The poster was a stark black and white study of the organization's officers. The men wore dark suits with skinny ties. The women wore the kind of dress that marks territory and exerts unlimited power over men. The figures were arranged in a semicircle that recalled a movie that has served as a touchstone for discussions of business and professional life. In the middle of the group sat Jorge, looking for all the world like the Godfather, Vito Corleone. Below him were the words "Welcome to the Family."

IN THAT ONE IMAGE, JORGE showed that he knew, consciously or unconsciously, something about professional life. It involved discipline, loyalty, competition, common knowledge. It wasn't something that could be turned into a desirable activity with some fun and games. Becoming a professional means joining the family, with all the rights, responsibilities, and requirements that come with membership.

Computer science has generally felt more comfortable with families of technology than with families of professionals. We have families of languages, processors, and operating systems. We generally conceive of technical families as a set of entities—either hardware or software—that implement a common set of functions. The value of such an approach seems fairly obvious. "By investing once in the common components, significant cost reductions can be achieved over a family of products," observed a pair of researchers. "This strategy has been used successfully in many industries, including computer hardware."

As with people of common ancestry, sets of technology are surprisingly hard to nudge into a common family. "Development of a product family adds complexity to the requirements capture and analysis process," reported two experts on software families. "There are many stakeholders, and each one has a different view and interests." Their individual perspectives make it difficult to understand the needs of others. "They feel that considering requirements in the context of the whole family is confusing, and the sheer volume of requirements and their variations is overwhelming."

The earliest examples of technology families within computer science show no effort to build consensus or to incorporate the needs of a large group. These families produced children that had common eyes and common noses but had substantial differences in behavior. Such a family grew from the first seeds of computation, which were scattered by the mathematician John von Neumann (1903–1957) in 1946 and 1947.

von Neumann was an indulgent parent, less interested in building a stable family than in distributing computing technology to the largest possible audience. Rather than make orderly plans for his offspring, reported his coauthor

Herman Goldstine (1913–2004), he took his design "to the United States Patent Office and to the Library of Congress with an affidavit from the authors asking that the material be placed in the public domain."

von Neumann's effort may have been chaotic but was remarkably fruitful. The family of machines became known as the "IAS family" after the Institute for Advanced Study where von Neumann worked. Depending on how you count the offspring, it may have as many as three dozen siblings and cousins including the Cyclone at Iowa State University, the Maniac at Los Alamos, the Muasino in Tokyo, the Weizac in Israel, and the IBM 701.

As a family, this group is quite diverse. Some of the machines fall pretty far from the tree. The Russian cousin, the BESM, deviates substantially from von Neumann's design. The Maniac may not really a full member of the group, if you believe its creators. It may be more of an irascible uncle who was swapped with another baby in the maternity ward. The Maniac was built "in parallel with the development of the IAS computer," complained its designer Nicholas Metropolis. "This error [that it is part of the IAS family] has been repeated so frequently in the literature that it may now be impervious to correction."

After these machines were knocked out of their tower at the Institute of Advanced Study, they quickly moved in different directions. None had any incentive to adhere to a common standard. They did not share a common instruction set and could not run a common program. By the late 1950s, any unity in the original IAS family was long gone. The only remnant of the group was the label "von Neumann architecture," which was applied, rightly or wrongly, to all electronic computers except for those that defiantly claimed to be "non-von Neumann."

Once the common family has been scattered abroad, it cannot be easily reassembled into a single social group. However, von Neumann's children had hardly established their place in the world before researchers began to appreciate the advantages of a single family of technology. By the early 1960s, IBM was investing most of its development funds to create a range of machines that operated in a single way. If one computer in the family could execute a certain program, then all could execute that program. This family would be called the System/360.

The original designers suspected that the task of creating a unified family would not be easy. "We knew that it was easy to build upward compatibility," recalled one committee member. However, downward compatibility came with a price. It would impose a "compatibility constraint on the design of each of the seven machines we envisioned in the family," acknowledged Fred Brooks (1931–), one of the lead designers. That constraint would impose additional costs on the smaller machines—costs they could ill afford "when we knew the competition would be after each with a rifle."

In determining how it would meet the challenge of competition, the System/360 design team spent some time thinking about how it would discipline the engineering staff. "The following ground rules should be imposed on the groups working on the logical structure of the proposed processors," it reported. "It is a fact that the designs of different groups will yield non-consistent products unless the programs are constantly controlled and measured against a standard."

THE SYSTEM/360 REQUIRED AN ENGINEERING discipline for the time. Each computer in the family was built by a different team. Each of these teams reported to a senior design group that maintained standards across the group. This committee extended its power beyond the machines it was building. When notified that the System/360 would affect other products within IBM, the coordinating committee responded, "The impact of any new family on current IBM systems will always be a problem regardless of compatibility." Like a misbehaving member of the Corleones, any product that threatened the viability of System/360 would be discretely separated from the corporate family and dispatched with sadness and regret and cold-eyed concern for the health of the organization.

Yet, the technical decisions for the family were hard because they influenced people's lives. They ensured the success of some workers and ended the career of others. Such facts are forgotten in the portraits of computer families. In them, we see a row of processor boxes scrubbed clean and shining for the camera. They radiate triumph rather than hardship, success instead of discipline.

POPULAR CULTURE HAS GIVEN US few good images of business, few stories that allow us to understand the problems faced by people in business. In *Wall Street*, Michael Douglas played to the caricature when he ranted and raved about the benefits of greed. His character lived in a world where there are no moral choices. In that world, success comes to those who desire wealth above all else and have no scruples about their actions. But most of us do have some scruples. We know that unshackled greed will rarely get us what we want. We hesitate to abandon our friends. We sometimes have to take a weak position to protect our interests. We often have to acknowledge that no amount of effort will salvage our current strategy. In such a world, we turn to other stories to express our ideas about business: mechanical aliens coming from another planet to take over our markets, a hapless baseball team trying to capitalize on its investments in a big game, a humble Italian family trying to conduct a little commerce on the streets of New York.

In choosing the Corleone family to serve as his metaphor for professional life, Jorge followed a path that has been trod by many. The language of *The Godfather* has permeated business. We talk of going to the mattresses, leaving a briefcase of money on the table, and making an offer that cannot be refused. Such phrases are so common that many use them without knowing their source. I am suspicious that Jorge did not know the original source of his ideas. For his generation, mobsters are sophisticated characters. They live in suburbs, send their kids to private schools, and have personal therapists. Yet, like the original Corleones, they worry about who is in the family and who is not, who offers respect and who keeps their distance.

Over the years, our professional societies have been concerned about membership in the family. They argued about who could be a computer scientist. Did they need to know hardware? Did they have to understand electricity? "Could they be that newer class of professional," asked the president of an early computing professional society, "who regards himself as a computer engineer or scientist rather than an electrical engineer?"

More recently, we have been more concerned about who was leaving the field. "There are efforts underway to define each of several flavors of computing disciplines," wrote one worried computer science educator. We "can accomplish more," she claimed, "if we avoid some of the effects of fragmentation and bring together all the computing-related disciplines as a large community rather than as a set of disjoint small groups."

The field of computer science is defined not only by technical accomplishments but also by those who take the name of computer scientist. As has happened in the past, and as will likely happen in the future, we are seeing both researchers and practical innovators question the value of identifying themselves with our discipline. Their answers will largely depend on whether they think we have anything to offer them. Unhealthy food and illicit drinks won't alter their opinion. Neither will prizes of expensive gaming machines nor the threat of vengeance for a child wronged.

It may seem odd that a profession, such as computer science, that has been so successful worries about its membership. However, that very success has put the profession of computer science in a precarious place. The fundamental ideas of computation have moved into almost every field of professional endeavor in much the same way that mathematics moved into those fields before it. Lawyer and doctor, financier and accountant. All of them work with computational technology and answer computational questions. None seems much worried about their relationship to computer scientists. Welcome to the community of technology. Welcome to the family.

02
Edward Elgar's Facebook

Like many an academic, I am truly sorry that Edward Elgar (1857–1934) had a well-developed social network.

Only if you have never attended an American graduation, be it a university, high school, or even kindergarten ceremony, would you be unaware of the fact that the final event of the American academic year has made Elgar's "Pomp and Circumstance No. 1" (D major, opus 39) the most ubiquitous piece of formal music on the planet. Beginning in late April and ending in early July, thousands if not millions of students march out of commencement ceremonies clutching a small record of accomplishment to the steady beat of Elgar's march. At those ceremonies, millions, or perhaps only thousands, of educators fidget in their chairs while trying to ignore the oppressively familiar music.

In 1901, when Elgar wrote "Pomp and Circumstance," he did not intend to write a piece of music that would be known to the American academic world as "The Graduation Song." Indeed, to the residents of Elgar's native England, "Pomp and Circumstance" is the patriotic song from the Edwardian age, "The Land of Hope and Glory." However, the fate of this composition was determined not by Elgar but by his social network.

As a prominent British composer, Elgar was part of an elite class that revolved around the aristocracy and royalty. It included a few distinguished artists, the right kind of wealthy industrialist, and those who married into the proper family even though they might be unaccomplished, powerless, and financially forsaken. For Elgar, this class stretched across the Atlantic Ocean and included a few Americans, such as the pianist Samuel Sanford, a pianist who taught at Yale University.

The American universities of the early 20th century were smaller than their modern counterparts and were only starting to move into their decisive social role. The "introduction of business principles into university policy," wrote Elgar's contemporary, the slightly cynical economist Thorstein Veblen (1857–1929), "has had the immediate and ubiquitous effect of greatly heightening the [school's] need for a due and credible publicity." One means of getting such publicity was to bring prominent individuals to graduation. Sanford was able to convince Yale to offer Elgar an honorary degree and then persuade his friend to come to the US to receive the honor.

The ceremony for Elgar was a beautiful affair. It had marching, colorful robes, and invocations by learned scholars. At the climax of the event, just as the assembled masses began to parade out of the hall, the college orchestra began to play the steady chords of "Pomp and Circumstance."

Perhaps Elgar's music is better than the reputation I claim for it, for "Pomp and Circumstance" favorably impressed those in the hall that day. Especially pleased were those who had come from other colleges to witness the ceremony. Two years later, the music appeared as the march at the Princeton graduation. It then moved to the University of Chicago. From there, it went to Columbia, then Vassar and Rutgers. By the 1920s, it had forever overwhelmed any other tune that might be used to accompany an American graduation.

At our graduation ceremony last spring, I was able to ignore "Pomp and Circumstance" for the first part of the event, as I had to shake the hands of all the undergraduate students. However, once the graduate students began to march across the stage and I retired to my chair, the music began to drum in my consciousness. The pace of the event began to slow as the graduate students, being more mature and hence less likely than the younger students to be drunk or hungover, took every opportunity to wave to their family or hug any professor they knew.

I looked for something useful to fill the time. Professor Lessen usually smuggles copies of the daily paper into the ceremony, but she was out of reach at the other end of the stage. Concluding that everyone was watching the students, I quietly took my cell phone from my pocket and began answering e-mail.

I had been working for no more than 10 minutes when a new message flashed on my screen. "What do you think you are doing answering e-mail during the ceremony?" it asked. "Don't you know that there is a graduation here?"

I scrolled to the bottom of the message and saw that it was signed by the members of my spring undergraduate class. I looked up and saw my charges in the back row of the auditorium, waving their caps and clearly gleeful to have caught me in the act of ignoring the ceremony. Like Elgar's social network, they were reminding me that they had some power over events. Even though they were in the back of the room and might not have been entirely sober, they were demonstrating that they could influence my behavior.

In just a handful of years, a tiny moment in human history, we have become a world of social networkers. Social networking tools, as seen in the various Internet sites, are part of our daily work and conversation. In embracing these ideas, we are starting to forget that we did not always view society as a nexus of friends and connections.

WELL INTO THE LAST HALF of the 20th century, we primarily viewed society with ideas and concepts that had been developed nearly 100 years before. We described our interactions in terms of familiar relationships, hierarchies, and lines of authority. Our ability to recognize and analyze social networks matured in parallel with our ability to build and manage large-scale data networks. At best, the social theory was only a step or two ahead of the technology.

In the early 1960s, Derek de Solla Price (1922–1983), a mathematician who studied scientific publication, concluded that the scientific community was not a single entity but a collection of loosely organized groups that he called "invisible colleges." Each of these invisible colleges looked at a common set of problems and used, for the most part, a common set of methods. "Not only do such groups form the natural units of which science is composed, but they are the main channels for the informal as well as the formal part of communications," Price explained. "We must realize soon that the existence of these groups is both natural and good."

From his idea of the invisible college, Price made many recommendations about how science should be managed. He thought that scientists and engineers should travel widely so that they could regularly meet with the other members of their invisible college. He proposed that real universities and research laboratories should have facilities that could be used to host wandering scholars from other institutions. "This is not just good-neighborliness," he wrote. "Such activity is not merely a preliminary to the desired end of producing scientific information."

Price also proposed that computer scientists should start building programs that would support the work of invisible colleges. "It is eminently possible, by citation indexing and other means," he suggested, to give invisible colleges "a custom-built information system to replace their own capriciously functioning system."

Many sociologists have disliked Price's concept of the invisible college. It seemed too rigid, too structured. It looked backward to an older age of formal hierarchies and social pressures to conform to a common ideal that might be embodied by a school in Cambridge, England, or Cambridge, Massachusetts, or even New Haven, Connecticut. It failed to account for the dynamic nature of scientific research. The typical scientific community "was not one which was tightly knit or closed to external influences," wrote one critic. "Outsiders played an important role in influencing the activities of members of the group."

The first theories about large social networks began appearing just as Price was writing about his invisible colleges and researchers in California and Massachusetts were starting to develop the technologies for a new kind of large-scale data network.

"Social links have been greatly facilitated by the drastic advances in communications," wrote one theorist. "Not only is it possible to see and move over great distances, it is possible to conduct intimate and important affairs over those distances: money can be sent by telegraph, jobs can be offered by telephone and so can consolation and advice."

Social network theory, as it started to be developed, was built on a simple foundation of communication. It ignored family relationships, hierarchies, and the division of labor. "Networks are defined as the set of persons who can get in touch with each other," according to one theorist. The connection could be direct or indirect, through fixed channels of communication or through one or more intermediaries.

The fundamental idea was simple, but it immediately posed a problem that would be recognized by anyone who prowled the data networks of the 1970s or 1980s. If connections were made independent of family and organizational ties, how would people meet each other? It was a conundrum that writer Henry David Thoreau had identified more than a century before. "We are in great haste to construct a magnetic telegraph from Maine to Texas; but Maine and Texas, it may be, have nothing important to communicate," he wrote, "as if the main object were to talk fast and not to talk sensibly."

The early theorists not only struggled with understanding how connections would be formed in a social network, they also realized that such connections would come in different forms. Primary. Secondary. Strong. Weak. Continuous. Discontinuous. They recognized that strong links would incur costs: a clear channel of communication and a daily message perhaps. They also grasped, albeit darkly, that weak links might have more value than strong ones. A social network's power might not lie in the few connections that you know well. It might instead reside in the vast multitude who will take your message, no matter how long it has been since they last heard from you.

In the late 1960s, the modern Internet was still 25 years away and the tools of social computing, such as Facebook, another two decades beyond it. The network theorists had only limited ways to observe how communications technology supported a community and even fewer opportunities to gather data that might test their ideas. Thus, their conclusions were highly tentative. Whether network theory "proves useful will depend not only on how viable the hypotheses turn out to be," wrote one sociologist in 1967, "but on its contributions to a more orderly conception of modern industrial societies."

AS A RULE, STUDENTS ARE not the strong links in my social structure. They depart from campus promising eternal loyalty to the old alma mater and enduring friendship to its professors, and then they vanish into the luminiferous ether. They may be forgiven as they are beset by many distractions. They have a place in society to find, debts to pay, and partners to attract. About the only time you can be sure that they will remember you as a dear and close mentor is when they need a letter of recommendation. "Dearest Professor," the e-mail will begin. "I've been wanting to contact you for so long." The text will be long or short as the case requires, but it will always end with the query, "Would you be willing to write a letter on my behalf?" The exceptions are always useful, the weak link that proves the power of social networking.

Shortly after my most recent exposure to "Pomp and Circumstance," I went on a tour of my invisible college, a group of distant colleagues that form my research society. Over the years, I have generally found that such visits are far less valuable than Price hypothesized. These trips generally center on a hurried lunch with a group of individuals who have been drafted for the occasion and have little interest in your scholarship. This gathering is followed by an inspection of the facilities, which lasts longer than the need requires and presents the institution completely out of context. At best, you will get 20 minutes to discuss your research with a sympathetic colleague at the end of the day—a brief human contact that comes with a price that involves 6,000 miles of travel.

Yet these inspection tours seem to have a purpose. No matter how much time we spend in electronic communication with our invisible college, we still need to see our comrades in person, no matter how arduous the journey. However, a recent visit to an outpost of my social network revealed a shift in my connections.

My discussions with scholarly peers was far shorter than I anticipated. We met for lunch. We swapped business cards. We toasted the field, each other, and all of our friends. Then they vanished for some important meeting with the promise that we would meet later in the afternoon to discuss things of great import. I again filled the time by answering e-mail on my cell phone. As I was sorting the messages, I realized that one was from a former student. In our last conversations, whenever that occurred, he was about to move to the city where I was visiting.

"Are you here?" I typed in desperation. "Because if you are, I need to be rescued. Respond as soon as you can."

I pressed send and waited to see if the links of the invisible college would prove to be weaker than the claims of the old alma mater, the physical institutions that still make some claim to order our lives with publicity, credible or not. Perhaps these connections would offer an evening of decent conversation and the promise of a good meal.

03
Spirit of Combination

I was surprised that Sean found my office. My place of work is a bit tricky to navigate, with its twisty corridors, structural pillars in the middle of hallways, lobbies that appear to be dead ends, distracting art on the walls—all of it donated—and not a helpful sign in sight. I used to tell people that my office was next to the giant photograph of Buzz Aldrin's footprint on the moon until I discovered that this piece of information was no more useful than the fact that my building is across the street from the only park in the city named for a 19th-century poet. While both items are true, neither is recognized by visitors to the area.

Yet, just as the forest will never confide to us about the noise made by trees that fall unobserved, so civilization camouflages the value of the truths it holds. You may believe that Walt Whitman was just an obscure writer you had to study in high school, but in the geometry of my neighborhood, the author who wrote that "We shall sail the wild and pathless seas" provides local pedestrians with the shortest distance between any two points.

Whatever time we gained by Sean's premature arrival, we squandered in idle chat. Sean is about to move to China and take a job in Shanghai, a topic that provides many subjects for lengthy discussion. When I asked him how he was preparing for his new assignment, he admitted that he wasn't doing much.

"I've been playing a game," he confessed.

"What kind of game?" I countered. I suspected and perhaps even hoped that Sean would provide me with a little insight into the amusements favored by young adults.

"It's silly," he said. "You start with two random pages in Wikipedia and see how quickly you can navigate from one to the other by using only the links on the page."

His quick explanation was so surprising that I forgot to give my speech on the improper use of the word "random," which is common among the youth of today.

"Really?" I responded. "Is this a global thing? Is there an organization for this game—a webpage?"

"I don't think so," he said. "Just a couple of us get together and play it at night."

At this point, I allowed myself to believe that I had discovered a new social phenomenon, a game that combined the contributions of the masses with a quest for knowledge that often seems absent in modern culture. It was a game in which Walt Whitman might indeed be on the shortest path from Mass Transit to Buzz Aldrin.

I started to sketch how I might bring this to the attention of the un-informed public. A note to my friend at the *Times*—maybe a Twitter campaign. I even had a name for the new sport: "Diderot's Discipline."

"Are you familiar with Denis Diderot?" I asked.

"No," said Sean, who looked as if he was a little sorry that he had raised the issue at all.

"Diderot (1713–1784) was a French philosopher of the 18th century," I explained. "He edited the first important encyclopedia in Europe and invented the basic concepts that define such a work."

"The word 'encyclopedia' signifies 'chain of knowledge,'" Diderot wrote in his discussion of the encyclopedia. "It is composed of the Greek preposition for in (εν), the word for circle (κύκλος), and the word for knowledge (παιδεία)." He hoped that this encyclopedia would transmit ideas to future generations, so that his descendants would become better instructed, more virtuous, and happier, so that "we should not die without having rendered a service to the human race."

IN 1751, AS DIDEROT PREPARED the first volume of the *Encyclopedie* for publication, he often thought about the future generations of the human race. He knew, all too well, that some of his work would be well-received, some would be replaced with better material, and some entries would slip into obscurity. "Opinions grow old and disappear like words," he observed, "the interest taken in certain inventions wanes by the day, and vanishes."

Diderot liked to compare scholarship to a "vast countryside containing mountains, plains, rocks, water, forests, animals, and all the objects that make for the variety of a great landscape. The light of heaven falls on them all; but it strikes them all in different ways." He described his work as proving a permanent path through this landscape. With such a vision, he was a perfect icon for Sean's new game.

Nonetheless, my vision for Diderot's Discipline faded quickly. As I did a few impromptu searches on the Web and traced the links I found, I discovered a website for Sean's game, a brief description, and a name for the contest: WikiAata. The website established that the game was neither Sean's invention nor a novel phenomenon waiting to burst upon the global consciousness. It was a modest contest enjoyed by a few hundred people, a simple pleasure created from the basic elements of the Internet, much like the games children create from balls, sticks, cardboard boxes, and patches of empty ground. If anything, the new game showed how thoroughly Wikipedia and the other novel institutions of social networking build on a foundation deeply rooted in our intellectual traditions.

IN SPITE OF ALL THE enthusiastic discussion of Wikipedia, the newest form of the encyclopedia is a relatively conventional extension of Diderot's original. While the managers of Wikipedia, the Wikimedia Foundation, have been able to use information technology to reduce the cost of encyclopedia production, they've done little to nothing to change the fundamental relationship between the workers who create encyclopedias and the knowledge that they organize. Like its predecessors, Wikipedia is prepared by authors and editors. Because of information technology, the authors number in the thousands, the editors in the hundreds, and none of them are paid.

Wikipedia has even left the basic structure of the encyclopedia intact, which was the heart of Diderot's invention. He argued that the *Encyclopedie* would consist of a collection of articles linked by cross-references that formed "the most important aspect of encyclopedic ordering." It is the "relation of ideas or phenomena which provides direction," he argued. By following the references, readers will get a fuller understanding of science and learn fundamental principles and common notions. These references would also serve to undermine unsubstantiated opinions and silly ideas. They will always, he stated, "have the double function of confirming and refuting, disrupting and reconciling."

Like many proponents of information technology, Diderot had great hopes for his invention. He thought that by leading readers through knowledge, his references would lead readers to discover "new, speculative truths, or to the perfecting of the known arts, or to the invention of new ones, or to the restitution of ancient, lost arts." He acknowledged that such work was something more than a mere mechanical connection between ideas. "Such references are the work of a man of genius," he concluded. "Happy is he who is able to spot them. He possesses the spirit of combination."

In spite of the deep foundations of modern life, we have a way of inverting ideas, of transforming the genius that produces a "spirit of combination" into the notion that anyone who spends enough time studying the combinations of an encyclopedia will become a happy genius. By the 1950s, American educational theorists were claiming that children developed best in homes "where continual reference to dictionaries and encyclopedias is taken for granted."

I must confess that I came from one of those families where encyclopedias were common and where we were encouraged to follow the chain of knowledge through cross-references. My brother and I were more than a little competitive on this point. We challenged each other to read the multivolume set from cover to cover, but we kept getting sidetracked by the cross-references. We'd start with airplanes, for example, and then jump to rockets. From there, we would go in quick succession to Cape Canaveral, to Florida, to the Caribbean, to the Windward Islands, and end at pirates. I should probably add that he also writes a column of wide-ranging topics and hopelessly obscure references. Perhaps the educational theorists of the 1950s were right in some sense, though I doubt that he and I represent the kind of happy geniuses that they were hoping to produce.

Diderot's system of indexed topic words and linked cross-references has started to show some problems as it has been adopted for modern information technology. A simple search of the 14.5 million Wikipedia entries can produce dozens of potentially useful articles and thousands of valid cross-references. With such a scale, the players of WikiAata or Diderot's Discipline can easily expect that every topic in Wikipedia is connected by a path of hyperlinks, no matter how intellectually distant. Black to white, good to evil, heaven to hell—there is a connection between them all.

As such, this wealth of information is often too large to help solve practical problems. "The information contained in Wikipedia is still unusable in many fields of application," note a team of German researchers. "There is no way to automatically gather information scattered across multiple articles." They also note that "the data is quite structured," but that "its meaning is unclear to the computer, because it is not represented in a machine processable" format. This group, like others, is attempting to expand the capabilities of Wikipedia through the tools of artificial intelligence. It's hard enough to employ these tools in static databases, so I imagine it's considerably harder to develop them for the dynamic nature of Wikipedia. However, if any of them are successful, they may well produce a substantial change to Diderot's approach to organizing knowledge.

I HAVE LONG FELT THAT it was better to guide students through the dangerous paths of this wicked world than to prevent them from leaving the house. Hence, I have long made use of the Internet in my classroom. On the first day of instruction, I appoint one of the students as the Wikipedia Lackey, WikiLackey for short, and direct all inquiries to him or her. (I once called this position the Search Engine Captain, but the title has been devalued as Wikipedia has made the task easier.)

Most students view the job of WikiLackey as something akin to playing a television game show. They believe that their success comes from finding an answer, hitting a button and phrasing the response in the proper form. In fact, the task is much harder than it seems, as it requires them to build a framework to assess the result of their search. The idea of mass transit may be linked to the mass of the moon that enables transit from the earth, but the two concepts are not interchangeable.

To impart the subtleties of search and its place in the intellectual process, I use a lesson that attempts to find the meaning in a certain popular song. The song is new enough for the students to be familiar with the tune, but none of them recognize it as anything more than a collection of beats that plays well at a party. The goals of a good party are usually devoid of intellectual traditions of any kind. Nonetheless, I try to get them to analyze the piece within four distinct frameworks (literary, social, historical, and musical) and search the connections among the ideas that they identify.

Of the four frameworks, the musical structure is the hardest for them to understand, as musical education has all but vanished from American primary schools. We start by developing a simple song model from Mozart, a near contemporary of Diderot. The model is simple. Verse, verse, chorus, verse, chorus, bridge, verse, chorus, coda. It worked for Mozart. It worked for Wagner. It worked for Irving Berlin, who studied the classics but wrote for the masses. It worked for Yip Harburg, who was looking for a way to the end of the rainbow. It worked for Lennon and McCartney, who, in the early days of their career, looked for a connection to a girl who was just standing there.

At some point, the class will usually identify our example as a song of alienation. The title suggests that it is about marching insects, but the lyrics express the complaint of a man who cannot communicate with his girlfriend nor his girlfriend with him. We quickly identify the elements of alienation songs and start identifying other examples. This task is harder, as there are many variations to the basic idea. The genders can change. The complaint can be expressed through imagery. The problem can be revealed at the end of the song. We ponder and identify a list. "Palo Alto." "A Day in the Life." "My Man." "Love Is a Losing Game." "A Case of You." Some work better than others.

The last part of the class comes when we notice that the music for our example doesn't correspond with the lyrics. If taken by itself, the musical framework would lead to a different conclusion than the one drawn from the literary frame. The words end with death and darkness, but the music ends in a climax that can only indicate satisfaction. How then could we search for similar songs? After a little thought, we begin to identify a process that establishes relationships among chord progressions and tempo and volume. If someone has been paying attention, he or she will notice that we also considered a Mozart aria that fits an identical structure. The words are sad, but the song is about triumph. The real triumph, of course, is the path that the students have assembled between the different pieces of information that they have found in the song.

THE CLASS OFFERS ONE FINAL lesson about the spirit of combination, though few students reach this level. When one of them finds the lesson, they usually discover that the intellectual process has more emotion than they anticipated. They arrive at class surprised or angry or perhaps a bit confused. The first to discover the lesson, Emily, entered the classroom filled with dramatic outrage and holing a small stack of paper.

"Colleagues," she announced, "We've been had." She then began to distribute her papers around the class.

"What do you mean," I asked with all the innocence I could muster.

"Not only have you done this lesson before," she said as she held a paper aloft, "You've written an article about it."

At the heart of her reaction was the feeling that I had betrayed them. I had led them to believe that they were getting a lesson that was prepared especially for them when that was not the case.

"How did you find it?" I asked.

"I was doing a little searching last night," she said, "and I started looking to see what I could find about the song from the lesson. One link led to another and soon I found that not only had you written about the subject but you had written about us."

The article is not an easy one to find. The title and key words suggest that it is about something else. To find it in the right context, you have to employ some careful queries, engage a little bit of imagination and approach the subject from the right direction. It requires patience, but it shows what the spirit of combination can accomplish.

04
Mental Discipline

It can be a barrier to entry. Even in my neighborhood, which occasionally leans toward a dictatorship of the proletariat, the political philosophy of the Running Dog Café can discourage patrons. The Running Dog was run as a Marxist collective. "If you find any word, item, or action to be racist, sexist, ageist, culturalist, or in any other way designed to undermine and divide the laboring classes," read the sign at the front door, "please notify a member of the wait staff, who will raise the issue at the next meeting of the Central Committee."

The stern warning camouflaged a lovely restaurant. The food was good, the atmosphere congenial, and the staff pleasant. It was a great place to hold a lunch meeting, provided you were willing to let other customers eavesdrop on your conversation. Apparently, many of the regulars subscribed to the philosophy, more associated with *USA Today* than the *Daily Worker*, that your business is my business.

At one of the last dinners I had at the Running Dog, I was subject to a running commentary from a young man who was trying to join our party. He laughed at our jokes, agreed with our remarks, and attempted to add his opinions to our discussions. Just as the dinner came to an end, he moved a chair to our table and sat next to a woman in our party named Carey, who seemed to be the object of his attentions.

He chose a bad moment to make his move. At that instant, the comrade-waiter delivered our bills, handing one to each member of the table. When we looked at the pieces of paper in our hand, we realized that each of us had received the wrong bill. Seeing his opportunity, the unfortunate young man asked, "Hey, what is the probability of that happening?"

We all paused and then immediately began searching for pens and pieces of scratch paper. With just a few minutes of work, we determined that there were three obvious ways of calculating that probability. You could enumerate the sample space, employ a combinatorial argument, or do a clever conditional analysis.

Carey led the discussion of the problem, as I recall. As she finished, she looked at the empty chair next to her and realized that the troublesome young man had disappeared. He had apparently retreated during our computations. "Such is the power of mathematics," she said. "An aid to the inquisitive, a comfort of man, and a protection to women."

Mathematics may not be the most universal way of protecting individuals from unwanted attention, but it has long served as a barrier to distinguish one group from another. First-year engineering students bond over their struggles with calculus, and economists wear their statistical knowledge as a badge of honor. The practice is as least as old as Napoleon, who required all his artillery officers to learn mathematics, even those who might not be expected to use it. "This particular shared body of knowledge," explained the historian Ken Alder, "distinguished the artillerists, as a body, from the general officers."

Yet, in the past month, I've been part of three conversations in which the participants honestly discussed removing mathematics from the engineering and computer science curriculum. A dinner with friends. A discussion with an engineering dean. The argument to remove mathematics is based on the claim that most mathematical analysis is now handled by computer programs.

"We would never do mathematics analysis by hand," the argument usually begins. "We would always use a mathematical analysis package, a structural modeling program, or statistical software. We would never trust any calculation done by a person."

As you can imagine, such suggestions are met by an explosion of emotion that can't admit to such a change. This emotion is usually followed by three objections, most forcefully made, for the retention of mathematics. First is the claim that engineers need to be able to double-check calculations. The second objection states that it's useful to estimate the order of magnitude for any calculation. The final, and most persistent, is the idea that mathematics provides a mental discipline for young engineers.

Mathematics will likely be retained but not for any of these three reasons. The first two are specious, and the last is an admission of defeat. If you don't accept hand calculation as part of the original analysis, you aren't going to accept it as a validation of machine-computed results. In many cases, it's difficult to compute even a meaningful estimate of a final answer, as the analysis can involve nonlinear differential equations or large matrices.

The third defense of mathematical education, the claim that it disciplines the mind, is the last defense of a dying field. The proponents of Greek, Latin, music theory, drafting, public rhetoric, and a host of other topics that were once required subjects of study have tried to retain a privileged place in the curriculum for their subjects by arguing that Ovid and Virgil and the sonata form were a good discipline for students. None of them succeeded.

In American education, educational historian Laurence Veysey argued the "idea of mental discipline contained inherent weaknesses as a conception," as it emphasizes the esoteric over the practical, subjects that are distant from daily experience over those that help students master physical and social experience. When teachers claim that their subject merely disciplines the mind, they're admitting that their ideas are no longer relevant for most students.

Still, our relationship to mathematics has clearly been shifting over the past two decades because of forces that computer scientists have unleashed through a process known as black-boxing.

BLACK-BOXING IS AN ACTIVITY THAT hides expertise. It takes a body of knowledge, incorporates those ideas in a machine, and then hides the inner operation of that machine behind an opaque façade. To use the knowledge, we operate the black box through a simplified set of controls.

Programming languages are classic examples of black boxes. They incorporate knowledge about computer architecture: memory, registers, machine codes, and all the other aspects of actual physical devices. They allow individuals who know nothing about the inner workings of a computer to utilize knowledge about computing logic and produce useful output.

Application packages such as spreadsheets, word processors, and games are other examples of black boxes, as they encapsulate knowledge about programming. Indeed, many if not most engineered products can be considered black boxes—thermostats, automobiles, mp3 players, and inertial guidance systems. All of them can be viewed as systems that hide knowledge. "Black boxes litter the societies of high modernity," notes sociologist Donald Mackenzie. "Increasing black-boxing may, indeed, be a passable definition of modernization."

While it's possible to trace the idea of the black box to the origin of the machine or the invention of interchangeable parts, we usually identify the concept with the electrical engineer Wilhem Cauer (1900–1945), who developed black box techniques to simplify the work of designing electronic circuits. Cauer's biographers note that during the 1920s, "engineering problems were typically solved in an empirical fashion by analyzing specific circuits instead of looking at classes or families of circuits." Cauer recognized that certain electronic functions could be isolated in a simple device that had only one or two or four connections to the rest of the circuit. Though he never used the term, the isolated device would be known as the black box.

In Cauer's day, black boxes would be filters, circuits that would block electronic signals in a certain range of frequencies. To build these filters, Cauer created a unified theory of filter design. Engineers could use this theory to design filters without worrying about the details of the construction. They could specify the filter and then grind through a series of equations to produce the design. "All known wave filters" of a certain class "are contained in the filters of the new theory," he explained. This "new theory has been carried through practically to find out the most economical filter for any practical purpose."

The black-boxing of filters is often treated as a technical achievement, but it's really a step in the division of labor, of engineering labor. "When a good circuit designer lays out a new circuit," explained a Bell Laboratories engineer, "he isolates those functions that are more or less self-contained," so it's easy "to partition the problem so that several people can work on the different parts." This partition allows for a division of labor. It lets a senior engineer assign simple tasks to less experienced designers. It also allows any designer to make use of expertise that a design team might not possess. If done well, the partition should allow the team to replace parts of the circuit with commercial modules. "Not only is this cheaper because of saving on design time," he continues, "but it may provide a better module than he could have produced. The function of this module may not be the designer's specialty, whereas the designer of an off-the-shelf module is likely to have been a specialist in that subject area."

Cauer's black boxes split the engineering community into two groups: specialists who could deal with specific problems and generalists who assembled smaller elements into a large system. The fundamental benefit of such a division was identified by Charles Babbage (1791–1871) in 1832. By "dividing the work to be executed into different processes, each requiring different degrees of skill or of force," he observed, an employer "can purchase exactly that precise quantity of both which is necessary for each process." Employers no longer need to pay for expensive skills when skills are not needed. Those skills can be the understanding of circuit design, the mastery of difficult computer languages, or even the mastery of mathematics.

We've long observed how black-boxing has reduced the demand for expensive mathematical skills in the commercial world. Just three generations ago, sales clerks needed to know enough mathematics to be able to sum a list of prices, to calculate taxes, to make change. Step by step, cash registers and point-of-sale terminals black-boxed that skill. Now most sales clerks need only know how to operate the box, how to aim a laser at a Universal Product Code, and how to record a credit card. A few senior clerks will have advanced training on the black boxes of the sales terminals and will know how to control their operation, but their number will be few.

As in the world of commerce, black-boxing divides labor in the world of engineering and computer science. Tools such as Mathematica, Maple, and Auto-Cad split the population of technical laborers into a large group that can take its mathematical skills from software and a smaller cohort that can contribute their knowledge to those black boxes. If we're to adjust the skills that we require of engineers and computer scientists, it will have to be done in relation to those tools rather than follow the argument that the rising generation needs to have its mind disciplined or that it needs the same kind of contact with mathematical symbols that we had, or our parents had, or, in my case, my grandmother had.

Of course, if we don't want to face the suggestion that our software has removed a fundamental set of skills from a portfolio of engineers, we can always retreat to the reasoning used by Napoleon and, I suppose, by Carey. Mathematics sets us apart—it's a barrier against the unwashed. Mathematics makes us special.

For Cauer, mathematics was a desperate tool of distinction. He spent his most productive years in Germany during the Nazi ascendency. His published writings suggest that he was able to find a refuge from the political environment of the age behind the mathematics of his work. The papers are abstract. They make no reference to military applications or social conventions. As they look towards the future, they pose problems that require only a journey deeper into the land of abstraction—more laboratory work, more improvement to theory.

Cauer met his end in a way that suggests he was no friend of the Nazi regime or at least someone that the military did not want to fall into enemy hands. Scientific knowledge is not an infallible barrier, either for issues of work or those of life itself. Still, we can accept the weaknesses of scientific knowledge as protection from undesired forces, but we reach for it all too easily.

Not that long ago, I embraced the social power of mathematics as I circulated at reception a certain government department. At one point, I found myself in the company of a former high-level government official who was very proud of his career accomplishments and was quite willing to share them all with me. He had been chargé d'affaires to a vital ally, ambassador to a dangerous enemy, undersecretary for important stuff, and special assistant for powerful people. He was with Reagan in Helsinki, Nixon in China, and Kennedy during the Cuban Missile Crisis.

I know that such recitals are best considered as evidence of insecurity rather than arrogance. I also know that they occasionally suggest interesting stories to be found. Still, after hearing the little speech, I succumbed to temptation. When he finally asked, "What I had done?" I responded, "Not much. I have a PhD in mathematical statistics."

With that sentence, the earth opened between us. He didn't slink away like the young man who was hoping to get Carey's attention. He talked for a moment longer about the problems in some distant and troublesome part of the world that he hoped to fix and then found a reason to leave my company. His parting words included a phrase about not being that good at mathematics.

I was probably the loser in the exchange. If the high-level official had really been with Nixon in China, then he may have had a good story to tell. High-level mathematics may have lost its ability to help us with common problems, it may have lost some of its value to engineers, and it may not be able to discipline our mind, but it can make us briefly special and occasionally can be used to discipline the minds of others.

05
Migration to the Middle

The future caught me by the shoulder last month when I received an e-mail from Freddie.

Normally, I don't have particularly well-developed foresight. After all, I've spent a career in a field that has had a remarkably dull narrative of progress. Each year, hardware gets smaller, cheaper, faster. In the same period, software has become more comprehensive and easier to use. Occasionally, the story is punctured by deadlines missed or budget overruns. Even if we add to this mix the free-floating bits of malware and other problems, we still have a history that's remarkably triumphant and projects nothing but progress. Only when we look beyond our immediate circumstances do we get a hint of the forces that have shaped our industry and get the briefest glimpse of the future.

When I last saw Freddie, he was leaving town with his guitar in hand to begin a career in popular music. I predicted that he would likely make his name as a producer, arranger, or composer. He possessed the skills to handle any of these careers and also knew that he was unlikely to become prominent as a guitarist. Though guitars had once been the dominant instrument of popular music, they were no longer the center of most bands. A guitarist, no matter how skilled, could no longer expect the kind of attention given to the likes of Jimi Hendrix or David Evans or even Jack White. No, the power in popular music was clearly in the hands of those who understood music theory and could make deals with capital.

Not long after his departure, Freddie surprised me with a photograph of his band playing on the stage of an influential music club in New York. It was a moment to be proud, as the club had been the original showcase for the punk and New Wave musicians of the early 1980s. It also evoked a bit of sadness, as Freddie was one of the last musicians to play in that venue. The club had been purchased by a real estate developer and was about to be converted into a retail outlet for well-financed children with discriminating tastes.

While students can be a difficult group to track, they tend to follow a predictable pattern. I heard nothing from Freddie for three or four years. During that period, he fell in love with a young woman, married her, and fathered a child. When he finally resumed communications last summer, he gave me a quick summary of his life that included the fact that he was no longer working as a professional musician.

"What are you doing for a job?" I asked.

"Technology," was his quick reply. "I'm doing IT for a hedge fund. Perl. Java. Configuration management."

I then asked him how he had prepared for this career, as I recalled that he had spent more time in music studios than in computer laboratories, more time with harmonic theory than mathematics. Freddie reminded me that he had originally taken a job managing a small network and had moved, step-by-step, to jobs with more sophisticated systems. "I did some studying on my own," he explained, "and learned from the work I did."

Freddie talked about his employer and the kinds of challenges he faced. He described situations that are all too familiar to anyone who has worked with software during the past 30 years: complicated interfaces, incompatible systems, unrealistic deadlines, inflated expectations.

As Freddie told his stories, I recognized that he might find some of these issues easier to address if he had additional training, access to best practices, or even more contact with peers who did the same kind of work. When I asked him who the senior technical staffer on his project was, Freddie paused.

"There really isn't one," he said.

"They all have the same kind of training as you?"

"Yes, but none of the others play guitar."

DEPENDING ON HOW HIS TIME as a professional but largely unpaid musician is viewed, Freddie has been in the workforce for a little more than a decade. According to the US Bureau of Labor Statistics, Freddie occupies one of the 855,000 jobs for computing professionals that has been created during that period. Those new jobs provide both an opportunity and challenge for the profession. As an opportunity, they demonstrate the world's need of technical skills. As a challenge, they demand that we recognize the forces that are changing the demography of the technology field, changes that are bringing new kinds of people into professional roles.

The demography of technological jobs isn't well understood, as the standard job categories for the field have changed rapidly over the past 30 years. The Standard Occupation Classifications for 1980, the categories that are used to track the labor force, included two job titles under the section Computer, Mathematical, and Operations Occupations. The first is "computer systems analyst." The second is "computer scientist, not elsewhere classified." The classifications didn't even include a category labeled "computer engineer." Such a job was assumed to be a position for specialized electrical engineers.

Of course, 30 years in the field of digital technology is a lifetime in any other industrial field. In 1980, the software industry had yet to be recognized by the business community. The term "software engineering" was just 12 years old and not widely used. Undergraduate programs in software engineering were few and far from standardized.

To understand why such categories are important, we only need to look at the demographic changes that occurred in agriculture during the 20th century. In 1900, fully 40 percent of the US workforce lived on farms and was engaged in agricultural production. A century later, that figured had dropped to 4 percent, and those workers provided food for a population that had increased by a factor of 3.5.

The farmers who left agriculture during the 20th century became part of the great movement of laborers who left the country and moved to the cities, where they became the new industrial workers of the era. It was known as the Prairie Brain Drain to the small cities of the west and as the Great Migration North to the sharecroppers of the south. "The major reason for the change," explained sociologist Daniel Bell, "was the huge increase in agricultural productivity during World War II and after, when the introduction of chemical fertilizers and pesticides raised agricultural productivity between 6 and 9 percent a year." Without these movements, the US would not have had enough labor to expand its industrial base during the 1920s and 1950s.

Nothing in the world stands still. The US experienced a loss of manufacturing jobs after the 1960s. While some of this decline was caused by companies moving production outside the country, more was caused by the increasing productivity of manufacturing processes. The autoworker of 1970 could accomplish far more than the equivalent laborer of 1930. The workers released from employment in factories moved into the service industries, such as financial services, programming, and software engineering. They left Detroit and Akron and moved to Redmond, San Jose, and Waltham. Without this migration of workers, the US economy could not have expanded into the IT sector during the 1990s.

HAVING WITNESSED THREE MAJOR MIGRATIONS of labor in the past century, we might wish to know if we are in the midst of a fourth. If we are seeing a new migration of technological workers, it is a migration to the middle, a decline in the number of people with either a great deal of training or almost no training, and an expansion of those who are modestly trained but still call themselves professionals.

While growth in the computer occupations category during the past decade seems substantial, it isn't uniform across the different computing professions. The jobs that require both the most and the least training have declined during that time. The number of positions for computer engineers has declined by 5 percent, while the number of openings for computer operators has declined by 38 percent. This change isn't surprising. During the past decade, the tools and standards that support both kinds of jobs have increased, and some kinds of jobs, notably that of computer programmer, have moved to lower-cost labor markets.

The three kinds of positions that account for the 855,000 new jobs are squarely in the middle of the field: network system analysts, software engineers, and systems analysts. As defined by the Bureau of Labor Statistics, these fields all require substantial training beyond the basic skills of an operator but not the scientific education of a computer hardware engineer.

It isn't necessary to have a bachelor of science degree to be considered a software engineer. According to the Bureau of Labor Statistics, a software engineer is the leader of a programming or system development project, not necessarily a trained engineer. "Occupations are classified based on work performed," explains the Bureau of Labor Statistics. Only in some cases, notably the most restrictive professions, does it consider the "skills, education, and/or training needed to perform the work at a competent level."

Indeed, the number of students who complete a BS in software engineering has declined steadily during the past five years. It's now below the level of graduates in 2000. In many cases, employers have filled the software engineering jobs by importing trained engineers from other countries or by promoting individuals trained in different ways.

"Computer science as an academic discipline," writes the historian Nathan Ensmenger, "and computer programming as an occupation have struggled with various degrees of success to establish institutional boundaries" that identify them as professional occupations. They have been unable to establish common standards for admittance to the field. Those who can do the work, no matter how they may have been trained, can generally find work. Freddie, for example, doesn't have an engineering degree, yet the Bureau of Labor Statistics considers his job to be a software engineering position.

We shouldn't expect to fill our software engineering posts from the ranks of musicians. Yet we're seeing more and more individuals who are training for software development in programs that look less and less like computer science departments. Perhaps the most rapidly growing technical program is that of computer game design.

Game design programs have become popular at associate degree colleges, public and private, and are increasingly found in major educational institutions. They're filled with students who see themselves in the employ of Electronic Arts or some other game developer, living the rest of their natural lives in the fantasy land of Donkey Kong and Halo.

Fantasies are lovely things, of course, but they must do battle with the monsters of economic reality. More often than not, the fantasy falls before the law of supply and demand, and we discover that the wonderful world of Adam Smith allows no extra lives, no resurrections, and no secret commands to unlock special powers. Only a few programs can place all of their graduates with computer gaming companies. The rest go into more prosaic careers: Web design, network analysis, and, if they can do the work, software engineering.

If we are faced with a growing cohort of computing professionals who did not have a traditional professional education, then we must ultimately consider the question "Who do we consider to be a professional?" The answer is not straightforward. If we make the criteria too stringent, current professional organizations for computer science could evolve into a small organization of highly educated people who have little impact on the application of technology. If we make the definition too generous, we might find that we have a large body of members who don't have a common vocabulary that would allow them to discuss the issues relevant to the field. If we do nothing, we may watch the technical world march forward and leave us little to do.

The march of the technical world materialized while I was attending a technical conference in Silicon Valley. As I talked with the other participants, I soon discovered that most of them had more in common with Freddie than with me. During a coffee break, I had a lovely talk with a technology entrepreneur who had been the lead singer of a New York band. "Straight up rock 'n' roll," she explained, "à la Sheryl Crow or the Pretenders." As far as I could tell, I was the only member of a traditional computing professional society in attendance.

ON A GOOD NIGHT WITH the band," explained Freddie, "you were grateful to take home $50, if you could even get that. There's no future there." He sees enough future in software to cast his lot and the lot of his family with the field.

Part of that future seems clear to those of us who work in the computing profession. If past is prologue, software will become more complex and more inclusive. Its services will be available to us on small portable platforms, in giant infrastructures hidden in the cloud, and on everything in between. In all, the world of software will be faster, more interesting, more engaging.

Yet the future of software also includes more than a few people who earn their daily bread from technological work even though they once believed they could command the night as popular musicians. From our vantage point, it's difficult to discern who will create the next generation of software, how those workers will be trained, and what organizations will support their work. Yet we must learn to answer those questions if we are to stay relevant to the field, if we are to look ahead to anything more than the life of a struggling artist who can't earn more than $50 from an evening's gig.

Exit
Newspaper Joe

One cold morning, I hurried out the front door to get the morning newspaper to prevent it from being snatched by Joe, who lives in the alley a couple blocks to the north of us. In the morning, Joe will pick up a paper from a neighborhood doorstep and read it, or perhaps pretend to read it, as he walks down the street. As he goes along, he drops pages. First the ads, then the sports, next the style section, then metro, and finally the front page. When Joe is done, the sidewalk is littered with a stream of blowing newsprint leading toward the doorstep where he found the paper.

As I stooped to pick up the paper, I saw a chalk circle, neatly drawn on the sidewalk with a few notes scribbled next to it. I thought it odd that someone would have drawn such a thing in the night. I looked up and saw similar circles in front of the other homes. The ones by Yousef's door and at Jeff and Marissa's house had no writing. Tim and Caroline's house was marked by a circle like ours. I stood outside long enough to realize that my feet were getting chilled and returned inside unsure of what I'd seen.

During the day, I found a few minutes to do a little research on the Internet but I found little that was directly relevant. The most interesting was an article on a symbolism that was used by hobos during the great depression. When a hobo "received a handout" from a home, he would "when returning to the alley, write carefully with his chalk on the garage door," a symbol to indicate that he had received a good meal from the owner.

For a moment, I concluded that the symbols were the work of Newspaper Joe, but quickly decided that this idea was wrong. While Joe might be the sort to draw chalk marks on the sidewalk, he probably wasn't capable of making the sophisticated drawings that I had seen. Furthermore, he didn't seem to be the sort to mark a home for the treatment, good or ill, that he had received at the owner's hands.

Expressing an impatience that I would not have tolerated from a class, I called a former student to see what she might know. She leads a computer security office and knew things about the technology community that are far beyond my experience. Because of the sensitive nature of her position, she does not like to let me use her name, so I generally call her X or Major X when I need to be formal.

I described to X the drawings that I had seen and waited for her response.

"It's called war chalking," X explained. "Those are marks that show the location of wireless routers in your neighborhood. Someone has walked up and down your block with a cellphone or a laptop checking for routers."

"What does it mean?" I asked.

"Some proponents of community networks believe that we should build large urban nets by opening our personal wireless routers to friends, neighbors, and pedestrians on the street."

"They can't be serious," I said.

"Yes they are," she replied before starting to discuss how such a strategy would have trouble with signal strength and scope of coverage. As she talked, I realized that our neighborhood was an unusual place. It was one of the first in the city to get broadband access, but it also contains a number of residents who could not afford the cost of such services. Since the houses were packed closely together, they covered the block with a strong set of network signals. I recalled Lauren's ability to borrow bandwidth from the neighborhood. I wondered who else might have tapped into our routers.

"Is there a security problem?" I asked.

X just laughed. "You know that wireless home routers are about as vulnerable a piece of hardware as you can buy. You can encrypt them, but, as the underlying signal contains a lot of public information, they are easy to decode."

After a moment she said, "You know that there are organizations that patrol your neighborhood to monitor router signals and look for sensitive information."

"What organizations?" I asked.

"Organizations," she responded.

A FEW DAYS AFTER THE call, I tried to talk to our neighbor Yousef about the chalk symbols. Yousef is one of the centers of local information for the neighborhood and often the first to take action when action is needed. He is also a heavy user of the local digital circuits, as he does most of his work for a company in New York. This time, however, he was hard to engage. The raccoons were expanding their presence in the neighborhood and were causing havoc. Yousef's yard had already been invaded by the newcomers.

"Do you know where they are living?" he asked without wanting a reply. "Betty's house. They have a nest in the porch at the back. We have to do something."

Of course there was something to be done and in the doing, it would overshadow any potential threat to our broadband service. Once, our neighborhood had been a working class area that contained enough industry and enough aggressive dogs to keep other forms of wildlife at bay. However, the needs of the local economy have changed, and with them, the geography of the neighborhood.

The house fronts have changed little over the years, but the homes they shelter have evolved radically. Once, this was a self-sustaining neighborhood with factories and grocery stores. Then it was collection of nice homes that were close to downtown. Now it is part of the global topography, where residences are close enough to comingle wireless networks and neighbors separated by jobs that are thousands of miles apart.

"Hoover Park: the neighborhood of Newspaper Joe, global workers, five increasingly aggressive raccoons, and free broadband for those who can find it."

Chapter II:
Of What We Speak

Introduction
Managing the Audience

Most parents shudder when I argue that few educational programs are as practical as a degree in theatre. They, naturally, equate the theatre with acting and immediately conjure a terrible and frightening scene. They picture their beloved child living in some filthy New York basement apartment with a filthy and frightening member of the opposite sex who spends far too much time with dubious characters and demands large sums of money for dangerous and illicit drugs. Their beloved child, unable to land steady work in any theatre of any quality whatsoever, is forced to work as a stock clerk in a bookstore, a job that clearly has no future whatsoever.

Still, acting is not theatre, and theatre demands a large collection of skills not normally associated with the liberal arts. As theatre majors, students learn to work with power tools and master the basic elements of both wood and metal fabrication. They learn project management, small group communication, leadership, basic advertising, budgeting, and bookkeeping. The list continues to include elementary circuit theory, human and customer relations, union regulations, and light design. To complete their education, they get a dash of liberal arts, including history, literature, psychology. Finally, they learn acting, which is the subject that really teaches them the principles of management.

"You can't be a good actor unless you are a good manager," explains noted Broadway actor Christian Conn. "You first have to manage yourselves. Every hour you spend in a job is an hour you can't be at an audition. Every dollar you spend on a luxury is a dollar you can't spend on a class to improve your skills at dancing or singing or speaking."

Even the craft of acting incorporates a fundamental process of management, the continuous improvement cycle. First you plan your performance. Next you perform. Third, you listen to the audience and assess what you have done. Finally, you incorporate what you have learned into your act and repeat the process. As a management principle, it may have been first articulated in 1939 by Walter Shewhart (1891–1967), but the basic idea had long been employed by actors great and modest. "If you don't listen to your audience," explains Conn, "you can't communicate that ideas that are supposed to be part of your performance."

In the modern theatre, the Shewhart cycle is employed with much of the same discipline that is used in industrial processes. In most performances, the show is actually controlled by a stage manager, who sits in a booth behind the audience, reads the basic actions or cues from a computer screen, and notifies each actor or stagehand of their appointed task, a process known as calling the show. If the show is small, they will be working it by themselves. If it is large, they will be joined by two or three assistants who will be working at computers that control the lights, the sound, and any special effects.

Computer technology was first used in the massive Broadway musicals of the 1980s—*Cats, Les Miserables, Phantom of the Opera, Starlight Express, Miss Saigon.* All of these shows had large mechanical sets controlled by desktop computers. "Stagehands are still needed, but the computer adds a layer of control," observed one commentator. "Twenty years ago, it was pulling a lever for each and every machine that had to move something. Today, it's hitting a Go button and making sure that nothing goes wrong."

For most theatres, computerized control is not as simple or as mechanical as hitting a button and watching the show unfold. The program for the show is developed during the technical rehearsals, which occur about three quarters of the way through the rehearsal process. During these sessions, the play advances by fits and starts as the stage manager sets each cue and checks the flow of instructions.

When the time comes to actually perform the play, the stage manager retains substantial control over the action. She or he can adjust the cues to respond to the audience or to unexpected events on the stage. They also collect information from each performance and present the information to the cast as notes so that they can assess and adjust their performance.

The connection between a theatrical program and a computer program is far from coincidental. The scientific managers of the early 20th century, the managers who were attempting to apply rigorous discipline to production, adopted the word "program" from description of events at a theatre and applied it to the production schedule of a factory. Shewhart incorporated it into his work on quality control. The early writers of software, who viewed themselves as controlling the production of a computing machine, borrowed the term program from factory managers.

While engineers were borrowing terms from the theatre in the 1920s and 1930s, the world of the stage was freely adopting the methods of scientific management to improve their shows. They ran experiments to test their ideas. When appropriate, they timed the audience reaction in order to get information that would help them better pace the show. Few were as systematic in the application of these techniques than a group of five comedians, the brothers Marx.

The Marx brothers faced the problem of transferring their act from the stage to film, from a venue that offered immediate feedback to one that offered limited responses from the audience. As their material depended heavily upon the success of the jokes, rather than any plot or character development, they had spent hours refining their ideas in front of a live audience. "Every day the writers rewrote their scenes," reported on of their biographers, "Groucho too spent hours changing lines, words, inflections." In one circumstance he tested a half-dozen different lines for a single joke before he selected the final version.

The success of the jokes depended not only on words but also on the timing of the delivery. Again, they worked to refine their timing on the stage, as they could not count on a consistent audience response from those who witnessed the multiple repetitions of the joke on the film set. "A stage director would take a stop watch," reported one of their biographers, "and would time how long the laugh would be," so that response from the movie audience would not overwhelm the next line of dialogue.

IN DISCUSSING MANAGERIAL PROCESSES, WHETHER in the theatre or in business, we tend to focus on the steps of specific procedures and forget humans who must add their judgment to the process. Human judgment is not a rational activity, else it would be replaced by a logical program and executed by a computer. Judgment engages the emotional side of management and demands character from those who would judge. It weighs competing interests, assesses the claims of the future against the needs of the present, and asks if the organization has sufficient moral strength to sustain its conclusions.

The Marxes were a strong group and were able to enforce their judgments against the ideas of many a prominent collaborator, including the most well known of their writers, the playwright George Kaufman. Kaufman disliked how the Marx brothers altered his scripts but could do little about it. At one rehearsal, he attempted, unsuccessfully, to mock them into submission by proclaiming, "Hush, I think I just heard a line from the script."

Strength of managerial character is needed from the start of any production, be it in a factory or theatre. "Stand by for Curtain," is the first command from the stage manager. When she judges the time to be right, she will start the play with the word "Go."

IN THAT MOMENT OF ARTISTRY, when the theatre darkens and the actors first walk onto the stage to cry for a muse of fire and a kingdom for a stage, we suspend our doubts and willingly accept the idea that we are watching real characters living real lives on stage. In so doing, we forget that a stage manager is sitting behind us in a darkened room and is actually controlling the show. "Stand by for sound cue 16," she will say into a microphone. A moment or two will pass as she listens to the audience and watches the action on stage. When she feels the moment is right, she will say, "Sound cue 16 now."

Last fall, I was sitting in the audience for the first production of a grand new theatre. I had had the opportunity to watch the company program the first minutes of the show during tech rehearsal. The first action rolled a coffin onto the stage. Members of the cast joined the scene in a specific order. After a moment of dramatic music, the dialog would begin.

On opening night, the coffin appeared as required and the first actors appeared as anticipated. However, as the scene expanded, an unexpected bit of music drifted into the hall. The tune was a 1920s jazz song and quite out of place for a funeral. I knew that they had not used this music during the rehearsal and was fairly sure that they would not have added it later. I speculated that the tune was coming from another part of the building but could not be certain.

The theme grew louder and louder as the scene progressed. It was carried by a pair of vigorous horns and supported by the beating of tom-toms. The sound of clinking glasses suggested that this music was taken from a party scene. As the sounds continued, the audience grew restless. Was this irony? A subtle reference to an ill-spent youth? The music grew louder, until it began to mask the voices of the actors. At this point, the audience had concluded that something had gone wrong, but it didn't know what to do. The actors, good troupers that they were, kept the show moving as best they could.

Finally, the lead actor took responsibility for the show. He touched one of his colleagues on the shoulder and moved to center stage. "Something has gone badly wrong," he announced. "If you give us a moment to repair it, we will reset and restart in a few moments, with your indulgence."

The director, who happened to be in the audience, stood up and tried to improvise for a moment, but he didn't have much to say, and the audience wasn't much interested in listening to him. He didn't have the humor of the Marx brothers, nor did he have the kind of data they gleaned from audiences. However, as he spoke, the stage manager fixed the problem. A sound cue had been misprogrammed. Instead of playing a file that contained a funeral dirge it had found the party music. In a moment, the correction was made, the cues quickly checked for other programming errors and the show reset. The stage manager then dimmed the lights, and when she felt that the audience was ready, pushed the button on her computer marked Go.

01
The Age of Accountability

Long before he started to cry, long before he bowed his head in a vain effort to recover his composure, you could tell that Akio Toyoda was in trouble. He was, to be sure, engaged in one of the more difficult rituals of the industrial world. When a company seems to be doing something wrong, when its products aren't working as advertised, we call its top executives in front of a congressional committee and ask them to account for their organization. We now live in an age of transparency. We believe that when decisions are made in public, or at least explained in public, they'll be more rational, more thoughtful, and best able to provide the greatest good to the greatest number of people.

Toyoda was making his public explanation because of a perceived failure of transparency. The prior months were filled with reports that his company's automobiles were experiencing failures of design or manufacture. A company representative identified a problem with a mechanical part and blamed a supplier. News reports suggested that an electronic circuit might have failed, or perhaps the software in an engine controller.

In a congressional hearing, a CEO must be transparent in an almost ceremonial way: humble, open to criticism, expressing gratitude to be able to speak to representatives of the American people. It's best to confess to problems that are vague and unlikely to draw legal action. In recent months, following an unfortunate appearance by the heads of the American automakers before Congress, a new step has been added to this ritual. In their testimony, CEOs must now make a statement that makes them seem like an ordinary citizen, a middle-class consumer of the company's products. The CEOs of the American car companies chose to drive their own vehicles from Detroit to Washington, DC, in penance for the mistake of flying on corporate jets to an earlier hearing. Toyoda decided to claim that he occasionally tested the company products. "I myself am a trained test driver," he explained. "As a professional, I am able to check on problems in a car and can understand how severe the safety concern is in a car."

But, of course, Toyoda is in fact a professional CEO responsible for the standard tasks of a corporate leader. He has to deal with stock prices, finance issues, coordination of production, strategic plans, and long-term investments. If he does that job properly, he would have little energy or attention left to devote to contribute to a proper test program.

The real sign that things were going to end badly came when Toyoda briefly opened his company doors to praise his employees and then slammed them shut before any questions could be asked. "At Toyota," he proclaimed, "we believe the key to making quality products is to develop quality people." It was a pleasant statement, a remark that identified him with the 200,000 individuals who work for his company. However, it was yet one more comment that attempted to be transparent without actually being transparent, to satisfy the form without providing understanding.

WHILE GOOD EMPLOYEES ARE BETTER than bad employees, employees good and bad are less important than a good organization—the collection of people, relationships, information systems, and protocols that are at the heart of a modern company. A good organization can get quality results from mediocre employees. A bad organization can accomplish nothing, no matter how talented its people may be.

Not long ago, a beautiful spring day brought a complete organizational failure to my front door. The people were skilled, well equipped, and possessed the best of intentions. Yet they lacked an organization that would allow them to accomplish the task that befell them.

The problem began when power failed at 3:00 in the afternoon. Computer screens went black, and hard drives ground to a halt with a stream of bad bits written across the most recently accessed files. The Internet dribbled a few last packets and then ceased to function. For a few minutes, 10 at most, the 200,000 people who worked in my neighborhood behaved like good employees. They sat patiently at their desks. They fiddled with the switches. They wandered into the department manager's office to see if anyone knew what was happening.

Had the technical problem been quickly resolved, we all would have missed a beautiful day and the subsequent excitement. However, nothing seemed to be happening, so, one by one, we all locked our desks, skipped into the lovely afternoon, and joined a traffic jam that wouldn't be cleared for six hours. Not only did the offices lack power, so did the stoplights.

Of course, plenty of good people on hand to fix the problem: metropolitan police, university police, park police and parking police (two very different groups), military police, security police, and even business district police, not to mention the crossing guards at the local middle school. All were well trained, and all had good equipment: white gloves, shrill whistles, and attitudes that could force an aggressive driver to cower in fear.

The police had all that they could want except for an organization that would coordinate their actions. They moved quickly through the streets and took command of the corner that was nearest to their regular duty station. They tried to move traffic in an efficient, orderly manner until they found that there was nothing that they could do. They couldn't see their colleagues at other intersections and hence couldn't make decisions that would keep the traffic flowing. The era of manual traffic control is long past—in the modern age, it's controlled by a combination of centralized servers, software models, sensors, and switched lights. A team of cops, no matter how well trained, can't improve that kind of organization.

In the aftermath of the great spring traffic nightmare, people called for investigations and more transparency in the police departments. For several weeks, they searched for a scapegoat, an individual who would take the communal blame. Perhaps someone had failed to give the right command. Perhaps someone had failed to develop an appropriate plan. Perhaps someone was eating a doughnut at a crucial moment. Transparency, they thought, would solve the problem.

While perhaps some strategic planning committee had indeed failed to imagine the crisis of that day, the failure was also organizational. At that time, our city's collected security forces didn't have an organization that could anticipate such problems and devise human structures that could address them.

IN MANY WAYS, THE AUTO industry has struggled with organizational structures that lingered over problems of the past rather than anticipated the needs of the future. For more than 60 years, the organizational model for the industry was provided by General Motors, which was assembled between 1915 and 1922 from a collection of small companies. Its leaders tried to create an organization that would minimize the complexity of manufacture by combining technical protocols with market forces. "General Motors has become an essay in federalism," wrote management expert Peter Drucker (1909–2005) in 1947. "It attempts to combine the greatest corporate unity with the greatest divisional autonomy and responsibility."

GM's structure was created by Alfred P. Sloan (1875–1966), who developed his ideas in response to the economic conditions in the early decades of the 20th century. He wanted a company that would contract during economic recessions, expand for growing markets, and rapidly change production for war. In the middle of the 20th century, Drucker argued that GM's organization "enables all units of the company to produce more efficiently and at lower cost than any of them could as independent units."

GM's corporate structure worked fairly well through the early 1960s, when its principle concern was meeting the demand for automobiles. However, the organization found it difficult to meet the additional demands that appeared in the '60s and '70s—specifically, it didn't know how to react to the consumer push for safer cars, and it resisted calls to reduce atmospheric pollution and increase gas mileage. "Where it should have moved long before of its own volition," wrote journalist David Halberstam, "the industry now slowly and reluctantly moved, forced by mounting public demand."

GM, along with the rest of the auto industry, reluctantly entered the digital age in 1980, when it installed digital controls on its products to comply with US air pollution and fuel efficiency standards. In general, the industry treated digital components as simply another part or subsystem. It was another bolt or gear or subsystem. Few in the industry thought that perhaps they should organize their cars around their information flow rather than their information flow around their cars. "While software modularity is commonplace in software engineering," observed a recent industry report, "it is far from practice in the automotive industry where the electronics system architecture follows company organization and automotive supply chains."

The senior engineers of the major auto manufacturers argued that they had good reasons for avoiding the modern tools of software engineering. They claimed that their methods encouraged "clear identification of responsibilities and liabilities." Hence, they clung to older information infrastructures, even as their products became more complex. Engineers learned to patch new elements into old systems, route multiple buses through a single connection, and gather extra information from an overworked sensor.

Organizations tend to make major changes only when they face a crisis. Hence, we may remember the financial unpleasantness of 2009–2010 as the event that created new organizational models for the automobile industry. Yet, a number of engineers and managers have been anticipating that they may need to create a new, more transparent information structure for all stages of the automotive life cycle—design, manufacture, distribution, operation, and disposal. Since 2000, they've been working on a new automotive information environment that recognizes that automobiles are multiprocessors on wheels that are part of a large, pervasive computing structure. At the core of this work is an initiative known as the Automotive Open Software Architecture, or AUTOSAR.

Like many an industry initiative, AUTOSAR is an effort to build a common technological environment in a way that lets everyone who contributes to that environment use it without paying royalties or worrying about patent infringement. While it identifies several common technical goals, such as a standard means of communication and a common development environment, it really has organizational goals. It seeks to end the isolation of individual engineers as well as the programs that they use to sense, store, and manipulate data. It gives them a flexible means of communicating and cooperating, so they're less likely to be an array of well-trained professionals who can't solve a complicated problem because the right hand can't see what the left is doing.

Perhaps most importantly, it changes the relation of the past to the future. For 30 years, the annual change of automobile models has been a barrier to improvement, forcing engineers to devote their effort to make new features work with existing software. "Mature reaction on component changes," explains one expert, "reuse of software, identical design rules across all users, concentration on the innovations and—last but not least—the safe handling of complexity is the target."

WE TEND TO LOOK AT initiatives such as AUTOSAR as merely technological development, new opportunities for gaining more control over the material world and using that control for our benefit. In fact, such things are also organizational projects: they provide us with new ways of dividing labor for the manufacture and operation of our products. As we conceive our cars around information, we'll structure our design teams differently. Owners will have new relationships with their mechanics. Manufacturers will have new connections to their fleet in the field. All of these connections will involve large amounts of data and will offer a new kind of transparency to the automotive world. It will be harder to claim that a car hasn't failed when data from the entire fleet reveals a problem. It will be equally difficult to ascribe the blame to others when this new transparency reveals dangerous driving habits or incomplete maintenance.

At the same time, this developing transparency will require outsiders to understand the nature of the data flow in the automotive environment. The data will have to be interpreted in the context of the organization that produced it. Furthermore, the time will come when we will again be reminded that we'll encounter situations that can't be solved by our definition of transparency—that some problem will develop within the system in a way that we couldn't have foreseen and can't address. At such a point, we'll see another auto executive sitting in front of a government board and trying to appear transparent. Following the script, he or she will be humble, open to criticism, grateful to speak to the representatives of the people, and willing to confess to a problem that really isn't much of a problem. Perhaps that person will cry—perhaps not. That may not be part of what happens in that particular age of transparency and accountability.

02
The Problem of Design

Dividing the light from the darkness. Pushing back the wilderness to make a place for civilization. Unpacking your worldly goods after a household move. All of these activities require equal amounts of energy. This is a fundamental principle of physics: Newton's fourth law of motion—the conservation of unrealistic goals. Yet, Tamara's voice gave no clue that she was surrounded by chaos.

"Boxes?" I asked. "You are standing in a room filled with boxes?"

"Of course," was her reply.

Tamara and her husband were about to embark on the great organizing task of human experience, that of bringing a baby into this world and nurturing it into adulthood. She was coming to this task later in life and hence had a fairly accurate idea of the effort that it would require. We talked for a bit about how she planned to fit her dissertation research into the two-and-one-half-hour time slots that babies offer their parents.

"I believe I can do it," she said. "Although I wish that I could point to someone who had done this already. It is, after all, a problem of design."

WHEN I FIRST MET TAMARA, she was not much interested in design problems or any other engineering tasks. She had studied human communication and was moving to California.

"It has the fewest cloudy days in the country," she explained. "That was my criterion for success."

Yet when Tamara began working, she found that many of her clients were involved with digital technology and that their communications problems were concerned with fitting an engineered product into a social and cultural context. Shortly after arriving in her new home, she attended a seminar on innovation that included the entrepreneur Phillipe Kahn as one of the speakers.

"Kahn spent much of his time dwelling on social issues," Tamara recalled. "He kept returning to the question, 'What is your consideration of culture?'"

Within the community of Silicon Valley entrepreneurs, Kahn was reputed to have a special insight into the interaction between human nature and engineered artifacts. That community tested such reputations with a scale defined by the values of business. A profitable business suggested a basic apprehension of social issues. A successful product fell higher on the scale, as it demonstrated a grasp of human habits.

An innovative idea that defined a new market, even an idea that was capitalized by others, held the highest place on the scale. Someone who could define a new market, so the reasoning went, must truly understand how human culture interacts with technology.

Kahn's reputation rested on contributions to all three categories of the entrepreneurial scale. He had run a profitable business and had marketed several highly successful products. He was also credited with creating the cell phone camera, thereby defining a new market for communication services. The tale of how he connected a digital camera to a cell phone has become a classic addition to the innovation literature, a story almost as famous as Alexander Graham Bell's urgent message, "Mr. Watson. Come here. I need you."

According to the story, Kahn constructed his cell phone camera in 1997 so that he could send pictures of his newborn daughter to friends and family. Connecting a camera to a digital cell phone was not necessarily innovative. Well before 1997, we knew that any digital device could be connected to any other digital device, even though the effort might require a substantial amount of programming and the result might not be particularly pleasing. However, the combination of the cell phone and the camera evoked a new set of emotions from people. New fathers, yet untested by late night feedings and still clinging to unrealistic plans for their new family life, looked upon these tiny devices and realized that they could share their moment of sudden transformation with distant family and friends. Adolescents, former newborns themselves, saw a slightly different idea in these new devices, one that recorded their growing independence and connections to nearby friends. The purveyors of photographic services, if they were paying attention, saw a warning in these little devices that looked nothing like a traditional camera.

BEFORE THE CELL PHONE CAMERA and its many smart siblings, new technology came in many shapes. Most of these shapes were three-dimensional, and a good number were beige in color. As the years have progressed, we have seen the shape of high technology converge to that of the unadorned rectangle. Phones, with or without cameras, are rectangles, as are laptops and desktop computers. Servers are more utilitarian rectangles that slide into frames, which are themselves large rectangles.

It is too easy to dismiss the current shape of high technology as the natural outgrowth of the underlying developments and forget that the design of devices is the product of both the inner nature of the machine and the outer influence of culture. "Form follows function," argued the great American architect Louis Sullivan (1856–1924), and the culture that uses an artifact ultimately determines its function.

Over the history of the computer, we can point to several machines that were consciously designed to be distinctive, to look different from common machines. Perhaps the most familiar of these examples is the original Macintosh (1984), but the most dramatic are the Cray-1 (1976) and the Connection Machine 1 (1986).

These were both high-performance machines and looked substantially different from the standard boxes of data processing machines. The Cray was a partial cylinder, a little less than six feet tall. Its power supply occupied a low ring that surrounded the machine and often drew comparisons to second empire furniture. The trade press occasionally referred to it as the "world's most expensive loveseat," but the comparison was undermined by a set of aluminum cooling fins.

The Connection Machine was housed in a set of interlocked boxes that attempted to mimic the architecture of the machines. The "company's president put a high priority on a package that would not only convince viewers of the machine's uniqueness," recalled the designer, "but would explain the nature of its architecture."

In fact, technical issues did not dictate the shape of either machine. The parallel architecture of the Connection Machine could easily have been mapped into a more conventional structure. The Cray hardware, though it needed to maintain short distance between its components, did not make connections across the ring and could have easily been fit into a cubic form.

If we look to the design of earlier computing equipment, we see a steady and conscious effort to make these devices look modern and to distinguish them from factory machines. IBM began thinking about the physical designs of its products in the 1930s. Company engineers modeled the shape of their accounting machines on Queen Anne furniture. They decided that the machines would have curved legs even though straight legs would have been cheaper to produce.

As IBM started to build more complicated computing machines, it hired professional designers to determine the outward appearance of its products. The most influential of these designers was Norman Bel Geddes (1893–1958). Bel Geddes had started as a set designer for Broadway plays and had established his reputation as an industrial designer by creating the General Motors exhibit at the 1939 World's Fair. Known as the Futurama, the exhibit showed fairgoers the world of 1960, including massive skyscrapers and high-speed freeways. "Each day of the fair," wrote one observer, "thousands of visitors waited for hours in lines up to a mile in length for the opportunity to experience the Futurama."

To convey the idea that an object was new or modern, Bel Geddes liked to employ the curved shapes that were found on airplanes, a concept known as streamlining. The curved shapes suggested not only newness, but also speed, power, and the conquest of nature. He applied streamlining to buildings, automobiles, and even to household appliances.

In 1943, Bel Geddes designed a streamlined shell for the Mark I calculating machine of Howard Aiken (1900–1973), which had been built by IBM. He created a shape that had curved corners, brushed aluminum panels, and brightly lit windows. "It gave poor Howard Aiken an awful pain, because it was fifty or a hundred thousand bucks for the case," recalled one worker. Aiken would rather have invested that money in the machine, "and that irked him."

During the 1950s, the streamlined style of Bel Geddes merged into the minimalist ideas of Elliot Noyes (1910–1977). Noyes was a junior designer in Bel Geddes' office and an army buddy of IBM President Thomas Watson Jr. (1914–1993). His friendship with Watson helped Noyes win contracts to design the shape of an IBM electric typewriter and the décor in Watson's office in the IBM building. He "stripped away the walnut panels and heavy curtains" of the office, reported one magazine, "replacing them with large sheer planes of color, and installing works of modern art throughout."

Like Bel Geddes, Noyes liked to create both objects and the spaces that were used to display those objects. He conceived the idea that computer machine rooms were actually display areas. He designed machine rooms for IBM that were clean, white, and marked by a rectangular grid. He wanted nothing in the room to interfere with the opportunity to view the machines. "If you get at the heart of the matter," Noyes wrote, "what IBM really does is to help man extend his control over the environment."

For the computers themselves, Noyes stipulated that they would be housed in simple white boxes with minimal decoration. As well as any IBM engineer, he knew that the computers did not naturally fit into rectangular boxes, but he did not want his design to give any hint that the IBM products were in any way mechanical. They would have no visible fans, no moving parts beyond the tape drives, not even a smell of lubricating oil if that could be hidden.

From his position at IBM, Noyes influenced the entire industry. Some vendors, such as Westinghouse, hired him to design their machines. Others, such as Burroughs and NCR, copied his designs. He injected his ideas into popular culture through the 1968 movie *2001: A Space Odyssey*. Noyes served as artistic designer for that movie and created spaceship interiors that looked like IBM computer rooms. These interiors had nothing in common with the spacecraft of the age, with their switches, dials, and utilitarian colors. They had bright white walls, undecorated surfaces, grid floors, and even the modernist furniture Noyes liked to purchase for IBM offices from the noted firm Herman Miller.

The computers of the 1960s did not look futuristic because digital technology made them look that way. They were presented in clean, simple designs because Eliot Noyes believed that such a design suggested the future of computing technology.

Noyes died in 1977, but he would appreciate the current design of computers. Black and silver rectangles. No wires, no buttons. That is the way the future should look. Tamara's future will begin in three weeks, when her firstborn son is scheduled to arrive. We hope that we will be able to continue our conversations, but such a goal will likely vanish in the presence of her new responsibilities. I don't know how she is preparing her new home in anticipation of the baby's arrival, but I suspect that she will be fully aware of the messages that her choice of decor will communicate. We cover the walls of nurseries with primary colors and images of characters owned by the Disney Corporation to signify that a baby lives in that room, a baby who will spend most of his or her life in the future.

Of course, a baby does not see the nursery décor as representing the future. If anything, children eventually come to associate the design of their nursery with the past, with the time when they were young, immature, and helpless. Eventually, they will demand that their room be redecorated with new colors and pictures of pirates, princesses, software engineers, or something that points to their future, their hope to make a name for themselves, to push back the wilderness, to overcome the law of unrealistic goals.

03
The Dictator and His Web Design

You come ready for a fight. A switchblade in a boot. A length of chain casually deposited in a briefcase. A pry bar hidden under a raincoat. After all, few settings are more deadly, more provocative, more ready to explode into a riot than a committee called for the purpose of redesigning a website. On three different occasions I have been part of such a committee, one of which was convened so long ago that it was probably charged with creating our first organizational website. On each occasion, participants joined the meeting warily, as if they sensed what was about to happen.

All of these meetings were chaired by some combination of technical people, graphic designers, and content editors. They tended to have a confident demeanor, as if the task at hand was the easiest thing in the world, even though they knew that the timelines were short, the resources were dear, and the deadlines were immovable. Each time, one of the leaders—usually the content editor—asked us to introduce ourselves. Around the room we went. "Hello, my name is…" "I've been with the company for one year, ten years, or no time at all." "I work for a unit that is identified by an acronym that is completely familiar to me but incomprehensible to the rest of you."

The preliminary discussion maintains the semblance of order. We smile and applaud. The first sign of trouble comes when we turn to the graphics designer for a suggestion of what is going to come. The designer, a starcrossed youth of 25 or 19 or maybe even 15, lacks the experience to know the magnitude of the fight that is in the offing. He or she, the gender does not matter, will try to guide the group through a few sample pages to illustrate the bright and bold concepts that will mark the new site. "This is not the final version," the designers always affirm with more confidence than they feel, "we still have a chance to make adjustments."

Good designers will do everything to avoid offense. They will craft a page for a mythical unit, the Division of Profitable Activities, although everyone will be suspicious that such an office is modeled on a rival group. The faux Latin text only increases suspicion among the committee members.

"Lorem ipsum blah blah blah," it reads. The text is derived from Cicero's treatise on the division between good and evil, "Bonorum et Malorum," but it actually dwells in that misty netherland between the two worlds. Nothing is good or bad but thinking makes it so.

At this point, someone will claim a fault in the design. "We have always had a direct link from the homepage." "We can't use this navigation structure." "We've always been considered an independent organization." "The design hides our workflow." Finally, the ultimate insult is launched into the air. "That structure will decrease our page rank." And so the fight begins. Offense is taken. Weapons are drawn. Blood is shed. The civil blood that makes civil hands unclean.

Such conflict is among the most confusing of modern warfare because it cannot be easily divided into a pair of conflicting sides. No Capulets and Montagues. No Sharks and Jets. Just a collection of rival warriors clashing over their roles in the organizational structure, roles symbolized by the links between webpages. In general, the committee leadership is powerless to stop the conflict. Should they attempt to discipline the group, they will find the combatants allied in a brief moment of unity against them.

Traditional management theories identify such fights as the second part of a four-stage development process for small groups, the forming-storming-norming-performing steps that psychologist Bruce Tuckman identified in the 1960s. "Group members become hostile toward one another as a means of expressing their individuality and resisting the formation of group structure," Tuckman claimed.

In Tuckman's model, committee members must go through a period in which they express their objections to the collaboration in emotional terms (the storming stage) before they can learn to work together (norming) and actually accomplish their goals (performing). Such an abstraction is useful in helping guide committees, even those involved with Web design, to complete their work. However, Web design is marked by forces that can agitate a committee and prevent it from completely focusing on the task at hand. Groups that design websites must deal with issues of identity. Each decision can affect the place that individuals hold in the organizational structure, the tasks they can perform, and the status they hold.

In my last bout with a Web design committee, I lost patience with the project directors. I felt that I didn't have time for such activities. We needed a stronger leader, I argued, someone who could march the group through the work and exact the needed compromises along the way.

The committee convener patiently listened to my complaints, promised a minor adjustment, and restated my assignment for the coming week. I ended the conversation with a feeling of self-righteousness, but that lasted only a moment. Had I actually won the battle, I pondered, or was my outburst just part of the process?

Not that long ago, in the month that marked the opening of the United Nations General Assembly, I had the opportunity to see how websites are developed in a more restrictive environment. At that time, I was asked to have lunch with the Web developer for a well-known military strongman, the Great and

Dear Leader of his people, a modestly prosperous but highly ineffective state that cannot maintain peace in its borders without a few strategically timed political assassinations each year.

The Great and Dear Leader had come to the US to explain his point of view to the citizens of the world and had decided to visit a few American universities, including my own, so that he might be in better touch with global youth. With the Great and Dear Leader came an entourage of about 30 individuals. It included several generals and ministers, the governor of a troubled region, a docile member of the political opposition, and an assortment of sisters, cousins, and aunts.

The entourage also included the Chief Information Officer of the Great and Dear Leader, who was assigned to my care. The Chief Information Officer proved to be an open and affable individual. He had just completed a personal website for the Great and Dear Leader and was most anxious to talk about his accomplishments. For ten or 15 minutes, he talked about the structure of the new site, the innovations that he had personally directed, and the tremendous response to the design.

"Did you design the pages or did you have a consultant?" I queried.

"It was mostly done by our staff in the London office," he explained. "All of our government's information technology work is done in London."

He further explained that he lived in London and visited the capital of the Great and Dear Leader only two or three times a month. As he talked, his voice slipped into a tone of reluctant disdain. He clearly loved his country but didn't think much of the workers employed in his government. He visited them only when necessary. He never went to listen. He only went to give orders that they would not accept over the phone.

That evening, I explored the Great and Dear Leader's website. It was a simplistic and silly site that compared badly to the Web presence associated with an American political party or even a regional plumbing supply business. It had clearly been modeled on a commercial site. All of the photographs looked like they came from advertisements. The persons in the photographs were unnaturally happy, unusually clean, and unapologetically trying to draw your attention to some accomplishment of the Great and Dear Leader.

I poked through the speeches, looked at the photo albums, and read the news releases. The site even had a store, where visitors could purchase memorabilia of the Great and Dear Leader, including photographs, desk sets, coffee mugs, and tee shirts.

"Click here to go to the Checkout," read the store page, "where you may purchase your goods to support the mighty revolution." When I finished, I concluded that the Great and Dear Leader's website was going to attract few visitors. Indeed, the visitor count on one page was barely into four digits.

AS WEB TECHNOLOGY MOVED FROM the laboratory to the public sphere, website design moved from being the product of a single person to become the responsibility of a group. Early "websites were often designed, built and managed by a single individual through sheer force of will," wrote two pioneers in the field. "The webmaster was responsible for assembling and organizing the content, designing the graphics," and writing all of the code.

The original developers of Web technology did not see a role for a Web designer. If anything, they felt that a website would naturally capture the structure of the organization that created it. "We should work toward a universal linked information system," argued Tim Berners-Lee, the original proposer of the World Wide Web. "The aim would be to allow a place to be found for any information or reference which one felt was important, and a way of finding it afterwards." In making his case, he downplayed those very elements of the system that would make it valuable in the public and commercial worlds. Generality "and portability are more important," he claimed, "than fancy graphics techniques and complex extra facilities."

Yet it was the combination of graphics and hyperlinks that brought emotional responses from early Web users. I recall a demonstration in 1992 or 1993 for senior administrators that drew audible gasps from the audience. They even burst into laughter when a link took the machine to a famous and slightly naughty work of art rather than to the homepage of the graduate student who was operating the demonstration.

Emotional responses generate experimentation. Emotional users were intrigued with the new Web technology and were interested in seeing what it could do. In some cases, the experiments produced new designs or even additions to the portfolio of Web tools. In many others, they led nowhere good. "When I first started doing Web work back in 1994, the <BLINK> tag was all the rage," complained an early Web designer.

"Everything had to blink, because if it didn't, it obviously wasn't important." Of course, these Web experiments included those that failed to produce anything of value, ultimately cooling emotional responses to the technology and starting the process of building standards for Web practice. Some of the first standards involved the process of developing new sites. "Start by assembling the people who will work on developing the site," recommended one handbook. "If this is just you, bring some other folks on board so you will have a broader set of perspectives to draw on."

By 2000 or 2001, the Web had ceased to be a global novelty and was no longer evoking the kind of emotional response that it had created eight or six or even four years before. At this point, formal standards for Web design began to appear. The IEEE released its standard in 2002.

"The recommended practices and requirements set forth in this [standard] are aimed to reduce the risks associated with webpage investments," it explained. "The value of Web-based operations is the delivery of the right information and services to the right persons at the right time with the least amount of effort."

Standards for Web design brought guidelines for employment as Web designers. Only a decade ago, those who were considering a career in Web design were pioneers and entrepreneurs, people who were equally interested in defining a new kind of job and in creating Web content. Such days have passed. Web development is now a standard job category with a standard description (US SOC 2010 15-1134). Perhaps more tellingly, teenagers are starting to consider Web design as an appropriate career, as a way for them to find a place in society.

RECENTLY, I HAVE MET TWO individuals who were training for a career in Web design: Ion, a waitress at the local coffee shop, and Jake, a farm worker who helped me build a retaining wall on my sister's property last summer.

Both have spoken about the kind of training they are receiving to prepare themselves for their future and the kind of certification they will receive when they are ready for employment. Both have prepared "standard portfolios" to advertise their skills.

As I have gotten to know both Ion and Jake, I have wondered if either of them would be able to control the kind of emotional outbursts that my Web design committees have produced. Ion may possess the character to do this kind of work as she has had to deal with the tantrums that come from customers who fail to receive the exact kind of sweetened coffee exactly when they want it. Jake is a bit of an idealist but he has seen enough hardship to know that the world is not easy.

Neither of them has talked about this aspect of their future careers, but both learned the nature of hierarchies from the bottom side, from clearing dirty dishes from the tables of rude customers and digging holes on mercilessly hot days. The two have faith that they will find a better place in society, a place with the authority they will need to do their work.

04
Bad Alignment

It wasn't working. Nothing was in alignment. The coffee was cold, the muffins were stale, and the software presentation was a forced march through a PowerPoint landscape denuded of life. Three hours had passed, and no civilization could be seen on the horizon. In command of the podium was a perky salesperson named Alena who led us through slide after slide with an inflection to her voice that suggested ideas of great magnitude where no new ideas could be heard. The eight of us on the committee sat in stone cold silence, praying that an all-merciful Divine Being would send a band of pirates to attack our meeting, seize this woman, and hold her hostage in a distant country.

We held no personal grudge against Alena. We could find no fault in her person or character. However, we could all see that the poor dear wasn't succeeding in the task assigned to her. As the representative of her employer, she was supposed to educate our committee and harmonize our aspirations with her company's goals, to show us that they would meet our needs when we met theirs. Such a task isn't easy, as it demands analysis, imagination, and more than a little empathy. These qualities aren't usually associated with pirates, but we were willing to take our chances. An open and unilateral statement of criminal assessment would have been far preferable to the presentation we were attending.

The problem of communicating the benefits of technology has bedeviled the industrial age from its inception. So often, new technology is conceived in terms of engineering specifications: processor speeds, data formats, power consumption, manufacturing costs. Rarely do potential customers see technology with the same eyes. They will be interested in new devices only if it somehow makes their lives better—if it moves them toward a goal they hold for themselves, their family, their company. As I watched the sales presentation, I could see that Alena had clearly been schooled in sales techniques that had clearly been derived from the classic sales cycle of John Henry Patterson (1844–1922), though she probably knew little about the origins of this approach.

Patterson, the president of the National Cash Register Company (NCR), was an early leader of the industrial age. He was one of the first thinkers to understand the problem of explaining new technologies to nontechnical audiences. His novel technology, the cash register, was a marvel of mechanical engineering and attracted as much attention as the personal computer of a century later. Yet initially, that clever engineering—the high-precision gears, the multiple linkages, the novel bearing designs—wasn't sufficient to attract more than a few paying customers. When new customers were first introduced to the machine, with its engraved case and polished brass, they would usually react with the simple question, "What's in it for me?"

Patterson developed a four-step cycle for connecting the technology of cash registers with his customers' goals and drilled this cycle into his stales staff. The steps were easy to remember: identify and propose, demonstrate and close. They were much harder to follow.

The first step in the process required the salespeople to listen to their customers and discover their human needs. Did they feel that they were in control of their business? Were they earning enough to support their family? Were they spending too much time at their work? After identifying such issues, Patterson's salespeople were to propose ways that cash registers could be used to solve problems and then demonstrate those solutions. For example, they could show how cash registers could reduce employee theft, simplify accounting, and track expenditures, which in turn would reduce anxiety, simplify labor, strengthen confidence.

The last step of the process, closure of the sale, brought the customer's goals in line with what National Cash Register had to offer. That was the most important part of the process for Patterson. "ABC," he told the National Cash Register representatives: "Always Be Closing."

ALENA CLEARLY UNDERSTOOD THE NEED to close a sale, but she didn't know how to work the other steps of the Patterson sales cycle. She started her presentation by saying that she wanted to listen to us and identify our needs, but she quickly proved that she was much more interested in identifying herself. In the course of 15 minutes, we learned about her academic credentials, the number of years she had worked for the company, the types of schools that had bought software from her, and, if memory serves correctly, the name of the Thai dressmaker who had created the suit she was wearing.

In telling her story, Alena was little different from the other salespeople who had appeared before us. As we listened to them, we had been regaled with corporate histories, stories of programmers who had developed their software, the revenue goals that had been met or exceeded by their regional office. Such stories were impressive at times but showed little analysis and less empathy.

Without identifying our needs, Alena and all the other salespeople had little to propose and less to demonstrate. They wandered through the remaining steps of the Patterson cycle like merchant ships lost on the stormy sea. They would tack toward one idea for a time before shifting to another in the hope that something might catch our attention. Eventually, they became lost and panicked. The first sign of trouble came when they started repeating the phrase, "The software will do whatever you want it to do."

The real evidence was seen in the acceleration of the PowerPoint slides.

At the start of the presentation, they lingered for 30 or 40 second per slide. After the first hour, this dwell time dropped to 15 seconds or 20 at most. As we approached the third hour, slides were flashing on the screen for no more than 5 or 6 seconds. These slides were detailed, technical graphics. Nested matrices. Symantec networks. Predicate calculus. Horn clauses. Each of these ideas flew past our eyes accompanied by the plaintive cry, "whatever you want." "whatever you want."

If Alena had asked me what I wanted to do, my response would have been unequivocal. I wanted to finish my service on the committee as quickly as possible. While I could see an obvious strategy that would have aligned that goal with Alena's hopes, I had to acknowledge that the result wouldn't have been entirely satisfactory to all concerned. Our committee actually had a more noble goal: It had been assembled for the purpose of improving the university's approach to assessment.

In the world of academe, "assessment" is the term for the more prosaic concept of "quality control." Although it's based on ideas that are considerably older, it has been part of higher education since the mid-1990s. It uses educational analyses that were developed in the 1950s and employs a basic tool of quality control, the Shewhart cycle of continuous improvement, which dates to 1931.

The Shewhart cycle is the familiar four-step process that shaped large parts of engineering practice: Plan. Do. Check. Analyze. Repeat. "We like to believe that there is law and order in the world," Shewhart wrote. "We seek causal explanations of phenomena so that we may predict the nature of these same phenomena at any future time." He knew that sometimes natural phenomena could hide its operations, but he also had great faith in the analytic powers of the human mind. To support this faith, he liked to quote the poet of the English Enlightenment, Alexander Pope:

> All Nature is but Art, unknown to thee;
> All chance, direction, which thou canst not see;
> All discord, harmony not understood;
> All partial evil, universal good.

Yet, Shewhart didn't accept the mechanistic view of the universal good that was shared by Pope's 18th-century contemporaries. He looked for universal good and hoped to find misapprehended harmonies, but knew that analytic reason couldn't always find them. We "are limited in doing what we want to do," Shewhart explained, because understanding every aspect of even a simple manufacturing task in its entirety "requires almost infinite knowledge." Therefore, quality control required the good engineer to "accept as axiomatic that we cannot do what we want to do and cannot hope to understand why we cannot."

Shewhart developed his cycle in conjunction with a statistical methodology that allowed engineers to search for problems in production and find ways of bringing those problems under control, at least for a short time. This method was well suited for Shewhart's employer, the American Telephone and Telegraph Company (AT&T), because it was a highly complicated business that followed a simple, well-articulated goal: universal service.

When AT&T began expanding in the early 20th century, its leadership concluded that both its customers and its investors would be best served by a company that offered a standard telephone service across the US and could dominate every market in which it operated. This goal required a uniformity beyond the scope of the accomplishments of any company operating at that time. Yet management argued that its goals required "standardized operating methods, plant facilities and equipment," as explained by an early company president, and also "complete harmony and cooperation of operating forces through centralized and common control."

AT&T's common goal simplified the human dynamics of quality control, making it easier for a team of engineers to empathize with the needs of their neighbor. As would any team of engineers, marching through the steps of plan, do, check, and analyze, they would need to understand how other units might view their proposal, which in turn required them to imagine how these units approached the goal of universal service. Of course, such a goal didn't eliminate differences within the corporation, as all employees would interpret universal service in light of their own opinions and aspirations. However, it gave a much stronger foundation for resolving disagreements than the goals found at most universities.

In words that have often been expanded and embellished, a university president once described the modern institution of higher education as a collection of rival, warring tribal factions united by a common heating system. Lacking a common heating system, our school was united by complaints about the parking lots. As most of the members of the assessment committee took public transportation, we were barely united at all.

In spite of our discontent, some of our committee members were comfortable with the academic ideas of quality control and even with the presentations by the software sales teams. In particular, the engineers saw how they might employ these pieces of software as they had the longest history with educational assessment. Engineering faculty began developing the concepts of educational quality control at roughly the same time that Shewhart developed his methods for AT&T.

In 1929, the Carnegie Foundation for Teaching established a committee to investigate the state of engineering education. To chair the committee, they recruited William Wickenden (1892–1947), who had been a senior manager at AT&T and was then president of the Case School of Applied Science in Cleveland. Wickenden created an extraordinarily detailed plan for his committee. A preliminary plan shows subdivisions of authority, lines of communication, data flows, and responsibility for outcomes. He had grand designs for the committee, "a comprehensive survey of the whole situation—students and graduates, faculty and facilities, curricula and methods, professional engineers and industry, and the economic and social significance of engineering."

In the end, Wickenden's committee produced a sympathetic report. Well before they completed their work, the members concluded that "there were no glaring defects in the contemporaneous policies and methods of engineering education." At the same time, the committee established the idea that education could be studied with the tools of engineering and that education needed to be treated as a process that requires continuous improvement. "There were many readjustments which were needed," the committee concluded. "The situation called not for revolution but evolution." It was a call to apply the ideas of Walter Shewhart: Plan. Do. Check. Analyze. Repeat.

I DON'T KNOW IF ALENA and her team did a formal assessment of their presentation to our committee. If they did, the feedback for their Shewhart cycle would have been swift, brutal, and obvious. We didn't buy their software. If they looked more deeply at our response, they might have discovered that the members of the committee responded in different ways to their presentation. The variations in these responses were determined not only by the different goals of each school, but also by the social structure in which each school operates.

The engineering school, by far the most sympathetic to Alena and her colleagues, is part of a complicated but unified social structure. This structure contains accrediting bodies, engineering societies, and professional exam boards. These groups are used to debating the nature of education and finding common ground among themselves.

By contrast, the International Affairs school abides in an anarchistic landscape and has little experience in working with other institutions to define the goals of higher education. The combative nature of the group is suggested by the titles of its courses: Civil Wars, Terrorism, Military Strategy. It even teaches classes in pirate theory, though we tend to call such courses "Transnational Security Threats" and limit the examples to the modern pirates of Somalia and the Strait of Malacca.

According to the best scholars of the field, pirates are most effective when they can control their operational goals, when they can build a strong bond of empathy among their band. To do this, they usually need the tacit approval of a nation-state, freedom from absent owners (usually achieved by stealing a boat or buying one with stolen funds), and assembling a team that accepts the twin goals of expanding plunder and avoiding capture. The situation doesn't quite parallel the AT&T of the 1930s with its goal of universal service, but it works tolerably well. In this circumstance, they have a simple debate over Shewhart's cycle. Will a new strategy increase the chances of gaining treasure? Will it make them more vulnerable to naval attack? They usually demand a full discussion of all hopes and doubts in such debates.

No pirate wants to worry about the concerns of others in the midst of a raid. Perhaps because of this, they are never available when you need them to disrupt a sales presentation that has gone badly out of alignment.

05
Investing in Ignorance

My younger colleagues would have called it a "random experience," a term they use to describe an event that is unusual or unanticipated rather than an encounter that is probabilistic in nature. I would have characterized the encounter as a harbinger of things to come. Neither description may have been entirely accurate.

I had just gone through the security station of a large government office building when a young man, not that well dressed, came running in my direction and pointed some kind of a digital device toward my face. Using a tone of voice that would be far more appropriate in a sports stadium than an office hallway, he yelled, "Secretary Peterson, do you condemn the Chinese actions on the London Currency Exchange?"

I looked at the device. It had a little red light. I looked at the young man. His glare clearly was intended to intimidate me into responding to his question. "Excuse me?" I said. It was the only thing that came to mind.

"Secretary Peterson," the young man exclaimed, "do you reject the efforts of the Chinese government to keep the value of its yuan artificially low?"

Other disheveled youths, some men, some women, were starting to gather around me. Each was pulling a digital device from a purse or pocket and aiming it at me in a vaguely threatening way. It took a moment or two for me to realize that I was facing an impromptu press conference. I was tempted to play the role that was being offered me and make some kind of grand pronouncement. However, I knew, deep in my heart, that I would only be compounding a mistaken identity with a misguided action.

"You've got the wrong guy," I said before I started to walk away.

I could see that not all within the group believed me, but they began to switch off their little data-gathering devices and put them away.

When I finally reached my destination, I quickly realized that I hadn't appreciated the nature of the day's event. I thought I had been invited to an informal discussion of how the government was supporting certain aspects of technology development. Instead, I was ushered into the building's large formal meeting room, one that had figured prominently in many a televised investigation. When I settled into the seat labeled "Dr. Grier, IEEE Computer Society," I wondered if I should lean into my microphone and intone the words, "The question is, what did the President know, and when did he know it?"

As I had earlier that morning, I resisted temptation. Judging those around me, I concluded that many wouldn't appreciate the reference to the distant investigation of Presidential misdeed. Those who would likely had heard others attempt to make the same joke. It's better to fail conventionally than to attempt to succeed unconventionally, especially if the odds of succeeding unconventionally appear to be low.

WE SOON SETTLED INTO THE day's work. A group of congressional staffers and consultants sat on one side of the room, asking questions and taking notes. The rest of us, experts we were called, sat on the other side and spoke our piece. Little time passed before it was fairly clear that the staff members were using us to test a certain hypothesis. The questions leaned a little too much in one direction and were prefaced with phrases such as "Don't you think the government should do this?" and "Wouldn't it be wrong for the Department of Defense to do that?"

The staff was probably right to use the meeting as an event to test ideas. Open-ended discussions are generally far too random to be of much good as they are simply the Brownian motion of the mind. Ideas ricochet around the room from speaker to speaker. They get sucked into the systematically placed microphones and eventually become the definitive footnote to support some crucial government policy.

At the same time, I could see that the structured nature of the day was leading our discussion into well-explored channels. I heard more than a few speeches, well-conceived and earnestly delivered, that added nothing to articles the speakers had published in Computer Society magazines or in the periodicals of other professional societies.

Midway through the afternoon, I became tired of the conventional direction of the discussion and decided that I would attempt to push it into a new direction. I spoke for a bit about historical lessons, organizational failures, and managerial issues that hadn't been included in others' presentations. The meeting halted for a moment as the participants tried to process my ideas, but it soon regained its momentum and continued on its prior course. I had spoken too late. The participants had already reached a consensus about the nature of the meeting, and nothing was going to change it.

Most research efforts deal with expanding quantities of information. More data. More calculations. More bandwidth. Yet, as we've learned all too well, large amounts of data aren't always a blessing. We can capture lots of data, but we can't always make sense of it. Using a phrase that was common among the early Internet developers, one researcher noted that the problem of our age wasn't learning to drink from a fire hose but "learning how to pick the olives from a flood of martinis being pumped through a fire hose." As clever as such a characterization might be, it misses a key point. Olive recognition is a relatively low-level intellectual task. It's easy to develop olive filters that can separate fruit from alcohol and even create refined versions that can distinguish between oil-cured and brine-cured olives, pimiento stuffed and almond stuffed, and even flag the occasional maraschino cherry that wanders its misplaced way through this analogy.

Data recognition is a median intellectual skill. It occupies the middle tier of modern taxonomies of knowledge. A recent discussion of educational objectives places filtering or matching on the third level of their six-level hierarchy. It's "perhaps the most basic of all aspects of information processing," they write. On the way upward, their scale passes through Knowledge Usage (level 4), Metacognition (process monitoring and goal setting, level 5), and self-system thinking (assessing importance and efficacy, level 6). As the scale advances, it introduces new difficulties and uncertainties. When working on problems of the highest level, such as setting policy goals or assessing the value of an entire process, it's easy to discover how uncertain judgments can be and how often they can be based on arbitrary or unanticipated knowledge.

Even the lower levels of intellectual activity can involve more uncertainty than we care to admit. Pattern matching, the kind of work that we do to recognize a melody, a picture, or the face of an influential member of the president's cabinet, is done with a fair amount of probability. Free markets, which we identify as a standard of transparency, can obscure as much as they present and force buyers and sellers to make judgments based on imperfect information.

IN RECENT YEARS I'VE BEEN following the growth of imperfect information markets that are known as blind or black-pool markets. These markets are the black boxes of trade, as they hide information to protect the value of some good or service. For example, an insurance company needs to dispose of a large block of stock, a country needs to buy an unusual amount of wheat, or a petroleum refiner needs to limit the fluctuations of its raw materials. In all of these cases, the knowledge that some entity was trying to buy or sell a large asset would alter the market in a way that would be detrimental to the entity that initiated the transaction. The insurance company would lose money against the book value of a large asset. The country would find it too expensive to feed its people. A refinery could find itself in a position of paying a lot of money for little guarantee.

Blind markets protect transactions by announcing only the possibility of a sale. Stock is available. Wheat is desired. Quantities aren't mentioned. Sometimes qualities are obscured and prices taken from other markets. Those who wish to participate in such a market can announce that they want to take advantage of the opportunity and state what quantity they have to buy or sell. The price is protected through ignorance. A participant will never know the identity of the other parties or how big the transaction might have been. In the past decade, such markets have become popular. A recent study estimates that they may account for 20 percent of the volume of equity trades in the US.

Of course, ignorance is a weak ally at best, even when it's bolstered by high-speed networks, large processors, and modern cryptography. It's an especially poor defense against those who need only a few small hints about the activity within the blind market. The strategy for getting information out of blind markets is similar to that of card counting in the game of blackjack. The rules of blackjack are such that the odds of winning vary according to the ratio of high-value to low-value cards that have been dealt.

Well-trained players can simply count the cards as they're dealt, categorizing them as low- or high-value according to whatever system they choose to adapt. When the odds go in their favor, the players bet heavily. When the odds are against them, they pull their chips into a circle and bide their time.

Card counting doesn't guarantee a string of wins at the card table. It only increases the probability of a win. Still, card counters who bet at a level that doesn't threaten their initial stake will usually end the day with more money than when they started. I should note that card counting is illegal in most gambling venues. Casinos can eject gamblers who they believe to be counting cards.

The strategy for dealing with blind markets is a little more complicated than card-counting techniques. It borrows heavily from the field of biostatistics and involves a process of proposing large transactions and then assessing the information of the final trade. It requires patience, a large stake, and an inclination that a certain proposed transaction might be sitting on top of a very large asset. It also requires moving quickly, as any advantage vanishes when the other partner in the deal realizes what you're doing. In the end, the best that you can hope to do is to beat the market, to make more money on the transaction than the rules of the blind market would allow.

Shortly after my governmental appearance, I was discussing the event with Michael, a colleague who's an especially energetic Internet partisan. He interpreted the event in light of the old saw attributed to American writer Stewart Brand: "all information wants to be free." In response, I argued that information is a fairly dumb beast that has neither wants nor desires but is more than willing to be kept chained to a post in the yard and fed a diet consisting of nothing more than a bowl of tepid water and a handful of parched meal.

Michael objected to this characterization and vigorously defended the new dynamic of the Information Age. He argued that digital technology has brought unprecedented amounts of information to the world at costs that were unimaginable even a decade ago. He even made a reference that compared the amount of material that circulates in one second on the Internet to the entire body of publications that existed prior to 1946, a remarkably erudite image. When I offered a compliment, Michael admitted that he found the reference on the Internet. Of course, information isn't always knowledge and usually falls far short of wisdom, as well as the more formal categories of metacognition and self-system thinking. The task of navigating that hierarchy is harder than we would like to think and involves more uncertainty than we care to admit.

While I certainly have an opinion about the market value of the yuan, I have to admit that this opinion is nothing more than a random thought, as we now use the word random. It is founded on certain ignorance and would require a substantial investment to raise it to the level of a useful idea.

Exit
On Top of the News

Once, Peter's work was easy to find: Front page of the daily news. Above the fold. Prime real estate for the best stories. His writing might be illustrated with a provocative picture or marked by a boldface headline containing a hint of a pun, but it was always signed with a byline that noted his name, his location, and the all-important title, "Staff Writer."

Such placement has become increasingly difficult to get. Step by faltering step, the front page has been vanishing from the American news industry. The members of the press have always admitted that their product had a limited lifetime, providing a source of vital information one day and a wrapper for fish the next. The laws of the marketplace have eroded the position of newspapers as a source of vital information, and public health laws have limited the role of the newspaper as a container for fresh food.

Day after day, we hear stories of papers firing their writers, merging with other organizations, stopping their presses. Long before this book was set in type, Peter's paper, after 100 years of operation, published its last paper issue, its last front page.

Many reporters have reacted to the changes in their industry by embracing the technology of the young, hoping that they can meld new tools with middle-age methodologies and somehow create a new audience. They Tweet. They blog. They post their ideas on Facebook. They rant about the state of affairs in YouTube clips.

"So what are you going to do to attract an audience?" I asked Peter the other day. I had just learned that his paper was going to continue operations as a 24-hour news site on the Web. I expected that he might have a different approach, one that rejected the fearful experimentation of his peers. He had taken a decade to embrace word processing and had never really been comfortable with the fax machine.

"I've been testing the Google and Yahoo news services," was his reply. "I'm trying to determine how to get a story positioned at the top of their lists."

The modern news services assess the success of a news story with a set of disciplined metrics. They count the number of links to a story and track the quantity of additional postings, unduplicated visits, and click-throughs. These items are similar to the information that traditional editors used to shape the print stories, information that included letters to the editor, subscriptions, and advertising sales. Despite their similarity, the new metrics differ from the old because of two properties that we have come to associate with the Information Age: speed and specificity. Judgment comes quickly, and it praises or condemns without mercy.

IN THE RISE OF THE Internet, many saw an opportunity for newspapers. "We feel that the delivery of electronic news is well suited to exploit the promised high bandwidth, switched, interactive communication facilities of the information highway," wrote one research team in those early networked days of 1994. This group foretold many of the features that we have come to associate with Internet news, including the selective delivery of content, individual collections of stories, and the inclusion of video. However, they failed to appreciate the importance of feedback to the news industry. They acknowledged that two-way communication allowed for "interactive and targeted advertising" and suggested that it might create new forms of "items as found in newspapers, such as bridge hands, crossword puzzles, and classified ads."

Yet, well before the Internet, both scholars and practical journalists had recognized that the news business fundamentally involved feedback. "In the communications process," wrote the pioneering scholar Ithiel de Sola Pool (1917–1984), "effects go both ways: the audience also affects the communicator." De Sola Pool argued that feedback need not be instantaneous. Information from readers could influence a reporter days or months after the original contact.

Prior to the latter part of the 20th century, most American papers gathered feedback from their community through a loosely defined network of people and connections. Most papers of the age were family owned and strongly rooted in a narrow geographic area. "Publishers saw themselves as guardians of age-old editorial standards," wrote media historian Elizabeth Neiva, "and viewed their papers as local institutions, not as commercial enterprises."

The publishers generally knew all of their major advertisers personally and were often acquainted, through friendship or animosity, with the major civic figures. Editors had learned the neighborhoods and could predict how a story would be received in each part of town.

As long as a paper was content to spread the news in its own backyard, it could rely on making decisions based on the opinions and gossip that flowed into its offices. Only those institutions that had national aspirations had to develop a systematic process of analyzing feedback from their readers. One of the early publications to develop an office to analyze the opinions of its subscribers was the *Literary Digest*.

Founded in 1890, the *Literary Digest* offered a compendium of stories culled from local papers and overlaid with self-congratulatory commentary that might have found a place in the modern blogosphere. Desiring the twin advantages of wealth and influence, *Digest* editors decided that they would attempt to expand the publication into a national periodical in the early years of the 20th century. To get a sense of their audience, they established an analysis office staffed with a dozen women and an equal number of hand-cranked adding machines.

Beginning in 1916, these women processed data from subscription records and from survey cards that were regularly inserted into each issue. These surveys asked for demographic information and also for opinions on the issues of the day: political contests, Prohibition, tax reduction. The *Digest* featured summaries of these opinions in an effort to draw readers. "We merely collect and tabulate the figures with entire impartiality and present them for what they are worth," argued the editors. These features were highly popular. The quadrennial presidential poll always attracted a new surge of subscribers.

From the analyses, the *Digest's* editors concluded that their readership came from the wealthier segments of the middle class. They believed that their readers were well-informed, had opinions on global events, and cherished ambitions to own the more expensive consumer items of the day: automobiles, home appliances, fine clothing. The editors were particularly successful in convincing the automobile industry to advertise in their publication.

Over 16 years, the *Digest's* analysis office grew bold in both scale and scope. "Literally thousands of people are employed in the colossal task of printing, addressing, stamping, distributing, and tabulation," bragged the editors in 1932. They also claimed that their work had an "almost frightful precision" and represented a "prediction of excellence seldom equaled."

As the 1930s progressed, the world turned. The smart young readers of the prior decade, the fine-looking swells and the fashionable women, had married, retreated into middle age, and accepted the constraints of the Great Depression. They were no longer buying Pierce Arrow automobiles or dresses from Lord & Taylor.

Nonetheless, the analysis office, with its burgeoning staff, could not see such changes. In the editors' assessment, the attitudes of the 1920s were still to be found among their subscribers. They lacked the technology and the methodology to see what was happening.

The advertisers were the first to grasp that the *Literary Digest* editors were no longer in touch with the nation. Seeing their feedback written in figures of profit and loss, they began to withdraw from the periodical. By the middle of 1936, the company was deeply in debt. It owed almost $100,000 for paper and printing costs alone. Its biggest asset was the information about its subscribers, which it leased for marketing and direct sales. The income from this information was not enough to stave off bankruptcy, which came after the *Digest's* analysis office badly misprojected the results of that fall's presidential election.

Although the story of the *Literary Digest* is usually told in terms of its failure to predict Franklin Roosevelt's victory in 1936, it also is a story of changing technologies and the valuation of intellectual assets. As the *Digest* was failing, other organizations were starting to produce analyses of consumer information by using punched cards, tabulators, and telegraph machines. These reports were less expensive and more detailed than the information the *Digest* produced. At its demise, the *Digest* had data on some 300,000 individuals that was summarized on mimeographed forms and held in manila folders.

Even a few years before, such information could be leased to a marketing firm for $15 per 1,000 records. Had it been punched on cards, it might have fetched a dime for a hundred names. In a form that had suddenly become outmoded, this information was worthless.

UNFORTUNATELY, THE *LITERARY DIGEST* PRESENTS no easy lessons to the modern newsroom. The *Digest* may have failed because the editors did not use the best information technology of its age to gauge the opinions of its readers, but it also failed because it didn't know what to do with the information that it had. Its staff did not have the ability to recognize the meaning of the data the *Digest*'s analysis office was collecting. Many periodicals have faced this struggle at some point in their history, and at least a few news organizations have found new information technology to be a destabilizing force, tools that make the company more vulnerable to market forces.

The punched card equipment that the *Digest* never embraced strengthened the power of advertisers at the expense of the newspaper. Advertisers quickly grasped that the reports produced by this equipment could identify not only the individuals who were likely to purchase their goods and services but also the readers who had no interest or ability to patronize their businesses. Pointing to this last group of readers as "waste subscribers," they would demand reductions in advertising rates.

Electronic computers further accelerated the demise of the independent newspaper. The acceleration was inadvertent, a side effect of an effort to reduce labor costs and make news organizations more efficient. The new efficiency, seen in computerized typesetting and automatic content management, increased the value of newspapers and encouraged owners to sell their business. "If you do not sell prior to death to put your estate in order," complained one owner, "your heirs will be forced to sell after your death to pay taxes." During the 20-year period in which small papers adopted this technology, the number of family-owned newspapers dropped from 1,300 to 700.

The Internet proved to be a particularly destructive force to the daily paper because publishers simply did not know how to fit it into their business operations. In the early 1990s, a half-dozen major newspapers concluded that they should not only publish information electronically but that their electronic publication effort should operate as a provider of Internet services. Customers would not go to the Internet to find their papers. They would dial into their paper to find Internet services.

It is not hard to understand why the Internet service model appealed to publishers. It had been validated by companies such as Compuserve and America Online, and it put their content directly in front of their subscribers. "We didn't want to be a storefront in someone else's shopping mall," stated one publisher.

In the summer of 1995, the *Washington Post* unveiled its version of the Internet service, which was called *Digital Ink*. The *Post* management advertised the service heavily, praising its benefits in the pages of their own paper, on the airwaves of local radio stations, and even on the sides of local buses. "If you don't get it, you don't get it," was their confident slogan.

However, few people ever decided that they needed to get *Digital Ink*. It began operation that summer slowly, and with faltering steps it stumbled through the fall, revealing its weaknesses to all. By spring, the *Washington Post* had determined that the service was unlikely to attract more than 11,000 subscribers and started to replace it with a conventional Internet webpage.

ONE MORNING EARLIER THIS YEAR, Peter called me to ask for some information. "What is the traffic like downtown?" he asked. I walked out to the edge of the sidewalk and looked up and down the street. A line of buses was parked in the curb lane, but cars were still moving easily. As I looked toward the intersection, I spied the familiar gray ball of a traffic camera. Peter could have gleaned all the information he needed from the district transportation website.

"Not bad," I responded, "but busier than an ordinary holiday. Probably more like a weekday."

"Good," he said. "We'll be heading downtown soon. Perhaps we'll see you."

"Us and two million other people," I added as we ended the conversation.

I was surprised when Peter said that he was coming to the city to cover the major social event of the winter, the inauguration of a new US president. He does not have a history of enjoying large crowds, and he has never spoken well of the trip from his home to the office. I assumed that he would be able to write his story for the day from the comfort of his home: Exile his boys to the backyard. Eject the beagles from his den. Download a few press releases. Watch events on cable TV. Fire up the computer, and pound out 650 words.

"It's the byline," he explained when I later questioned his reason for coming to the city. If he wrote the piece from his home, he explained, the byline would have to say "Quaint Ethnic City" rather than "Important Global Capital." No one would credit a piece that admitted to being written at a distance of 50 miles from its subject. It wouldn't be on Google's top list. It wouldn't be on the front page. It wouldn't be above the fold. It wouldn't be read. Feedback. Not a cancelled subscription or an inflammatory letter to the editor—the feedback of the Information Age. The feedback that can get you to the top of the news.

Chapter III:
The Exercise of Power

My God.
That'll be the second power station I've paid for this winter.

Absurd Person Singular (1974)
Alan Ayckbourne

Introduction
Doug the Rocket Scientist

The problem was fatigue. The goal was rest. The solution was easy. All I needed to do was to stand up and take my leave. All of us were ready for sleep. I had just taken a five hour flight from the East Coast. Doug the Rocket Scientist had scheduled a bicycle ride for the morning. Chery, whose diurnal schedule follows the orbit of the news rather than the rise and fall of the sun, was just a few hours from the ringing alarm that would start her commute across the darkened city. Yet I didn't move, and neither of them gave me any encouragement. We were living in that moment of addictive friendship, those times when every word that passes around the circle is sweet. You dare not leave the conversation because you fear that some beautiful lesson will be offered and that you will never have a chance to learn of it again.

Finally, the conversation began to flag as the old devil of entropy began to pull us into his grasp. I suggested that it was time to get some rest. Doug seemed to agree and mentioned the hour when he would meet his cycling partner. I was starting to stand when Doug added a remark that seemed to end the evening.

"I need you to look at something tomorrow," he said.

"Sure," I replied. I had long served as a witness for Doug's technical ideas. I assumed that I would find a fat envelope of descriptions and sketches at the breakfast table for me to review.

Doug looked at Chery and then back at me and said, "It's my testimony for the City Council."

"Really," I said. "Testimony about what?"

"Green energy," was the response.

"A noble cause," was my remark. "What are you trying to do?"

"Get them to understand the value of environmentally friendly energy production so that they will make good decisions in the future," Doug said.

It was my turn to look at Chery. I am not always the best at discerning her thoughts, but I guessed that the two of them had disagreed about this subject and that I was being asked to arbitrate. If that was true, I had a choice between two outcomes. I could stand for virtue and the rest that we all needed by declaring the day at an end and heading for bed, or I could choose the hypocritical strategy of attempting to teach Doug the basic lessons of public decision-making so that he would not make a fool of himself in front of a minor civic body in southern California.

I chose hypocrisy. One always does when one is with friends.

As my text for the lesson, I chose Sam Rayburn's famous line about Texas politicians who take your money, drink your whiskey, steal your women, and vote against you anyway. The original quote is slightly more vulgar but I didn't feel that the extra emphasis would have done anything to convince Doug of its truth. I merely wanted Doug to understand that in practical politics, you don't care if people agree with you, or reason as you would reason, or even like you. All you want is for them to vote for you.

There, of course, is the hypocrisy. I was trying to teach Doug that he should not attempt to teach the city council. Do as I say, not as I do. Perhaps it was caused by the hour of the night. Perhaps it came from the fatigue of the flight. Perhaps it had no cause beyond the delusions of human friendship.

We argued for two more hours into the night. Doug argued, as idealists always do, that well-informed leaders make well-informed decisions. I pointed to all the obvious examples, but nothing would move him. Finally, unable to keep the lesson going any further and facing an unwilling student, I resorted to the strategy that I should have accepted at the beginning.

"You're plan is very brave," I said.

"Brave?" he asked. "How? I thought you said it was misguided."

"That was early. I now believe it brave," I repeated. "You're going to hazard all your potential influence when the council has no decision before it or perhaps only a minor decision. As I see it, your goal is to be influential over the long term. If you make a fuss now, you will risk being classed with the supplicants who are there to complain that the schools are painted the wrong color or that the red-tailed squirrel should be named the city mascot or that the Motor Vehicle Office should be a perfume-free zone."

"But those are silly issues," he complained.

"Yes," I acknowledged, "but yours could be considered silly as well. Important issues are those that involve large amounts of money, two compelling alternatives, and the likelihood that they will look like idiots if they make the wrong choice."

At that moment, we had a serious decision to make. I called the question and stood. Hearing no one vote in the negative, I slowly walked to my room and embraced the solution of sleep.

SOMETHING SHIFTED IN THE NIGHT. While Doug never entirely accepted my theory of politics, he did start to adjust his own goals. Clearly, he wanted to gain long-term influence and avoid being labeled as a narrow-minded complainer. Yet, the desire to teach still lingered in his mind. He wanted to demonstrate the physical truth behind his position and lead the city council in the way of the angels.

A week or so after my visit, he made his first appearance before the city council and talked about environmentally friendly energy generation, the extended benefits to the city, and a state program that might help support the city in any effort to reduce its electrical consumption. The council was friendly and willing to engage him but clearly not interested in taking any action based on his presentation. It was a lesson that he would have to work harder to engage the group.

At his second appearance, he identified two issued that directly affected the city: utility rates and the city energy budget. He decided that he could not do much about the utilities in the short term but that he could devise plans for reducing electrical consumption in city buildings and in the lights at public parks. These were not the grand ideas that appeared in his diagrams and sketches of new electrical systems. Yet, they were not silly either. They bought him some credibility with the council and achieved my goal of keeping my friend from looking stupid. They may have even saved the city some money, though I cannot guarantee this last claim.

DURING MY SUBSEQUENT VISIT, PERHAPS six or eight months later, Doug and I spent an afternoon walking through a local arboretum. Neither of us is particularly interested in flowers, but we accepted the activity as a strategy for avoiding the fatigue that came from late night discussions. We would divide the day. I would spend the morning with Chery while Doug rode his bicycle. She and I had been friends long before she had met Doug. In the afternoon, Doug and I would go for a walk while Chery attended a yoga session and dealt with other issues. The easiest destination was the neighborhood arboretum.

Far from providing a genial commune with nature, the arboretum encouraged the two of us to engage in our common bad habit: the dissection of mysterious pieces of machinery. I cannot speak for Doug, but I acquired this problem as a child. Time and again, I would be caught with the elements of some device scattered on the floor. Anticipating adult disapproval, I would claim that the thing was obviously ill-constructed, for I had merely been holding it in my hands when it "came apart." Doug may have come by his habits more honestly. When we first met, he kept a metal lathe in his living room and the plans for a high-altitude rocket in his study.

At the arboretum, the park's electric tram presented itself to Doug and me. It was parked next to a small outbuilding and plugged into an electrical outlet. Doug led this disassembly project by asking a simple question: "Could the tram be charged by solar power?" We searched our pockets for tools and found a battered Swiss army knife and a couple of cell phones. Doug raised the hood to look at the motor and told me to slide underneath the tractor and photograph the vehicle specification plate. "It is my new universal way of collecting documentation," he said.

While I was on the ground, he asked me to photograph the electrical connectors, so he could see how it was engineered, and the springs, so that he could estimate the gross weight. When I emerged, he had just finished measuring the roof of the cars in units of cell phone length and was about calculate the amount of power that a set of solar cells could deliver. However, at this point, a park ranger appeared. Her face had frozen into an expression that suggested she was anxious about confronting two well-dressed adults who appeared to be preparing to vandalize her tram.

At this point, Doug behaved as he never would have done in a city council meeting. He did not quite flirt with the ranger but did everything in his power to make her feel comfortable and important. Out came a smile and a business card. He said that he was a member of the Friends of the Arboretum, that he was very interested in helping the group become more environmentally conscious, and that he was very pleased to see the new water recycling systems on the park's toilets. He was on familiar ground.

He guided the ranger by her shoulders and showed her the various parts of her tram. As he identified the batteries, the voltage regulator, the controller, he softly pushed the idea that it would be wonderful for the park to cut its tram free from the electric grid. She was clearly enthralled and seemed more than eager to be his advocate to the management of the facility. The conversation ended with a discussion of park programs and the new garden along the north border.

"Do you think they'll actually add the solar panels?" I asked as we headed home.

"Don't know," he said.

"Do you think it will actually benefit the park?" I continued.

"Sure, it will get them off the grid and save a little bit of fossil fuel."

"Will it save them money?"

"Probably not," he said.

"Will it be a wash?"

"Maybe," he said. "If they run the tram only half full and keep it parked in the full sun rather than under the trees, they might recover the investment in 16 to 18 years. "

"Is that a good deal?"

"Some may not think so," said Doug. Nodding back towards the ranger, he added "But I believe that she does."

"But that doesn't mean that she can do anything about it," I started to say.

"No," he agreed. "We now need to work on the board."

01
The Society for the Promotion of Goodness

The schedule is tight, but I have disciplined it into a workable routine. I leave my office five minutes before noon and march north toward the Society for the Promotion of Goodness as quickly as I can. Whenever possible, I stop at Leo's deli to grab a sandwich. If I don't have something to eat during the lunchtime discussions of technology policy, I will get testy and say something I will later regret. At Leo's, I'm likely to meet one of the other participants in the day's discussion.

Often, I will see Alyssa, a legislative aide to Senator Dingbat, who never tires of reminding the group that she is a scientist; or Leonard, the associate editor of the *Digital Anarchist,* who can recite the entire US Communications Act of 1934 as amended by the Federal Telecom Act of 1996; or Scott, who is the executive secretary of the Transportation Electronics Association and honestly believes Charlie Wilson's dictum of "what is good for General Motors is good for America."

During the discussion, I often take a seat next to the Wikimedia representative. This individual seems to change with every session. It's a young woman one day, a guy with tattoos the next, and a lobbyist in a skirt suit on the third. After the fourth or fifth change, I began to wonder if they had high turnover among their staff or if they allowed the general public to edit their policy representatives like they edit the entries in their encyclopedia.

These discussions are democracy in action—they are the forums where technology policy is debated. At each session, some great thinker will present a new idea that is intended to strengthen the American lead in technology, release industry from the trammels of regulation, promote innovation, or deliver new and important services to ordinary men and women. Following the formal discussion, the members of the audience begin their work. They identify weaknesses, expose favoritism, and propose alternative ideas, which might or might not be any better.

It's a brutal process, but it refines the strategies for the nation's technology. If your idea can't survive the lunch crowd at the Society for the Promotion of Goodness, it will never see the light of day. Several years ago, the topic at one of the Institute luncheons was a proposal to replace the US telecommunications regulations with a new global system based on the open systems interconnection (OSI) reference model. The idea was presented by an individual who could have passed for a professor. He wore a tweed jacket, a striped shirt, and a tie that didn't quite match either.

He spoke softly, but logically, about how telecommunications was now organized in layers that followed the OSI model, and hence we needed to have regulations that also followed that model. He proposed that we establish one set of
independent regulations for the physical layer, another for the data-link layer, a
third for the network layer, and so on. An independent organization would manage each of these sets of regulations. The tweedy little professor was very compelling. His ideas had a force of logic that seemed inevitable. The audience was
quiet, perhaps too quiet. When the presentation came to an end, no one raised
a hand to speak. This calm was a false peace, a pause that suggested a successful
presentation instead of the exact opposite. After 10 or 20 seconds, one member
of the audience stood to make the first assault. Others quickly followed. No part
of the proposal was spared. The economic benefits were torn to shreds. The technological advantages were swallowed in a gulp. The simplicity of administration
was gone in a moment. By the end of the meeting, nothing was left of the carcass
for the vultures to pick.

In common with most debates over technology policy, those discussing the
OSI model fell into one of three camps. The first are the technological determinants, who generally believe that there is a natural law of technology, not unlike
the law of gravity, and that society must shape its goals and policies to fit these
laws. One of the determinants gave a speech that compared the two current versions of the Internet protocol, IPv4 and IPv6, that continued for a much longer
time than one would have anticipated. The oration seemed to have no point beyond suggesting that no technology is a permanent fixture in our world.

The second camp consists of the policy analysts, the aides that will actually be
shaping the legislation that governs the development of technology. This group
believes that engineers are painfully naïve and have not the slightest understanding of how government needs to balance the conflicting political forces that rule
the world. Legislation is a complex thing, they argue, and it can't be trusted to
ignorant individuals. This group was well represented at the debate over the OSI
model. Their representatives would begin their comments by citing a sacred
verse from US telecommunications law and arguing that no technology, no matter how good, had any right to interfere with the law of the land.

I once took an elbow from this crowd as the discussion turned to Internet
governance. I suggested an alternative approach to handling this, one that
would correct a serious flaw of the current system. Barely had the words left my
mouth when I felt the jab that pushed me off balance. Rather than addressing my
ideas, the speaker accused me of slandering the current leaders of the Internet
on national television and that my unwarranted accusations clearly came from

a wicked and evil mind that was bent on destroying civilization as we know it. His comments were supported by two or three others, who agreed that my evil thoughts and intents should be publicly rebuked and punished. Fortunately for me, these discussions were not broadcast on national television but only streamed over the Internet. I knew from talking with a friend at the Institute that few of my colleagues would be watching my humiliation, as the number of viewers of the discussion were in the high two figures. Still, I didn't like being taken to task in a public forum, and I sat out of camera range for the next several sessions.

The final group of participants are the representatives of the trade associations or, as they like to style themselves, members of the advocacy industry. Generally, these individuals are former policy aides who have a dozen clients, a rented office, and a webpage. They are often difficult to understand, as they tend to talk in the jargon of their industry, but they deliver an unmistakable message: "Don't touch my people." Ultimately, this group doomed the fortunes of the OSI policy that had been promoted by the professor in tweed. None of them embraced the idea. They all understood how the current system worked, for good or ill. No one wanted to abandon that system for a new one with unknown consequences.

SOMETIMES, THE LUNCH TIME POLICY discussions are led by a captain of industry, a senior officer of a major corporation. Often, these talks combine the weaknesses of the three major groups that constitute these discussions. They are often full of technical details, marked by aggressive political moves, and underscored by the hint that the world is on the road to ruin because it has not recognized that the interests of the people are indeed one with those of industry. The worst of these talks are those held in the main meeting room of the National Academy of Sciences, which resembles a Masonic Temple. Surrounded by symbols of knowledge and power, the captains will spew forth a 90-minute concoction of opinion and whimsy that benefits no one but themselves.

Thus, I had low expectations when I walked to the Society for the Promotion of Goodness to hear an address by the CEO of one of the major Internet companies. At best, I hoped for a partisan talk on the way the Internet could be used to improve government operations. The captain had been an advisor to one of the recent US presidential candidates. In case the best was not to be my lot, I sat on an aisle so that I could leave early and get back to my office.

The initial signs were not promising. The person to my left was an enthusiastic young man who praised the speaker with words that bordered on the embarrassing. According to my seatmate, the speaker was a man of unparalleled vision and was responsible for the greatest change to civilization since the invention of fire.

I nodded and let his remarks fall to the ground. So this must have been what it was like, I thought, to have been in the audience when the Beatles played for Ed Sullivan or when Frank Sinatra took the stage with Tommy Dorsey. The emotions of the crowd were engaged in a fundamental way that were connected to the popularity of the speaker rather than the logic of his message.

Most of the talk was modest. Praise for the value of the Internet. Hope for the future. Careful avoidance of the legal and policy issues that touched on his company. No comment about the new presidential administration. In spite of the cautiousness of the talk, the audience remained excited. Many erupted in applause during the speech. Several held cell phones aloft to record the event for friends stuck in the office or loved ones remaining at home.

However, eventually the speaker got to a more interesting subject, the distribution of electricity. At first, I dismissed the treatment as obvious and partisan. His firm needed a steady supply of electricity, both for itself and its customers. However, the speaker soon moved into a discussion of a new way to think about electrical transmission. He began explaining this idea with a piece of business hyperbole: "We transmit electricity with the same technology that we had in the 19th century." His point was true, but the idea he used to support it was technically false. The US actually has a much more sophisticated national network than it did 110 years ago, but it still thinks in 19th-century terms. We generate electricity at one point and transmit it to another point, where it is consumed. Over the years we have developed newer and more efficient technologies to generate and move power. However, we have done nothing to broaden our concepts of electrical generation. We still think of it in 19th-century terms.

Our model of generation has been slow to advance. As late as 1930, virtually all electrical utilities were isolated from one another. "Baltimore, Denver, Duluth, Kansas City, Minneapolis-St. Paul, New Orleans, Portland (Maine), and New York have no connections with other power systems at present," reported the Institute of Radio Engineers. "In the case of New York City, while the power systems in the city are interconnected, a large part of Manhattan is supplied by direct current." Policy makers were concerned about these isolated systems not because they were inefficient or vulnerable but because they might limit the spread of a new technology: television.

One of the more promising designs for television required the transmitter and receiver to be synchronized by a common 60-cycle electrical power grid. New York has "no tie-in with either New Jersey or Long Island," one report complained, hence "any station using Manhattan's power supply for synchronizing cannot render service to the neighboring populous districts of New Jersey, Long Island, and Connecticut."

No one was prepared to unify the national electrical grid at that point, so engineers found other ways of synchronizing TV signals. The electrical utilities were remarkably slow to pull their transmission lines into consistent power systems. Even today, the US still has three distinct electrical grids: one that serves the area east of Wyoming, a second that serves Wyoming and land to the west, and a third that serves Texas. Assembling the system into three grids is a substantial accomplishment. "The electricity transmission system is one of the greatest engineering achievements of the 20th century," bragged the US Department of Energy.

Still the accomplishments of one century, no matter how grand, can easily fail the next. The same government department that praised the work of one generation has noted that "there is growing evidence that the US transmission system is under stress." At the Society for the Promotion of Goodness, the captain of industry argued that we needed to abandon old ideas and think about generation in new ways. He invited us to think about the power grid as a dynamic system, a smart grid that could give energy to anyone or accept energy from anyone. The comparison, obvious to him, was the Internet, which has a standard open design that can be connected to any data device that meets a certain minimal set of requirements.

Of course, the task of building a dynamic power grid is substantially harder than the job of building the Internet. Tolerances are narrow, and the consequences of failure can be large in terms of infrastructure damaged, businesses destroyed, lives lost. A recent study begins its list of engineering specifications with "Reconfigure the flow of electricity to minimize the effect of an outage due to a fault in a quarter of a cycle," and then lists requirements that include load control, voltage control, price information, and system isolation. It's a list that could not easily be achieved without the experience of building the Internet.

The real problem, of course, is that of cooperation, of getting a common agreement among a large collection of engineers, investors, policy makers, corporate executives, and voters. We will need some kind of consensus from this group about the nature of a new power grid if we are to see any progress on this issue. As a group, these individuals form a dynamic system of their own, one that is perhaps just as unpredictable and dangerous as a national power grid.

As I have learned at the lunchtime meetings of the Society for the Promotion of Goodness, anyone can add a bit of energy to disrupt that system of stakeholders in power transmission, but few can get the results they want. Only a master can overcome the constraints that each individual poses on the system and move the group to a desirable outcome.

When the captain of industry finished his remarks and moved to take questions, he found himself talking with people more interested in the Internet than in the generation of power. He answered the questions graciously, without trying to push the subject back to the electrical infrastructure. He was playing the role of being in the vanguard, the leader who raises an issue to attract the right stakeholders to the debate.

As the captain of industry spoke, several organizations were getting ready to jump into the fray. They had prepared position papers and webpages and videos that were all intended to charm the US Administration. They offered studies by engineering conferences, recommendations by policy organizations, and advocacy statements from trade associations. Some are complete. Some are gathering final comments. Many are old reports that have been updated so that they seem to be current when the debate really started in Congress. This is how technology meets politics. This is where policy is tested. This is how we promote an agenda of goodness.

02
Celestial Navigation

Many couples have testy discussions about golf. Or tennis. Or rock climbing. Or soccer. But my friends Doug and Chery are the only couple I know who have had an awkward conversation about rockets.

Chery and I have been friends since childhood. Our fathers worked together at the old Burroughs Corporation. When she told me that she was marrying a rocket scientist, I was both pleased and intrigued. I was happy to see her find a partner and interested to learn what sort of person a rocket scientist might be. Like many an individual who has followed the American space program, I speculated that someone who sends machines to navigate beyond Earth's atmosphere might have a special view of the world, that earthly concerns might have a celestial tint. I quickly found that the opposite was true, that celestial activities were tied to those of common life.

"I'll be back in time for dinner" were the first words I heard Doug say.

The three of us had agreed to meet for coffee at a restaurant near Chery's apartment. I was visiting their city on business and had taken an extra day to meet Doug and to share a year's worth of news with Chery. Both Chery and Doug had arrived before I found the place, and the two were already in the midst of a vigorous discussion.

"It's two hours out there," said Chery, "and two hours back. You won't be home for dinner."

"I'll leave early," replied Doug, "I'll get back in plenty of time."

At this point, I was certain I understood the conversation between the two of them. The subject was clearly golf. Doug and his buddies had a tee time for noon at some distant course. Chery doubted that her then fiancé could finish the game, drive home, take a shower, and arrive on time at the place where we were all to have dinner. I was so confident of my judgment that I made a misguided attempt to defuse any anger. "Playing a round this afternoon?" I asked after we were introduced.

"No," replied Chery, "he's going over the mountains to fly rockets."

"Oh," I said, grasping the fact that Doug the Rocket Scientist was also Doug the Rocket Hobbyist.

"I finished this one last weekend," Doug interjected. "We think we can get it up to 35,000 feet."

There was not much more to say, though many words continued to be spoken. As a couple, Doug and Chery were still in a relatively early phase of their relationship. They had not yet combined households, merged their social goals, or even found a common way of discussing their needs. Their conversation analyzed every aspect of Doug's schedule for the day, the potential problems, and the need to be back in the city at a certain time. It ended, as such things do, on an awkward note.

Doug was resolved to get his rocket flown. Chery was not convinced that he was going to be able to arrive on time for our reservation at the Bayside Restaurant at 6:30 p.m. We could only hope that all things would work for good and that the day's events would not be disrupted by poor planning, a shifting wind, or the happenstance of traffic congestion on I-405.

DOUG THE ROCKET SCIENTIST IS technically Doug the systems engineer. He oversees the design and construction of digital systems for large spacecraft projects. His job is to make the individual boxes that constitute the spacecraft electronics work as a whole. The process is tricky and fraught with problems. He can specify the basic functions of a system in planning documents, but such documents still leave a great deal of discretion to the people who are building the basic components.

"You can't design everything yourself," he explains. "You have to trust the other engineers to articulate what they can do, explain the shortcomings of their design, and suggest what can be done to make a system work."

Trust is a difficult thing to engineer, as it involves history, character, and an ability to put aside your own goals for the good of the whole. It requires participants to recognize when they are indulging their own curiosity rather than creating a solution, even an unusual solution, that meets the needs of the group.

Entering into a project and assuming that all parties automatically trust each other is like entering into a marriage without acknowledging the fact that you are about to share a bathroom with someone who has a very different idea of how such a facility should be used. It's all too easy to claim that the gender which sees little reason to return the toilet seat to the horizontal position has a deep character flaw or that those who believe that shower rods were invented as a place to dry underwear have a moral shortcoming. But such claims do little to help a marriage meet its design goals and do nothing to build trust.

Once, while I was sitting in Doug's office talking with him about nothing in particular, he picked up a cable from a side table and threw it across his desk. "This," he said, "is an example of extreme silliness. No one is willing to take responsibility for the cable and its problems. My component group says, 'That's a cable, and we don't take responsibility for cables,'" remarked Doug. "But the cable guys say, 'That cable contains a transformer, so it's a component and not our responsibility.'"

We often try to solve such problems with an overall plan, but such plans can have failings of their own. You can establish a budget for power, time, or weight and make the different units compete for their share, but in the end you might have a device that only fosters more problems.

Doug once worked on a large project that divided a satellite's outer skin and tried to make sure that each component group got the share it needed. The component groups fought hard to get prime real estate on the spacecraft. "In one design, two key devices were only 10 degrees apart," Doug said. It was an efficient use of the skin, but it posed a serious problem. "One device was a navigation sensor that had to find the sun. The other was a scientific experiment that would have been destroyed if it absorbed large amounts of solar radiation." Each group tried to blame the other for the poor decision. Neither was willing to trust someone else to find a solution.

SILLINESS IS, OF COURSE, IN the eye of the beholder. Irresponsibility is also not easy to identify. When you're close to a design, you usually can't imagine that others don't see it as you do. In engineering organizations—indeed in many organizations—we try many different techniques to get people to articulate their needs, to listen to each other. Ultimately, we hope to understand and trust each other. We have team social gatherings, take our staff on retreat, play team-building games, give everybody imprinted sportswear with a common logo. Such things might not directly build trust, but they give team members a common experience, and common experiences can be used to build trust.

In the first spring of a difficult war, the engineer and aviator Charles Lindbergh (1902–1974) looked to common experiences to rebuild some trust in his marriage. Lindbergh was living apart from his wife so that he could work on military aircraft, but he was also feeling that his marriage was distant and strained. Their relationship had been rubbed raw by 15 years of intense public scrutiny. Every activity of Lindbergh and his wife had been reported in the press. After the Japanese attack on Pearl Harbor, that press had been especially critical of the couple because of their isolationist politics, a stance that argued that the US should stay out of the war.

Once the fighting began, Lindbergh had concluded that he needed to support his country and had offered his technical skills to any organization that would have him. This act had proved more humiliating than he had anticipated as it had drawn scorn from the general public and angry disapproval from his wife. Eventually, Henry Ford had offered him a position in his aircraft factory. Lindbergh accepted this position and left his home for Michigan.

After several weeks at his new job, the Lindberghs took the first steps to reconnect. Anne Lindbergh (1906–2001) began the process by writing to her husband and grew frustrated when he did not reply. When he did reply, Charles

Lindbergh offered a small token to show that he was ready to rebuild their relationship. "The moon is at Bathurst takeoff height," he wrote to his wife. Such words could be taken as an attempt at poetry, an effort to charm his wife through pretty words, but they were actually a shorthand reference to a common experience, a time when they had learned to work together.

In the early years of their marriage, they had flown all over the world to survey air routes. They had gone to Europe, Asia, and Africa, where Bathurst could be found. Even though Lindbergh was the skilled engineer, he had split the work with his wife. In particular, she was responsible for navigation and communication. At Bathurst, they had a difficult departure and had to work together to get the plane airborne. Each had to shoulder responsibility. Each had to trust the other. No one else could help.

The dynamics of a marriage might be either easier or harder than those of an engineering team. A marriage can be sustained by social forces that are never quite captured by a contract or a design deadline. Occasionally, as in a national emergency, in the pursuit of a grand goal, or in the mere joy of doing something for the first time, an engineering team can find an extra bit of commitment that binds a group or team together, but most often, trust is built upon history and common experience.

Doug the Rocket Scientist often struggled to find enough of those qualities to hold a project together.

"We were once working on a fairly complicated spacecraft," he told me, "for which we contracted with two different firms and got two very different results."

Both firms followed the specifications and both built instruments that ultimately worked. However, one firm devoted most of its resources to building their sensor, while the second spent more time thinking about how their device would communicate with other satellite systems.

The first firm "created a 'roll your own' interface for its sensor," noted Doug. "They argued that they had no incentive to follow one of the military or civilian network standards, as they would never build enough of the sensors to recover their investment. It's not as if they were building a laser printer and could recover their costs over a production run of 100,000 units."

The firm delivered its device well before the deadline, but Doug's group could not make it talk with the other satellite systems. "We had a hard time making that thing work. We continued to debug that interface after we delivered the satellite to Cape Canaveral. We were working on it until liftoff."

"The second company spent less time on its instrument, but it connected its work to a standard interface. Its machine was late. The company had to deliver the sensor directly to the Cape, but we plugged it into the system, and it worked fine the first time."

"We weren't worried about it," Doug reported, "because it talked in a standard way. We could trust it."

Not all group events are common experiences, and not all of them build trust. Early in my career, I was part of a software group that went on a "team and trust-building" retreat. We listened to a talk about the company. We played a few games. We were encouraged to speak freely about our feelings. We all were asked to wear tennis shirts marked with the company logo and some heartening phrases, such as "Best software in the known universe."

At some point, I noticed that the women in the group were not especially enthusiastic about the day's events. When I asked how they were feeling, I got a bit of an earful in return. "Someone hasn't thought much about what we're doing," remarked one of my colleagues. "We're wearing men's clothing and playing men's games. I feel like I'm wearing a flour sack and being the sympathetic soul at a high school track meet. What's in it for me?"

On that day I met Doug the Rocket Scientist, I think he probably had a clear idea of what "was in it for him" and for Chery in their relationship. I don't remember if he arrived at the restaurant on time that night or if he had had a shower, or if the moon hung over the horizon, but I do recall it as a wonderful evening.

03
The Rev. Swaminathan's Ashram and Software Institute

Originally, I had hoped that I might be able to spend two or three weeks visiting the industries of Bangalore, India. With that much time, I would have been able to explore the city in detail, meet civic and industrial leaders, and really begin to appreciate how the region operated. However, when I eventually concluded that I would be able to stay in the city for only two days, I carefully planned every moment of my visit. I determined where I wanted to go, who I wanted to meet, and how I would arrange transportation from the airport.

Almost immediately, my plans began to fall apart. I found my car at the air terminal, threw my bag in the back seat, pulled out my map, and told the driver that I wanted to see a group of technology businesses that were east of downtown. The driver carefully examined my map as if it were some kind of sacred text. He rotated it in his hands and turned it over so that he could study the back. Finally, he folded the document, returned it to me, and looked me in the eyes.

"Shopping?" he asked.

"No," I responded. "I want to see the software companies. Computers."

The driver pondered this idea for a moment. "Ah," he finally said, putting the car in gear and starting on our way.

I sat in the back, taking notes and following our progress on the map. The driver made decisions with confidence. A left here. A right there. We were going through an area with modern offices that bore the trademarks of well-known Western companies. In about 15 minutes, he stopped the car in front of a large and ornately detailed blue building.

"Here," he said. "What is this?" I asked. "It isn't a software company."

"Temple," he said. "It is very important."

Under other circumstances, I would have been more than willing to tour the temple. Religious practice has been the pattern for so much of human activity. The monasteries of medieval Europe refined the division of labor, the coordination of shared activities, and the management of common resources, such as land and water. Although I suspected that the temples of Bangalore might have provided me with some insight into India's commercial culture, I felt that I could not devote any of my precious time to them.

"No," I said. "Software. Computers. Industrial park."

"Ah," said the driver, and off we went again.

As we drove away from the building, I saw a small sign over one door that suggested that this building might be more directly connected to the technology industry than I had believed. "The Reverend Hiram Swaminathan's Ashram and Software Institute," it read. "Java!" "Peaceful Programming!" "Software Enlightenment!" "APL!"

By the time we reached the large concentrations of software companies, I had learned several lessons about the area. First, like the cities of Bombay and Calcutta, Bangalore had reclaimed its pre-British name of Bengaluru. Second, the city was also the home of the Indian aerospace industry, so many local companies dealt with metalworking and machine tools. Finally, the digital technology and software firms were all connected to the high-tension electrical wires that crossed and recrossed the landscape.

We spent a day making an improvised tour of the various technology firms that shared the common landscape. Big firms stood next to small firms. Global companies were connected to local suppliers. Research laboratories were across the street from discount retail outlets. During a respite in our travels, we stopped at a fruit stand that stood by the entrance to a major hardware developer and watched a group of young boys and small goats play some kind of organized game in the company's parking lot. The game seemed to be a variation on cricket, and the rules apparently favored the goats. As darkness began to spread across the sky, I told the driver that it was time to head to my hotel. The communal air, now cool with the evening breeze, mingled the perfume of curry spices and burning cow dung from the fires of 10,000 kitchens.

The traffic slowed as we returned to the city center, choked by a parade in honor of a local goddess. The driver, growing increasingly nervous, suddenly stopped the car next to the temple of the United Theosophical Society, opened his door, and dashed into the building. At this point, I was more intrigued than worried. I had yet to pay him for the drive, and I owed him a substantial sum. After missing the opportunity to see Reverend Swaminathan's Ashram and Software Institute, I was inclined to look inside the Theosophists' building. Theosophy had played an intriguing role in late Victorian India by combining the religions of Asia and Europe. We shall "unite firmly a body of men of all nations in brotherly love," wrote its founder, "and engage them in a pure altruistic work, not on a labor with selfish motives."

I left the cab and headed for the building, but stopped when a loud flushing sound told me that the Theosophists controlled a public resource far more important to Bangalore taxi drivers than "a body of men engaged in altruistic work." My driver returned refreshed, calm, and ready to get me to my hotel.

On the whole, the software industry has given little thought to the allocation of public goods. The giant players in the field have never debated the access to the

Dardanelles, fought over the coalfields of Alsace, or argued about the farms of the Yangzi Valley. If anything, we often believe that we exist outside the restrictions of shared resources and geography. Our ideals and aspirations, as recorded in the advertisements of trade journals, suggest that we can conduct our business from an isolated beach in Brazil or a trout stream in the pristine wilderness. In such places, we are all masters of our fate and need never worry about shared resources.

In fact, the software industry actually requires few common physical resources. Buildings can be constructed anywhere. Computing equipment can be shipped to any corner of the globe. Skilled workers, when offered adequate incentives, can move across political and cultural boundaries. Of all the resources the software industry consumes, only electricity ties the field firmly to Earth. Until software companies can derive their energy from sunlight or spin it from the Earth's magnetic field, they will be dependent on the entities, public and private, that generate and distribute electrical power.

IN INDIA, THE PRODUCTION OF electricity tested the country's ability to build a modern industrialized society. In 1966, after nearly 20 years of independence, India still had no national power grid, no unified process for creating and delivering electricity.

"Dried cattle dung," wrote one engineer, "contributes as much to total energy consumption as does electricity."

The story that takes India from the electrical infrastructure of 1966, the infrastructure that compares badly to burning cattle dung, to a modern infrastructure 40 years later is a parable for the free market. It begins with the government of the first Prime Minister, Jawaharlal Nehru, which distrusted capitalism and looked to the ashram and temple and the people's collective for guidance in building a modern economy. Nehru's government stressed traditional Hindu values, such as the "renunciation of gain and the submergence of self for the good of all." Government ministers connected these values to the managerial techniques of the Soviet Union. Only "a revolutionary plan can solve the two related questions of land and industry," Nehru proclaimed. He also stated that he was "inclined more and more to a communist philosophy."

The communist philosophy brought technical sophistication to India. It allowed the country to build modern airplanes and to develop a nuclear bomb. At the same time, it failed to build the Indian economy as Nehru had envisioned. Critics argued that the country's economic plan misidentified the economy's structure, directed funds to inefficient industries, and failed to address key problems with the country's infrastructure. "It may be pointed out that [the government's] discussion of Indian economic planning," wrote one critic, "is almost entirely lacking" in several important issues. He claimed that it would produce less wealth than other ways of handling the economy and that it would ensure that "a large amount of investment funds will remain idle."

The Indian government tried to refine and improve its methods of planning the economy but with only limited success. "We are far from adequate optimizing models," noted an observer in the 1970s, "especially for a country as large and as complex as India." The electrical infrastructure was in especially poor shape. According to critics, it was marked by "endemic power shortages, poor operational performance and [the] precarious financial condition of the State Electricity Boards."

India began to abandon economic planning in the 1980s, and it started reforming the electrical industry in 1991. It opened the market to private suppliers, reorganized the transmission network, allowed new firms to distribute electricity, and restructured the government's role in the market. The process was not fast or easy or painless. India's reforms were often compared, not always favorably, to the steps taken by Latin American countries. Yet, by the middle of the decade, the electrical infrastructure was clearly improving. By 1995, private firms were starting to generate electricity and sell it on the country's power grid. In some years, they were adding more capacity to India's electrical infrastructure than the state-run utilities.

Without the reforms, the country would not have had enough power for call centers in Mumbai, radiology offices in Kolkata, or software firms in Bengaluru. Even with the reforms, the electrical industry needed substantial investment to keep pace with growth. As the year 2000 approached, analysts noted that the country would need to build 10,000 megawatts of capacity per year to keep pace with the country's economic growth.

Of course, the market's lesson is that projects will attract investment if the rewards are great enough. With the strength of the Indian technology industry behind it, the market delivered the capital needed to sustain the industry. At the same time, some investors began using those same markets to circumvent the problems of the Indian electrical infrastructure. They built economic ashrams, private industrial parks with private roads, private buildings, private housing, and private sources of electricity.

Private electricity, like the private resources of a monastery or an ashram, is in the hands of like-minded organizations that have separated themselves from the world. If you believe the advertisements, the tenants of the Indian industrial parks are spiritually inclined businesses that would not misuse the common resources. In these parks, companies are motivated by "pride of ownership," customers come for a "delightful experience," and employees receive the blessing of "fulfilled aspirations." It might not be "peaceful programming" and APL but it does seem to be a good place to get away from the problems of the world's infrastructure and do a little business.

On my second day in Bangalore, I was awakened by the sound of a ringing phone. "Your driver is here," said the voice on the other end of the line. It seemed early for me to begin the day's work, but I pulled myself from bed, quickly dressed, and headed downstairs. At the doorman's suggestion, I had hired a hotel driver to get me to my appointments. "Our staff is more knowledgeable than the local taxi drivers," he said. "They won't get lost."

Yet, as the day progressed, my new guide seemed little better than the previous day's driver. He didn't seem able to read a map and repeatedly had to stop and ask directions. On one leg of the journey, we twice passed the Reverend Hiram Swaminathan's ashram, although we received neither peace in programming nor enlightenment in software. In the middle of the day, when we were out on Mysore Road, I had to flag a policeman and ask his guidance. We returned to the hotel in darkness, after the obligatory stop at the Theosophists' bathroom.

When I entered the lobby, a doorman ran up to me and said, "You didn't come down for your car this morning."

For a moment, I didn't know what to say. "Yes, I did," I stated. "The driver is just leaving the hotel." The doorman looked through a window and said, "That's not a hotel car, that's a private cab."

"What do you mean?" I asked.

"That was not the driver we hired for you."

Needless to say, this last remark led to a lengthy discussion with the doorman. In this discussion, each of us had a different goal. I wanted to learn how that rogue driver had called my room, and the doorman wanted to learn how I was going to reimburse the hotel for the car I had never used.

As we were working in the context of a market economy, I, as customer, had more power than he, as supplier. The doorman cancelled the debt and gave me a reasonable explanation for the day's events. He said that the driver had probably been in the lobby the day before, had heard me make arrangements for a car, and had decided to capture my business before the hotel driver arrived. A clever exploitation of a free market, I suppose, but a market that I would prefer to avoid.

04
This Is the Way We Would Build a Barn

There was no question about it: It was an invitation to a barn raising. My friend Doug the Rocket Scientist had sent an e-mail to a group of his friends asking if they could spend a weekend helping him install a solar roof on his house.

It was a call to community service that we rarely receive in our age: a chance to help a friend; an opportunity to work with a team of interesting and talented individuals; a job that would make a real, substantive impact on the world rather than merely another 10-kilometer charity walk to raise funds for some modest cause with a guilt-provoking name, such as the Association to Make the World Better for Oppressed Children, Tropical Hardwoods, and Arctic Seals. This was different. This was tangible. With two days of work, we would cut his home free of the local power grid and release a few kilowatt-hours for others.

Had not my presence been required elsewhere, I would have strapped on a tool belt, picked up the nail gun, and rushed to the Rocket Scientist's side. My time with the Rocket Scientist generally becomes an advanced seminar on engineering problems. He delights in uncovering how little of the technology I actually understand, even though he still asked me to serve as a witness on his drawings for patent applications. I take great pleasure in asking all the unanswerable policy questions while I admire his ability to convince others of this rightness of his cause.

The solar roof has been an ambitious project that has tested the Rocket Scientist's full set of skills. Through e-mail, I have followed the challenges of obtaining building permits, design approval, and project finance in addition to enduring several cold weeks with no roof and no heat. He has had to make cross-city trips to find specialized hardware and relied on friends near and far to get specialized devices. By the time of the barn raising, the project had become the kind of educational experience that was once afforded only by the communal construction of large farm buildings.

Before we had formal engineering education, before we created learning outcomes and pedagogical standards, communal barn raisings offered the opportunity to learn structural engineering. Even after the founding of the first technical schools in the middle of the 19th century, American communities taught their youth how to build buildings when they pooled labor to construct large animal shelters or threshing barns for private farms. Three or four times a year, the able-bodied members of the town would gather to help one of their neighbors create a building frame, raise that frame from the ground, and complete the outer walls. These events reduced the cost of construction by 40 to 50 percent while also transmitting a great deal of practical knowledge.

At a barn raising, children would learn the basic skills of shaping wood, driving nails, and hanging doors. Adolescents would learn how to design a truss, distribute load, and raise a frame. The young adults would get their first taste of management by coordinating labor and leading a team.

When the students finally became teachers and claimed authority over new projects, they would reproduce the traditional designs they had learned in the manner that they understood. In most regions, farm buildings had unity of form and purpose. They were not "haphazardly thrown together by inexperienced amateurs looking for a hasty shelter," noted one scholar, but "were carefully built by men who had the benefit of both past experience and forethought."

Communal barn raisings began to vanish in the middle of the 19th century. By 1870, they were being replaced by more systematic ways of transmitting technical information, such as textbooks, university experts, and engineering diagrams. By the start of the 20th century, they had largely disappeared from the rural landscape. "Modern barns should replace those of ancestors when necessary," explained a 1909 report on the farm economy. "Because a barn answered the purpose of our grandfather is no reason for us to pattern after it."

It's not likely that Doug's project will soon be repeated as a means of teaching communities how to build a solar roof. The body of knowledge that forms the basis for alternative energy is already too technical to be transmitted from generation to generation by means of a communal activity and a weekend of apprenticeship. When we look at how we provide information to programmers and software engineers, we quickly realize that we are barely a generation away from a time when we transmitted ideas with informal methods and that our field has been hampered by confusion over the value of formal and informal means of communicating the lessons of experience.

We must let time communicate these lessons. The 19th-century farm buildings represented 200 years of experience with wood construction on the North American continent and at least a millennium of similar work in Europe. The initial generation of programmers could call upon no such legacy. Engineering provided little relevant experience. Mathematics offered even less. Equipped primarily with energy and vision, those programmers created several ambitious and difficult software projects, including the Semi-Automatic Ground Environment (SAGE) control system of the US Airforce, the Fortran compiler, the operating system for the System/360, and the Multics mainframe timesharing operating system.

The first generation of programmers was an impatient lot and generally felt that they should have gained more experience from the first software systems. "Software production today appears in the scale of industrialization somewhere below the more backward construction industries," complained a software designer in 1968. "We undoubtedly get the short end of the stick in confrontations with hardware people because they are the industrialists and we are the crofters."

Experience alone would not turn programmers into software engineers any more than it would transform crofters, small-scale Scottish farmers, into industrial managers. If anything, two decades of experience in software development suggested that programming might never be transformed to an industrial scale. "Production of large software has become a scare item for management," noted a Bell Laboratories researcher. "By reputation it is often an unprofitable morass, costly and unending."

SCHOLARS GENERALLY IDENTIFY 1968 AS a key date in the history of software engineering. In October of that year, a group of 60 senior programmers met in Garmisch, Germany, to talk about the future of their field. They discussed many topics that have become staples in the discipline: system specification, design, implementation, testing, documentation, and maintenance. They also asked how people would learn to be software engineers and how they might ever learn to master the problem they called "programming in the large." "Is it possible to have software engineers in the numbers in which we need them," asked Carnegie Mellon professor Alan Perlis, "without formal software engineering education?"

No one proved to be willing to answer this question with an unqualified "yes." Several participants wanted to distance the idea of software engineering education from both computer science education, as it was then taking form, and also traditional engineering education. "I am convinced that much of the game in which we are involved is one of making the best of the world around us, understanding what the world wants, and matching what science can offer," argued one attendee. "That to my mind is truly engineering."

Most of the group concurred that software engineering education required more experience than could be gained from traditional textbooks and classes. Students would need to serve a term as a crofter on the land—seeing the problems faced by large programming projects.

At least one professor, Edsger Dijkstra (1930–2002), was reluctant to embrace this idea, although he did not want to be an advocate for book learning. "We have a Dutch proverb, 'One learns from experience,'" he began. To him, these words suggest that learning happens automatically. "Well, this is a lie," he observed. "Otherwise, everyone would be very, very wise."

Dijkstra advocated a form of system development that he called "structured programming," and he argued that the principles of this approach should be applied to education as well. Educators should not deposit students randomly into programming projects and expect them to learn. These experiences needed to be structured so that the students would "learn as much as possible." Software engineering education, Dijkstra claimed, was based on practical activities, but those activities needed to be well engineered.

The Garmisch conference had been called for the purpose of designing a software engineering curriculum, so the attendees considered all the usual concepts of higher education: courses, goals, assessments, and the like. However, they were unusually attentive to the task of structuring a programming team so that each member could learn all the information needed to complete the job. One professor described how to use seminars to transmit information through a group. Another suggested that programming teams should always be assembled of close friends, "because then they will talk together frequently, and there will be strong lines of communications in all directions." Others had ideas for techniques that involved three-ring binders, old steel file cabinets, and documentation protocols.

Arguing on a more abstract level, Djikstra kept returning to his fundamental idea of structure. He claimed that programmers were best able to learn from their work when the software product was well structured and "this structure is reflected in the structure of the organization making the product." In such a structure, authority would be well delineated, and the young would learn from the old. The inexperienced would learn basic skills. The novices would study algorithms. The oldest apprentices would gain an understanding of system design.

At the Rocket Scientist's barn raising, all parties fulfilled their roles. The technophobes carried batteries. The weekend mechanics bolted panels to their frame. The Rocket Scientist proved that he was the master of his vision. "Whoopee!" he typed in the e-mail reporting that the roof was done. "It was heavy overcast and raining, but at 10:32 a.m. we generated power."

Filled with gratitude for the accomplishment, Doug launched into a litany of thanks for the people who had helped him. His gratitude included 40 people, all with specific tasks. Looking at the list, I began to appreciate the complexity of the task, the challenges of the design, the difficulty of construction, and the requirements of local regulation. I also saw that my name would have fallen into a category on the list vaguely titled "overeducated manual laborer." I'm certain that I would have spent a good day with good people, but I would not have learned much about the system. Black panel. Black cable. Black bracket. Lift and carry. Keep moving so you get the job done by sunset.

I had not been able to be part of the solar barn raising because I was in the land of the crofters, dealing with problems that could only be solved by the method of crofters. Instead of raising structures, I was planting words and teaching a new generation of software engineers to do the same.

There are, in fact, rules for writing clear stories and persuasive arguments, but they are better learned by placing the tools in your hand than reading about those rules in a book or on a webpage or watching a video presentation. The young must learn technique. The adolescents get structure. The leaders on the edge of adulthood find management.

As it happened, I taught these lessons in a rural classroom that stood on the edge of an old farm. The barn, which held ground at one side of the parking lot, had clearly stood for six, seven, or maybe eight generations. It had once sheltered draft horses but now served as a storehouse for hotel supplies. The beams had obviously been cut by hand, and the frame had an asymmetric design that indicated it had been raised by a team of workers who had not been taught the technical aspects of construction in school. Not a nail was to be seen in the structure.

The children who had learned to pound pegs with a hammer on this project undoubtedly had taught other children to do the same when they built their own barns in other corners of the village. So the pattern continued, with generation following generation, until one child went to school to learn engineering, and the grandchild of that child decided to learn the engineering of software and raise barns of code.

05
Attention to Detail

Nothing demands a more detailed accounting of our actions than a roaring prairie fire, a glowing wall of energy that stands ready to take all that we might have to offer. Such fires occasionally occur in the region that holds my family's farm, a picturesque 12 acres in the dry foothills of the American West.

The farm has an emergency electrical generator to provide water to fight the flames. Even a modest fire could cut the connection to the power grid and make it impossible to pump anything from the aquifer that lies some 30 feet below the surface. The generator can deliver 15 kW in a matter of seconds, but it can't begin to satisfy the full demand from the farm. The water pump takes almost 3 kW by itself. That load is compounded by the power required by other essential equipment: the air conditioner, barnyard lamps, and hay loader. If you want a hot shower and a cold drink after defeating the fire, you'll need to add a couple more kW for the refrigerator and the water heater. Without an accurate account of the electrical load, the generator will grind to a halt long before you can bring its power to bear on the fire.

In that moment before you throw the switch, when the circuits are still part of the local power grid, nobody has to make a detailed load calculation for the farm. The power demand for every family in the hills is aggregated into a single quantity. The local utility cares nothing about your individual needs until it comes time to settle the bill at the end of the month. You might need a little more electricity or your neighbor might require a little less. From the utility's point of view, these fluctuations are lost in the aggregate demand. It manages the local infrastructure for the aggregate not for the individual. This may not be the most efficient way to manage electrical power, but it has worked fairly well for almost a century.

More than any other issue, the ideas of aggregation and markets lie behind the current discussions of electrical infrastructure, the discussions that focus on the concept we now call the smart grid. We tend to view this as a technological problem. "Using digital sensors, computing modeling and real-time data, a smart grid would revolutionize our antiquated" electrical power system, explained a recent article in the *New York Times*. Yet, the smart grid really involves a radical change in how we view the market for electrical power, a change that will require us to be more responsible for our own actions and more dependent upon our neighbors.

For most of its history, the power market has involved a dialogue between two parties: centralized generators and aggregate populations. In its earliest days, this dialogue was best described by utility magnate Samuel Insull (1859–

1938). After starting his career as an assistant in the company of Thomas Edison (1847–1931), Insull launched his own firm to create the large electrical utilities. In forming those utilities, he recognized that aggregate demand was more uniform than the demand from any individual household and thus "the fundamental basis of the profit-making of an energy-selling company."

Insull promoted his ideas with a set of charts and diagrams that became well-known in the early electrical industry. Aggregating demand from small consumers produced a more uniform and predictable demand for electricity, he argued. "The characteristics of an individual are therefore of interest only in that they form a contribution to the characteristics of the group," he explained. Consequently, "we can sell these small customers at a profit as a whole whereas any engineer who knew the facts could demonstrate to me that each one by himself is a loss to us."

The financial markets lavishly rewarded Insull's ideas. His utilities were the largest and best financed of his age. He used these resources to build the control structure that we currently associate with electrical markets. This structure divided the electrical supply into three parts: generation, transmission, and distribution. He moved generation into large, centralized plants because they were more efficient. By contrast, his competitors were generally building regional or neighborhood plants.

To aggregate demand, Insull created large distribution grids that were controlled by regional substations. These stations kept statistics on electrical usage, projected demand, and monitored the actual consumption of power. The stations were connected to generators and to one another by dedicated phone lines. The stations could use these phones to call for additional power or report that the demand for electricity wasn't as great as anticipated.

The last element, the transmission lines, linked generators to grids. Initially, the utilities owned these lines as well as the grids and generators. However, by slow and steady steps, they became part of a market for bulk electricity. By the 1930s, this market included the generators in government hydroelectric projects. By the late 1970s, it had expanded to embrace a substantial collection of government, private, and public entities. However, this market still operated according to Samuel Insull's principle of aggregate demand.

As CURRENTLY CONCEIVED, THE SMART grid will bring us the tools to start thinking about individual electrical consumption rather than aggregate consumption. Just as social networking has given people the ability to exchange ideas as individuals rather than as members of institutions, the smart grid allows entities to participate in the electrical markets as individuals. These markets will provide new information for controlling the grids, calling for power from transmission lines, and ultimately projecting the requirements for electrical generation.

The proponents of smart grids argue that this approach to power management will let them accommodate new technologies, such as electric automobiles. The "idle capacity of today's electric power grid," reports a study by the Department of Energy, "could supply 70 percent of the energy needs of today's cars and light trucks without adding to generation or transmission capacity—if the vehicles charged during off-peak times."

This aspect of the smart grid discussion parallels the ideas of Insull, who used statistical methodology to incorporate the demand from electrical railroads into his utilities. "If you consider it merely as a fraction of the supply of energy required by a community for all kinds of purposes," he observed, "the demand from railroads is found to be simply an incident."

THE TASK OF BUILDING A smart grid requires us to solve two kinds of problems: technical and social. Of these two classes, the technical problems may be easiest to address.

Much of the fundamental technology is based on well-tested ideas, such as those found in the Internet's hardware and software. Some have called for research to create radically new technology to support the smart grid, including new means for transmitting and storing power. No matter how radical these ideas, most of the research builds on existing technology.

By contrast, addressing the social and managerial problems may be much more difficult. Many of these problems come from the segmented structure of the nation's electrical infrastructure. Although this infrastructure involves several large government entities, such as the generation plants of the Bureau of Land Reclamation or the Tennessee Valley Authority, local agencies control most of the system. As they should, these local agencies consider only their own interests when they make policy. As a consequence, they tend to reject plans that require them to make sacrifices on behalf of the greater good. This is perhaps best illustrated by the problems of building new transmission facilities. "It is becoming increasingly difficult to site new conventional overhead transmission lines," explained a recent US government report, "particularly in urban and suburban areas experiencing the greatest load growth."

Yet the construction of new facilities is only one aspect of the social problem. The plans for the smart grid propose an infrastructure that can operate in a unified manner. Such plans will require large investments and force the public debate to concentrate on the problem of controlling financial risk rather than on the value of radical innovation. No one, as Samuel Insull knew well, wants an expensive infrastructure, no matter how large a market it creates, if that infrastructure has a high risk of creating a financial loss.

The task of focusing investment on the right aspects of the smart grid will be tricky, as the new electrical infrastructure might create markets that can't deliver all the benefits their supporters claim. Many reports note that the smart grid will be able to handle new suppliers as well as consumers; thus, any small investor could purchase a generator and add power to the network. However, that idea will work only if the market can set a price that will reward small investments. The current electrical infrastructure can't reward a family that wants to put solar cells on its roof or chooses to place a spinning turbine next to its barn. It's far from obvious that the smart grid will do a better job of providing incentives to such projects unless it substantially increases the price of electricity.

Any market, can, of course, be shaped by initial investment, technical and operational standards, subsidies, and early demonstrations. Currently, much of the technical work on the smart grid involves these issues. "The Smart Grid will ultimately require hundreds of standards, specifications, and requirements," explains a report by the National Institute of Standards and Technology (NIST). In addition to standards, NIST is creating a plan—a road map—to shape the industry and encourage investment. The Department of Energy is supporting research to develop the smart grid's basic technical elements. Agencies in Europe and Japan are addressing similar issues as they work to create their own version of the smart grid.

Among those hundreds of specifications and requirements, one item is repeatedly identified as central to the task of creating a smart grid: securing network information. If markets run on information and if bad information can destroy markets, then the markets that the smart grid forms will need to protect their data streams. "Cyber security must address not only deliberate attacks, such as from disgruntled employees, industrial espionage, and terrorists," notes the NIST report, "but also inadvertent compromises of the information infrastructure due to user errors, equipment failures, and natural disasters."

WITH ALMOST 25 YEARS OF experience in dealing with the problems of data security, we've learned that cyberattacks can embarrass organizations, damage credit ratings, disrupt government operations, and destroy industrial machinery. Records of electrical usage may not be as sensitive as our medical history or our credit information, but they still build an intimate record of our lives. The utilities know when we're sleeping, and they know when we're awake. They know when we watch television or open the refrigerator to cheat on our diet. Conceivably, they'll know about the unexpected trip that requires us to charge the electric automobile.

Of course, we have a long experience with trading information for better industrial products and more efficient services. Overall, the exchange seems to have been beneficial, producing more value than it has claimed. Still, we don't really know all the ramifications of living in a more active and individualized electricity market. It might have little impact upon our day-to-day lives or put us in a position of revealing to our neighbors more details than we'd like them to know.

Even though he managed his utilities with aggregate statistics, Samuel Insull would certainly have wanted to know more about his customers. "At his fingertips," noted one biographer, "he always had an impressive array of statistical data." He argued that the value a community received from a stable source of electrical power was well worth the cost of the information. As Insull explained in 1912, "There is no greater problem in the industrial world today than the proper method of producing energy and distributing it in a given area."

Exit
Human Comfort

Like many an engineer's office, the chaos of Doug's office was misleading. Admittedly, it offered little in the way of human comfort. It had no place to sit and none to stand. The floor was covered in packages, paper, and engineering handbooks. The book shelf, packed with official histories of NASA, tottered as if to remind the casual visitor that this was earthquake country and to suggest that the chaos was caused by accident, not design.

Yet, like many an office of an engineer, the place was not a space for work but a machine to organize memory. You could point at anything within its walls and get a story in return. An introduction, a development, a moment of climax, and a resolution. Sometimes, the story might tell how the item worked or when the item was acquired. Always, it communicated why the artifact was important to the owner.

The cable resting on a hook? The solution to a problem of satellite design and management. The skull in a Ziploc bag? Part of an opossum skeleton he found while he was doing the final wiring on some power system. The breadboard circuit mounted on a ½" piece of pine? The physical remnants of his doctoral dissertation, the first time was able to keep the interests of bits and amps in working balance. The solar cell in a little clip? The prototype for an electric roof.

Only a few engineering offices have been preserved and most no longer express the stories that they did with such chaos in life. The last office of Bill Hewlett (1913–2001), in Palo Alto, California is clean and neat and suggests nothing of its original occupant. Apparently it is used as a meeting space. Thomas Edison's lab in Greenfield village more closely captures the spirit of a working facility. When it was moved from New Jersey to Michigan, the transportation crew even excavated the office's landfill and brought it to the new site. The office of W. Edwards Deming (1900–1993) in Washington is a favorite, as it has some of his papers scattered on the desk and his original books on the walls. Yet, like the others, it is a shrine and has lost some of the personality of its owner.

I would like to have helped dismantle the office of a colleague when he retired. It gave the appearance of a spare parts dump and looked thoroughly unstable. Old linkages sat on the floor. Books were piled high to the ceiling. Wires, that may or may not have remained connected to power sources, lay causally on a table. My colleague started his technical training in the Drama School of Yale, where he studied stage engineering. I have always been suspicious that the room was artificially dramatic.

Offices are an index to memory, a place to organize a life. You point to an object and ask "What does this do?" In reply, you will get the story that says "This is what it means to me."

Chapter IV:
The Global Life

He's run off into the wide world
When he could have stayed here under my protection.

Lie of the Mind (1986)
Sam Shepherd

Introduction
Statisticians from the Maldives

The interview was very formal. We arrived mid-day, dressed in business clothes, and answered about our home, our ideas about various cultures and our personal contacts in different countries. We had to demonstrate that we were trustworthy if we were to be allowed to host distinguished visitors to the United States.

As the interview came to an end, the committee across the table gave us a gentle hint that we had passed and asked what sorts of people would we be willing to take into our home. At that point, we made the decision that has made all the difference thus far.

"What sorts of people are the easiest to place in American homes?" we asked.

"Political leaders from Europe," came the response. "They generally come from the ruling party or the top ranks of the legislative opposition. Americans generally find these people the most interesting."

"Wonderful," we said. "We'll be the host to anyone who is not a political leader or not from Europe."

So began our brief career of hosting foreign visitors for the State Department of the American Government. We held dinners for a Japanese television crew, a newspaper columnist from Nigeria, a calligrapher from Korea, an Estonian poet who was researching government proclamations at the Library of Congress, and every single statistician employed by the Maldive Islands.

Of course, we can never be certain that we met every single Maldivian statistician. The commonly accepted philosophy of science, due to Karl Popper (1902–1994), would suggest that we cannot gain confidence in the conclusion that we have seen all Maldivian statisticians, we can only increase the doubt in the claim that we failed to have some to dinner. Still, the Maldives are not a big place and do not have a large cohort of statisticians or any other occupation. With only 396,334 citizens, the country occupies 298 square miles of landmass that sits, on average, 7' 7" above the mean height of the sea.

The second Maldive visitor, or perhaps the third, dropped one of the traditional statistical jokes at dinner. "Data," he said, "equals the model plus noise." It is a phrase that captures the premise that all measurements follow an underlying pattern but are always corrupted by some kind of error or noise. "The rest of the world is the model," he continued, "while the Maldives are the noise."

I suspect that the comment was intended to convey the role that the Maldive Islands play on the world stage. Its culture borrows heavily from southern India; its economy is based on tourism; and its military forces cannot even threaten its nearest neighbors. However, the words actually conveyed the fundamental challenge that is posed by any effort to understand a distant culture. So much of such efforts traffic solely in noise, as the work required to grasp the fundamental trends of a civilization is difficult.

The combination of cheap airfares and free blogs has meant that many a traveler has left a detailed record of their voyages. These records, occasionally entertaining but often predictable, tend to go through three stages of life, which are four fewer than the English Bard offered for the lives of his characters but still enough to allow us to understand contact across cultures in the Internet age.

The first stage of these records is that of the child. In this age, everything is novel and exotic. The traveler gapes at a world that is new and captures the experience with actions that are both naïve and slightly offensive. They tell of surfing in Malaysia, hiking in the Atlas Mountains, playing with the penguins on the Ross Ice Shelf. They post photos of silly dances in front of the Taj Mahal, lewd references at the temples of Angkor Wat, and scenes from American popular culture on the steps of Cristo Redentor. It is a period that carries the potential for long-term embarrassment but is usually mercifully short.

The second stage is that of the adult, which is attempting to understand the world. It is filled with jumbles of words that attempt to chronicle any quality that seems to be unique. In thousands of words, it attempts to explain how grocery stores in Moscow differ from their counterparts in Atlanta, how Tokyo fathers give special treatment to their daughters, and how the Robben Island prison uniquely shaped the character of Nelson Mandela. These descriptions are rarely read because they contain little to read. They are lists of words and nothing more.

The last stage is that of declining faculties, of a world shrunk too small. Running out of novel experiences and growing impatient with lengthy descriptions, the correspondents struggle to provide additional information about their experiences. The excuses come and are always the same. "I have done nothing new." "Nothing new has happened to me." "I have done nothing new to report." They have no further observations about the noise. Their prose dribbles for a while and then stops. Sans novelty. Sans exoticism. Sans anything.

The best of the correspondents choose a different approach that recognizes that they have never left the main trend of their lives. They have gone to a new country only in body. Their spirit, or at least part of it, remains in a community or family that resides at home. For them, the ideas that they need to communicate are not those of novelty or exoticism. They are the stories of growing up in a community that is both familiar and new, both here and there. It is Emily trying to make a Thanksgiving Dinner in Novosibirsk, Mark in Moscow courting Janelle in London, Melanie keeping alive a love of an English literature that has nothing and everything to say about her days in the l'Extrême Nord du Cameroun.

Underlying the global power of digital technology is the old Internet mantra: "drinking from a fire hose." It is a phrase which claims that volume can be equated to knowledge, to utility, or perhaps to amusement. It suggests that a certain amount of bandwidth will be able to carry distant experiences across land and ocean to share with friends and family.

While this idea is an honest attempt to describe the amount of information that can be passed through digital connections, it overlooks the fact that most people never even attempt to drink from an operating fire hose, and those who do find the experience unpleasant if not painful. Large volumes have their benefits, but they tend to push us in common directions. At first, such directions seem to represent a major trend or insight, but soon enough they break apart into a shower of droplets that reveal nothing but spray, nothing but the noise that is left when the important trends are gone.

The impact of digital technology is at least as fundamental as the changes wrought by its predecessors: high-speed printing, submarine telegraph cables, satellite television. At the same time, it reveals trends that are small not large, timeless not novel, universal not exotic. Statisticians, even in the Maldive Islands, are engaged in mundane tasks, no matter how fancy their technology may be. They are describing a society—cultural, political, and economic—that holds the lives of 396,334 souls who live on 298 square miles of real estate, a homeland that is only 7' 7" from the overwhelming tide. Should that tide rise, and it very nearly did during a recent holiday season, we hope that we have the stories that show how this country was connected to the rest of the world, how it was connected to the global model that underlies all the data that we can collect.

01
Managing at a Distance

Even though Erin was certain that we would talk about her, Dan and I never once mentioned her name in our conversation. Erin is convinced that the two of us hold strong opinions about her life, her plans for the future, and the young men who clamor for her attention.

Erin claims to have solid grounds for her concerns. Dan is, after all, her father and has more than 20 years of stories about her life that range from the merely embarrassing to the tragically compromising. I was her teacher and could relate a similar set of events that occurred as she passed through those last steps of transition from senior adolescent to young adult. If any two men on this Earth possess information that could control Erin's life, they are Dan and I.

Erin needn't have worried. Dan and I both know that we have no power over her. We both know that we couldn't begin to understand her life, though we might like to think that we could. We have no real information about Erin's situation, her choices, or her plans, hence we have no practical ability to redirect her life.

Besides, Dan and I have far more enjoyable subjects to discuss.

Dan's recent visit gave the two of us a brief opportunity to discuss the world's problems with no constraints, no calendar, and no budget limitations. Dan runs a large laboratory that has been operating for some 60 years. The organization has been a leader in the development of modern technology, including important applications for computers, but many observers feel that it is nearing the end of its useful life. Within the next few years, they claimed, the lab will cease to contribute anything of value to the world.

At that point, the managers will be faced with a large, unutilized workforce that will be tormented by the memory that they once did something important. The managers might have no choice but to shutter the building, put a historic plaque on the gate, and turn the engineers onto the street to beg for spare change to pay their professional dues.

As I have never worked in Dan's laboratory, I had not been disciplined by the nature of the situation. I was free to invent any operational detail I desired and to manipulate those details at will. Lines of control, departmental resources, operational routines, production metrics—all of these things came freely from my imagination as I speculated on ways to reorganize the institution.

For a little more than an hour, Dan and I indulged in fantasy management, directing not the real laboratory or even a useful abstraction of the truth but an institution made of words and lies and wishful thinking. We finished our time together with that burst of adrenaline and camaraderie causing us to believe that we had conquered time and space even though we had no evidence to support that conclusion.

Despite all protests to the contrary, Erin was convinced that her father and I had spent the hour talking about her. "Dad had a very good time," she noted.

"We have a lot in common," I responded.

She looked at me as if I had just confessed to her worst fears, but our conversation quickly moved to a discussion of her job and her effort to establish a career. She works for one of those firms that describes itself with the phrase "new media." It is a company that is trying to make money by selling advertising on webpages that contain some minimal amount of information. We chatted for a few minutes about revenue streams, click-throughs, demographics, and strategies. Then suddenly, a troubled look flashed across her face.

"My boss is moving to California," she said, "and is going to have her second baby in October."

"So who will manage your office?" I asked.

"My boss," she replied.

I paused at this point, understanding neither the changes to her office nor the issue of concern to her. To probe the situation, I started asking questions that would get Erin to answer "yes." It's a strategy I learned from my mother, who was a primary school teacher. "You learn nothing from children," she would say, "until they say 'yes' to three consecutive questions." It is a strategy that is useful for conversations with people of all ages and cultures.

"So are you moving to California?" I began.

"No," she said, "I'm staying right here."

"Will someone new oversee the daily operations of your office?"

"No," she repeated. "My boss will still run the group. Over the Internet. After she delivers her baby."

At this point, I felt that I had learned nothing, but I continued. "With no local manager?"

"None," she said before uttering the phrase that would explain the entire situation. "Except perhaps for me."

Erin, by her nature, wants order and discipline. With her manager on a distant coast and preoccupied with a new baby, Erin saw the responsibilities of running her office falling on her shoulders in the most chaotic and disruptive way possible. She doubted that her colleagues would get the work done on their own. She doubted that e-mail was an adequate tool to convey the complexities of daily operations. She feared that her boss would be unable to follow the tasks of the office. Chaos and old night were descending upon her. In addition, Erin knew this as certainly as she knew that Dan and I had spent an hour together conspiring to manage her life.

THE TECHNOLOGIES THAT WE HAVE deployed over the past two decades have given us new ability to manage activities at a distance. Engineers use them to manage production workers; schedulers use them to coordinate distribution channels; fathers use them to manage daughters, though I suspect that efforts in this last direction are less effective than most fathers would like.

In looking at the problem of distant management, we see that a good communication mechanism is only one of the tools that we need to control distant activities. We also need to be able to abstract the nature of those activities, determine the best measures for describing workflow, and create ways of ensuring trustworthiness. Ultimately, all of these elements play a role in determining the success of the new managerial scheme.

I had not thought much about the changes in distant management until a friend, Yugang, told me that he had started a new business in China.

"So does this mean that you've left California?" I asked.

"No," he responded. "I love San Diego and never want to leave."

"Do you travel to China often?" I asked.

"No," he replied. "About once every three or four months. I don't much like the long flight, though it does give me the opportunity to read all the technical publications that have been accumulating on my desk."

"So you have someone there who handles the day-to-day management," I concluded.

"No," he said. "I do it all myself over the Internet."

YUGANG WENT ON TO EXPLAIN that his firm deals with a single, highly abstract class of technical problems. Using a set of software tools, his Chinese engineers search for viable solutions. Once they find a good solution, they log it into a database.

From his desk in California, Yugang can easily track the work being done on the other side of the Pacific. He can verify the validity of the solutions, determine how those solutions were created, and even learn how much computer time each solution required.

After Yugang explained his process, I noted that many programmers far less skilled than his engineers had found ways of appearing to keep a computer busy when in fact they were merely spinning the disk drive and flashing meaningless symbols on the screen.

Yugang laughed. "It hasn't happened yet," he said. "So far we've been able to produce the work we need without using excessive resources."

ALTHOUGH COMPANIES LIKE YUGANG'S TECHNOLOGY business are relatively new, the phenomenon of distant management has an extensive history. For centuries, a good way of making money has been to create goods in one market and sell them in another. When the distance between the two markets precluded daily contact, merchants employed other strategies to manage their business. They looked for partners who could be trusted with resources and would reliably report the business conditions in the distant market.

"Well into the nineteenth century," wrote the business historian James Beniger, merchants managed their distant operations with "whatever communication they could manage, which usually meant hiring and distributing family members in key commercial centers," relying on "a traditional code of family and commercial 'honor.'" Sons could often be loyal representatives in distant centers, as they stood to inherit the accumulated wealth. However, they could easily have a sense of entitlement that caused them to challenge their father's leadership or even to squander their inheritance in riotous living.

Impoverished nephews were better, as they had fewer options for independent action. Ambitious sons-in-law were often the preferred representative, as their loyalty was ensured by the wife and children who remained at home.

Modern communications technologies reduced the need for capitalists to have large families with dutiful daughters and loyal sons-in-law, but they did not entirely solve the problems of distant management, for they uncovered the hidden problems of trust. It is far easier to lie to someone distant than to someone nearby, especially when a political or cultural boundary lies between the sender and the recipient. The telegraph, the telephone, and the Internet have only served to spread the three great lies of business, the misrepresentations that begin by claiming that "The prospects here are good," and then move to claim "We will easily meet our goals for the quarter," before ending with the classic falsehood, "The check is in the mail."

MOVING IN PARALLEL TO THE growth of communication was an expansion of abstraction, of using numbers and formulas to describe the activities of business and business relationships: cost accounting, production reports, financial statements, sales figures. The "language of quantification is a technology of distance," wrote the philosopher Ted Porter. "It exacts a severe discipline from its users, a discipline that is nearly uniform over most of the globe."

Of course, numbers by themselves do not necessarily represent truth, as British Prime Minister Benjamin Disraeli (1804–1881) noted when he classed statistics with the more obvious forms of misrepresentation of "lies" and "damned lies." However, quantification came with abstract models of business, rules for gathering data, and acceptable forms for presenting conclusions.

"It may be admitted that office work is difficult to measure," wrote management consultant William Henry Leffingwell (1876–1934), yet without it the manager "cannot know whether he is managing the office efficiently, or is keeping on the force more clerks than are actually required."

Leffingwell was one of the management consultants of the early 20th century, a group of individuals who worked to discipline manufacturing procedures and reduce the expense of operations.

Often called "efficiency experts," or scientific managers, these consultants are not normally included in the pantheon of those contributing to the modern computer, as they did nothing with electronic machinery and had only a passing connection to programs and algorithms. Yet by providing the ways to standardize business information, they opened the way to control commerce with stored programs.

"Control," wrote Leffingwell, "involves a very extensive knowledge of numerous details which... cannot be remembered by any ordinary individual." He argued that such details needed to be abstracted into a routine or an algorithm so that the manager could verify that the work was being done "without the necessity of personally knowing all the details that are involved."

The abstract routines of the efficiency experts allowed business activities to move across political and cultural boundaries. Knowing only a few basic facts about the routine, managers could make decisions about the allocation of resources and the scheduling of operations. They did not need to know the location of the office or the nature of the workers. Cost, speed, amount of product—that was all the manager needed to know, and that information could easily be transmitted over a wire.

Among the 20th-century notables in this field are a few familiar individuals, including Henry Gantt (1861–1919), who invented the project schedule chart that bears his name, and Frederick Winslow Taylor (1856–1915), who is considered the founder of the faith.

The best known of these management experts are Frank (1868–1924) and Lillian (1878–1972) Gilbreth. Their daughter, Ernestine, and her brother, Frank Jr., recorded the Gilbreths' story in the book *Cheaper by the Dozen*. The younger Gilbreths tell of a family that was "sort of a school for scientific management." It had standard ways of washing dishes, a sealed bid system for awarding household jobs, and a process chart that organized the events of the day and allocated precious resources, such as time in the bathroom. "It was regimentation all right," remembered the two siblings, "but bear in mind the trouble that most parents have in getting just one child off to school and multiply it by twelve."

Most parents have at least a little in common with the Gilbreths, as they often attempt to abstract their child's life into a weekly schedule, a list of tasks, or a chart of goals. Some have speculated that such techniques, when combined with a good Internet connection, might even allow them to manage the distant life of a grown daughter or son. Perhaps such control is possible, although, in my experience, it has never worked any better than the managerial plans we create when we gossip about failing sports teams, dissolute celebrities, or aging laboratories in need of reorganization.

02
Drinking with the Dinosaurs

Before the morning was over, I despaired of getting anything out of the conference. The gap between me and the participants seemed far too great. The translator was making a valiant effort to make sense of the Russian language but was stumbling over a litany of acronyms and technical terms. Her words, tinged with anxiety, lagged behind the slides by as much as five or ten minutes. As I knew only the pleasantries of the language, I could do nothing to help her beyond a laugh of sympathy when one of her translations slipped into the unintentionally obscene. When she uttered an unusual variation of a common vulgarism, I realized that she meant to say "re-entrant program library."

The conference had been organized to examine the technical contributions of the former Soviet Union and to compare them with developments in Europe and the United States. The speakers of that morning, most of them retired Soviet engineers, were arguing that they had created a computer industry independent of the West. I was intrigued to learn what they had done and was willing to let them make their case, but I found their evidence blocked in the gray haze of the translation.

Late in the afternoon, one speaker told a story so compelling that his words momentarily shone through the dull fog. He spoke in a hurry, as if he had to complete his narrative by a certain deadline. Unable to keep up with the words that tumbled out of his mouth, the translator was reduced to briefly summarizing the pictures that flashed on the wall. "Aircraft intercept," she said. "Digital signal processing." "Capitalist enemies from the NATO countries." "Missile targeting." "Destruction of imperialist intruders." Long before he showed us his last slide, a photograph of a destroyed American spy plane, we all knew that this man was describing the air defense system that the Soviet Union had deployed in the 1960s.

In taking questions from the audience, this speaker expressed regret about the things that he had not been able to accomplish. He told about his hopes to build a stronger system with better technologies and a more efficient design. His work had been thwarted by the enemies of the Soviet Union, enemies that dwelt within the bureaucracy and within the government. Ignorant bosses. Inefficient staff. Biased government planners. Corrupt officials. To the general approval of his peers, the presenter spat out the name "Gorbachev" as if it were mouthful of rancid potato soup.

When the talks were over, this speaker was one of two dozen individuals who retired to the clubhouse in the Academy of Science building to celebrate the day's events with an evening of drink. The Russians' beverage was vodka, the sort that should not be exposed to open flames. Mine was a local designer water, Molotov Springs according to my transliteration of the name.

The theme for the evening's discussion was the failure of leaders and the sacrifice of comrades. Each speech was followed by a toast, which pulled the group into the shared bond of melancholy. One speaker gave an elegy to the fallen of the Great Patriotic War, and we took a drink. Another recited Dostoyevsky, and we took a drink. A third sang a mournful hymn to failure, and we took a drink. After a time, the room grew quiet, so I stood to respond.

"I cannot recite Dostoyevsky, and I cannot sing a hymn," I said, "but I can at least offer the words of the great English poet."

> That time of year thou mayst in me behold
> When yellow leaves, or none, or few, do hang
> Upon those boughs which shake against the cold,
> Bare ruin'd choirs, where late the sweet birds sang.

I don't think they understood the meaning of the verse. Shakespeare's sonnets can be hard enough to understand without the added burdens posed by language and alcohol. Yet, the spirit of the poem caught the Russians' attention. They rose from their chairs. They applauded and hugged me and kissed my cheeks. "You have the soul of a Slav," they said. "You understand our lives. You are one of us."

Our hosts, tired after an emotional day, were being overly generous. I can make no claim to understanding either the spirit or the letter of the culture that shaped their lives. At the same time, I could see that we shared one experience in common. The Russians talked about technical projects that had been canceled with no explanation beyond the bland announcement that the decision was "good for the motherland and the Party." I, too, had once worked on a project, now some distance in the past, that was abruptly terminated "for the good of the company."

At the time, I had been a young programmer, freshly out of school, who specialized in system measurement and metrics. Had I been more experienced, I might have seen the signs that our project was in trouble: A boss suddenly reassigned to a "future studies project" where he had no line control over the development. A customer walking away from a substantial deposit. A financial manager demanding an immediate demonstration of all working features, "whatever they might be." They were signs that said our project had been weighed in the balance and found wanting.

WE ARE TOLD THAT WE must learn from experience. We are told that we learn from failure. "The notion that learning from failure is desirable is difficult to dispute," writes one pair of management consultants. "Agreement with this principle, however, does little to foster its enactment in the face of persistent psychological and organizational barriers."

In trying to learn from the death of our project, my colleagues and I first erected the barrier of self-protection. We were certain that the failure was caused by the misjudgment, malfeasance, or stupidity of one individual. We were equally certain that the individual who caused the failure was not one of us. It might be a product manager. It might a financial officer. It might be a technician who tested chips. It was not us.

The senior management never asked us to complete a final report on the project. I doubt that we could have done it honestly. Even in the best of circumstances, such work is difficult. A colleague of mine once wrote a review of how his office had operated during a difficult time. Their work had been successful, but they had encountered numerous problems along the way. He had circulated an intermediate draft to his coworkers and asked for comments. "Every one of them," he said, "wanted to rewrite some section to make themselves look better. No one defended the actions of someone else."

Beyond the desire to allocate blame elsewhere, we desired a simple explanation for the project's failure. We wanted a chain of causality that began with a simple mistake and led directly to our ruin. "For the want of a nail," wrote Benjamin Franklin (1706–1790), "the shoe was lost; for the want of a shoe, the horse was lost; and for the want of a horse the rider was lost, being overtaken and slain by the enemy, all for want of care about a horseshoe nail."

As we advanced to new jobs and new employment, we never moved beyond the notion that a single error had caused our downfall. We blamed the complex instruction set, the nonstandard compiler, the weaknesses in operational management, the lack of finances. All of these ideas gave us the comforting story that the failure was not our fault.

Years would pass before I realized, to my own embarrassment, that my reports might have contributed to our problems by exaggerating our competitors' weaknesses. I would require even more time to begin to understand the various layers of causes that might contribute to a project failure.

THE FIELDS OF LAW AND medicine both identify different layers of causes. Often, they work with three such layers, which they name in turn: the exciting cause, the predisposing cause, and the remote cause.

I have always found it easiest to distinguish these three layers in the example of the Chicago fire of 1871. This fire, which burned three square miles of the city, was a disaster far beyond any product failure of our age. According to legend, the fire was started when a cow, belonging to Mrs. Catherine O'Leary of DeKoven Street, kicked over a lamp. This story has been questioned by both historic and contemporary scholarship, but it is still a useful device to explain causality.

In the traditional story of the Chicago fire, the cow is the exciting cause. Her action led directly to the conflagration. The predisposing causes are many. The first is that a lamp was placed within striking distance of a cow. It is followed by the fact that the buildings of the time were constructed of highly flammable dried pine. A third was the lack of an effective fire department.

The remote causes are harder to identify and are often speculative. The O'Leary cow might have been anxious because it hadn't been milked the night before or because the neighbor children had teased it or because Mrs. O'Leary, angry from an argument with her husband over city taxes, had whacked the beast on the side.

In trying to learn from failure, we usually dismiss remote causes as too distant from our activities. Likewise, we ignore exciting causes by claiming that they are too arbitrary and too hard to control. If Mrs. O'Leary's cow had been brought under control, we might have had the same fire being started by a child playing with matches or an adult throwing a lit cigar into the wrong gutter.

We tend to focus our attention on the predisposing causes of failure and attempt to correct them. The citizens of Chicago instituted a new building code that required more fireproof materials. They redesigned the city to make it harder for fire to spread. Finally, they reorganized and strengthened their fire department.

The exciting cause of the failure that began my career was a missed deadline. A date fixed by the project designers for the demonstration of the central hardware came and went with no obvious sign that the system would ever work. However, by itself, the missed deadline would not cause the death of the project. "Objectives are missed and schedule and cost targets overrun with distressing regularity," observed a president of the American Federation of Information Processing George Glaser (1931–2006). Yet from that missed deadline came the calculation that our project was not likely to produce an adequate return on its investment. Vice presidents met, compared figures, and decided that the end had come.

In the end, the predisposing causes for our failure were all linked to the market for our product. First, other firms were establishing a position in that market, reducing the opportunity for us. Second, the customers in that market were starting to adopt standards that were incompatible with our system. Finally, we concluded that our competitors would be offering more powerful and less expensive systems about the time that ours would be ready for delivery.

Yet, pointing to the market can be merely another way of deflecting blame. It can also make an organization too conservative, unwilling to develop a new product unless market conditions are far better than they can actually be in real life.

In our case, the market pointed to our own technological failures. We were entering a new market and had neither the intellectual ability to design the proper system for it nor the technical ability to implement a good design. "Projects that depend on technological breakthroughs for their success present special management problems," wrote Glaser. "Despite the high risk of failure, such projects are common in the computer industry." He added that "a few are successful, largely because survival is a strong motivator, but typically casualties are high."

"Despite the importance of learning from failure, it is more common in exhortation than in practice," wrote two business scholars, "and our understanding of the conditions under which it occurs is limited."

LIKE MANY OTHER YOUNG PEOPLE, I was largely untouched by the failure of our project. I packed my bags and moved to another city, hoping that a fresh environment would give me the opportunity for success. Chicago, which was a young city in 1871, responded in a similar way, though of course it was geographically bound to the southern tip of Lake Michigan. The city rebuilt itself and looked for success in the future rather than lessons from the past. Barely two decades after the fire of 1871, Chicago hosted the major cultural event of the century's end, a world's fair that, among other things, unveiled the mechanical tabulating machines of Herman Hollerith (1860–1929), the founding technology of IBM.

The dinosaurs, the name I have come to apply to those Russian electrical engineers, were remarkably untouched by our melancholy evening of poetry, song, and drink. They arrived at the conference the next day happy and eager to talk. I tried to engage a few of them in a discussion about project failure, about what they had learned from the ultimate fates of their project. Not only were they not interested in discussing such a subject, they seemed unable to understand my questions.

ONLY LATER DID I REALIZE their response to my approach was honest rather than an effort to hide technical incompetence. After all, they had spent their careers in an environment where market success was unknown and value was measured by the ability to support the country's leadership. They had seen that environment vanish, and now all they could do was hold their accomplishments to the light, like little fossilized bones, and say to anyone who would listen, "This was good. This was important. And we could have done something even better."

03
Open Borders

Had the decision been in the hands of the lab's senior leadership, I would never have been given a pass for the day. The department heads were anxious and not especially interested in leaving the security of its compound to talk with someone who was naturally curious, asked lots of questions, and knew enough physics to make sense of the photographs that were circulating on the Web. Those photographs had shaken the authority of their leadership. The images showed the results of a recent accident in their major particle accelerator. They included twisted beams, crushed concrete, and mangled equipment. If they had been able to muster the power, the senior managers would have closed the lab to outside visitors. However, managers rarely have all the power that they feel they deserve. Neither superior technology nor the authority of science allows them to act as they please. A graduate student took pity on my request and granted me a pass to his office and the computer center.

The student, Rashid, met me at the front desk of the lab, the Organisation Européenne pour la Recherche Nucléaire or CERN, and escorted me back to the computer buildings. We were exchanging the usual pleasantries for such a situation: our academic background, the work that we had done, the people we knew. As we approached the computing complex, Rashid remarked that we were crossing the national border from Switzerland into France.

"Really," I said. "Technically, don't we need visas to cross legally?" The Swiss had voted to deactivate their border stations but had yet to implement the decision.

"Probably," he responded before resuming the previous topic of conversation.

I scanned the area and spotted a couple of security cameras hanging from poles. If the lab did not require visas, it at least knew where we were. In all likelihood, the cameras were installed to protect the facility's assets. The lab does not do national security work and is proud of its policies to circulate technical information freely. These policies are derived from a set of fundamental agreements among the national governments that support the organization. Such agreements are the detailed work of national science officers. They describe and protect activities that scientists believe are fundamental to their field. They serve as reminders that there are no such things as natural rights for science and that our approach to science is governed by human decisions about what is open and what is not.

I HAD COME TO CERN to get a sense of how its computing facilities operated. I knew that this division could not claim the kinds of innovations that had been developed at American physics laboratories. It was a service organization that provided the means of processing large amounts of data that came from the facilities. I expected to find large, powerful machines that were part of highly organized and well-disciplined systems.

I was aware that CERN could claim at least one major innovation. It served as the midwife for the technology that became the common interface into the Internet, the ideas of HTML and network browsers. This accomplishment occupied a central place in the lab's museum. Surrounded by remnants of old experiments, clever demonstrations that attempt to educate the youth of today, and one of the world's more impressive cosmic ray detectors, stood a display case that contained an old Unix workstation and a well-thumbed cross-indexed encyclopedia.

The encyclopedia had been the muse to the originator of the World Wide Web, Tim Berners-Lee. He had owned such an encyclopedia as a child and had been enchanted by the way that it took a reader from one field of knowledge to another. He had contemplated how he might implement such an idea in software and had been led to a particular brand of Unix workstation. This system was sold with the source code for much of the system software. Rather than write his index system from scratch, he could borrow large pieces of useful code from the machine itself.

CERN's MACHINE ROOM SAT ABOUT four meters into French territory. If there had ever been a problem transporting data across national boundaries, it was clearly at a disadvantage. At one point, it had been a traditional, centralized computing center with large scientific super computers carefully deployed so that visitors could be impressed with their large physical presence. However, this center no longer displayed the old totems of a scientific computing center. Nothing looked particularly impressive or even distinctive. What I saw in front of me was the picture of a typical corporate computing center with racks upon racks of servers.

"How many processors?" I asked mechanically, hoping that the number might suggest an interesting story of innovation.

"About 40,000," was the reply. The tone suggested that no one was interested in an accurate census.

Across the front line of the machine racks stretched a rope on stanchions. A sign suggested that it was deployed to keep groups of computer tourists at bay and protect the machines from the unpredictable actions of marauding school groups. If such was the intent, it was misguided in its application. The racks contained nothing of interest. No aspect of the little gray processor boxes or the orange and yellow cables would tempt anyone, young or old, with the hunter's curiosity. The only objects that interrupted the landscape of digital agriculture were a red cylinder in the far corner of the room and a black cube in the center.

The cylinder was the facility's Internet connection, which also served the local region. I originally mistook the black cube for a vending machine, but it proved to be a digital storage facility. It contained hundreds of hard drives, neatly arranged in little slots. These drives were manipulated by a large mechanical arm, which selected a disk, placed it in a data port to drain the appropriate content, and then returned it to the proper resting place. The cube might have attracted the eyes of a young visitor for a minute before revealing the disappointment that it did not accept Euros and did not dispense chocolate.

Rashid explained that the center's life had been drained by the rise of virtualization. With virtualization, researchers did not need a large computer close at hand. In fact, they did not need to have any specific computer at all. Instead, they packaged their programs and software into virtual machines, programs that simulate the operation of a physical computer. They then sent those virtual machines around the world in search of physical resources. The researchers never knew which physical devices were doing their work.

Virtualization grew out of the earliest efforts to divide the full resources of a single computer among several individual users. As with so many technological developments, it looked backward rather than forward. The roots of this idea "are most deeply entwined with the style of use of the computing machines of the 1950s by scientists and engineers," wrote one commentator. "In those days, the machines were used as personal tools, much like their predecessors, which had been designed and dedicated to specific applications."

Programmers knew how to develop code for a single machine, so they devised a system that appeared to be a single machine even though many people were actually using it. The result was a system that isolated programs from each other. The programs could detect nothing else on the computer and hence did not realize that they were sharing a processor, memory, peripherals, and even registers.

An IBM research group did most of the original work on virtualization in 1964 and 1965. This group had been organized to create a comprehensive system for sharing computing resources. The leaders of IBM had anticipated that it would be the prime contractor on the US government's effort to develop such systems, an effort that would be known as Project Mac. Much to the surprise of the IBM group programmers, their proposal failed to win the contract. With few options in front of them, they rewrote their proposal, pitched it to their corporate leadership, and started the work of developing their own time-sharing system. This system would be a collection of three programs that would be known as VM for Virtual Machine.

From the start, VM fell on a different side of the border from Project Mac. Project Mac began with the process, the indivisible bit of code, as its fundamental unit. It built an environment that allowed processes to operate independently. This environment came to be called Multics and was an example of a timesharing system.

The IBM group began with the fundamental ideas of the machine and tried to preserve its fundamental features for all users. The group got its system working in about 18 months and presented it to a decidedly cool corporate leadership. The corporate officers were not especially impressed with the VM system, but they were willing to let it become a minor product, the kind of system that has no official support from the company but is sustained by a vocal group of loyalists. "We did not know if the system would be of practical use to us, let alone anyone else," confessed one developer. It was "only a small step toward the goal of making computers easy and convenient."

In this period, the company was beginning to grapple with the issues of software and how it differed, as a product, from hardware. The researchers recognized that VM occupied territory that was quite different from the realm of Project Mac and that it had little in common with the time-sharing systems of the day, so they relegated it to a back pasture for programs that would receive little promotion and less support. This pasture nourished many other pieces of unusual IBM software, such as the language APL.

Something there is in the information age that dislikes a wall. Programmers saw enough of VM through the fence to install it on their own machines. They also demanded that IBM support the system and invest in it. Through the 1980s and 1990s, a time when programmers could easily purchase an entire machine for one person to use, the VM advocates kept the product alive.

VIRTUALIZATION FURTHER UNDERMINED THE BORDER that split the CERN facility and overleapt the fence that surrounded the lab. It freed researchers from any dependency on specialized hardware. Instead of waiting for time on super computers in the lab's machine room or even super computers at other physics laboratories, it compressed data and programs into a software package called a virtual machine and sent that package out into the network in search of any kind of computing resource. It could run at another laboratory. It could run on surplus cycles that had been donated to science. It could utilize commercial services that might otherwise be used to support a retail store.

Indeed, while visiting CERN I received an e-mail from a physics laboratory in the United States that was using a commercial service to process experimental data. The lead investigator was quite proud of her accomplishment, though she acknowledged that many would find it difficult to understand the challenge in using machines that were designed to support webpages for scientific calculations. I thought that I might share with her the story of the British Nautical Almanac, which adapted commercial accounting machines to scientific calculation in the 1930s. However, after a few moments of thought, I realized that the experience of the Almanac office would only confirm her worst fears. No one thought the story newsworthy, as few of them understood the difference between counting pounds, shillings, and pence and the calculations to predict the movement of the planets across the night sky.

It is something fundamental that does not like a wall. From the very start, researchers wanted computers to move, even though the task was quite daunting for many of the early machines. "I predicted that the computer would never work again after reassembly," recalled an engineer who worked on one of the first programmable machine. The move had to be treated as a complex engineering task. The machine had to be disassembled, crated, moved, tested piece by piece, reassembled, and validated by running programs that had once worked at the old site.

"In reconnecting it I discovered a wiring error that was in the original drawings," reported the engineer. He corrected the error and tested the machine once again. It required substantial effort but the machine ran "successfully for another ten years." Virtualization needs no testing, no reassembly, no crating and uncrating. The machine simply moves over the Internet.

WHEN I LEFT CERN, I took a trolley back to the city and found the cars packed with people. There were young adults dressed for a night of drunken reveling, families with children in their hands, and portly middle-aged men dressed as 17th-century soldiers and carrying a variety of weaponry that is not normally allowed on trams. A torch. A long rifle. Some kind of grappling hook. A broadsword with very nasty edges.

I must have appeared confused, for the man next to me asked if I knew what day it was.

"I have no idea," I said.

"It is the night of the Escalade," he responded. "The night that the Protestant troops repulsed the last major attack of the Counter Reformation." He then asked his daughter to show me her chocolate pot and tell me the story of Mere Royaume.

Mere Royaume lived in a house that was perched on the city wall. On the night of the Escalade attack, she was making soup in a large pot. When she spied the French troops climbing the wall, she opened the window and flung her pot at the attackers. She killed one, sent a platoon into retreat, and provided a moral to children that could be illustrated in a chocolate treat. She reduced all the great questions of the age, questions that hung on contradicting opinions about humanity's relationship to the divine, to a little virtual pot packed with candies.

Walls and borders have their place. They define responsibilities, protect action, and allow the careful study of complicated ideas. Still, we celebrate our ability to circumvent these boundaries by championing the open flow of scientific information, promoting the movement of virtual machines, and rejoicing in a little pot of chocolate that is held by a little girl with a shining face.

04
The Digital Jolly Roger

Even though it prominently displays a city vendor's license and health certificate, I am hesitant to purchase anything from Eddie's food cart. You just don't know where his food has been. Sure, most everything is sold in sealed packages, but many of those packages look as if they were snatched from the back of a pickup truck that was idling at a loading dock. Still, Eddie serves a good cup of coffee and has a loyal customer base, including limo drivers who are waiting for their employers to finish their power lunches at the nearby Costosi's restaurant.

I was chatting with Eddie recently when he suddenly asked, "Do you need some software?"

"Excuse me?" I asked. It never occurred to me that Eddie might be doing some computer system design work in his spare time.

"I was just wondering if you needed some software," he continued, "because you look like the sort of guy who might. And I know a guy up in Columbia Heights who could get it for you cheap."

Perhaps it was neither the time nor the place to be inquisitive, but I couldn't resist asking, "Is it the real stuff or is it pirated?"

Eddie grinned in a way that almost made me believe he might be a survivor of the golden age of the Caribbean buccaneers. He then gave me a quick description of how the copy protections of a major software vendor could easily be circumvented. He spoke as if every 12-year-old shared this knowledge. "The software works perfectly well," he added. "It doesn't have any documentation, if that is what you want, but who cares about it anyhow. Price is $20."

So Eddie belongs to a pirate gang, I thought. As I was trying to phrase a response, Eddie misinterpreted my silence as a bargaining tactic and lowered his price to $10.

I laughed and declined his offer. Software piracy is a strange business to operate on one of the city's busiest street corners, but the world is a confusing place. He has operated his food cart there for years, despite Costosi's efforts to stop him. Likewise, I suspect that he will be able to peddle his software for years no matter what the software giants attempt to do.

OF COURSE, EDDIE'S CART IS only a tiny part of global software piracy. The Software & Information Industry Association estimates that that the industry lost US $28 billion to pirates last year. A report from the Business Software Alliance notes that across the globe, $1 in illegal software sales is racked up for every $2 in legitimate sales. In some countries, such as Albania and Zimbabwe, virtually all software is pirated. In several big markets, notably Russia and China, more than 80 percent of software is illegal.

Software piracy, like the classic Caribbean piracy of the 17th and 18th centuries, is a crime against a distribution network. The Caribbean pirates preyed on the wealthy but fragile transportation route that connected Spain to its Central and South American colonies.

The pirates extracted great wealth from this vital link, which carried weapons and manufactured goods to the colonies and returned millions of silver and gold coins to Spain. They operated freely in the region until the European powers took deliberate, organized steps to eliminate their bases of operation.

The growth of the British navy in the 17th century greatly reduced piracy in the region. Nonetheless, pirates vanished from the Caribbean only when the region ceased to host an important distribution network.

Compared to their ocean-going counterparts, software pirates will be harder to eliminate, as the information industry has given them a technology that lets them hide their activities far better than William Kidd (1654–1701) or Henry Morgan (1635–1688) could hide their ships on the deserted beaches of unknown islands. The struggle against piracy will be one of the defining periods of the information age, as it will test the software industry's ability to project its power, to control the actions of reclusive pirates in distant lands. Just as Spain began to falter when it lost access to the mineral wealth of the Americas, this industry will find itself in deep waters should it lose access to the rich revenue streams that it enjoys.

LIKE SO MANY PROBLEMS OF this world, software piracy has existed almost as long as software itself. One of the earliest computer pioneers, Calvin Mooers (1919–1994), noted that the software markets of his era were "characterized by a kind of anarchic morality in which all software is fair game for outright rip-off."

Then, as now, many considered the problem to be one of ethics. They claimed that people stole software because they didn't know any better. "Computer software and data are intellectual property," wrote one educator. "The problems start when people cannot, or will not, make the mental transition from physical to intellectual property."

Yet piracy is not merely a failure to recognize right and wrong. Mooers noted that the early pirates were "not only individuals; among them, in fact, are a few of our largest and most highly respected corporations."

Companies have many reasons to encourage piracy, reasons that can cause them to take actions they know are illegal. In a piracy case of the mid-1980s, two different firms copied a well-known piece of system software and marketed it as their own. At first, neither acknowledged that they had done anything wrong. Instead, they claimed that they were merely making a shrewd, though admittedly aggressive, business decision.

A friend of mine, who worked on the software before it was stolen, decided to approach the problem as a missionary among the lost souls, just as the European churches sent emissaries to convince the pirates of the errors of their way. This friend tried to stop the piracy by organizing a conference for all parties to the complaint to discuss the foundations of morals. Sabers and cutlasses were to be left at the door.

In addition to the usual round of lawyers, principals, and mediators, this conference included a Protestant minister and a Buddhist monk to lead the discussion. At the meeting, one of the firms had a change of heart. Light shone from the heavens. Scales fell from their eyes. They recognized the evil of their ways and immediately repented.

The other firm, however, didn't react in quite the same way. They found the talk of right and wrong interesting, in an abstract, intellectual way, but they still insisted that they had behaved by the rules of the market. In the end, this defense was no better than the claim that pirates make the market more efficient by redistributing surplus wealth. The officers of the corporation ended their days in the jail, guilty of theft on the high seas.

IN THE GRAND ERA OF Caribbean piracy, the most effective pirates were not the lone ships preying upon the Spanish, but national pirates, privateers whose ships were sanctioned by the United Kingdom or the Netherlands to attack foreign commerce.

The most famous of these privateers were the buccaneers, the Brethren of the Coast. "They formed a seafaring republic which did as much as any nation to erode the Spanish dominance of the New World," observed one historian.

To defend against the privateers and buccaneers, the Spanish had to build a substantial infrastructure in the region. They created a navy, a string of heavily armored forts, and a communication network to keep the residents informed of actions in the area.

The buccaneers of software are not from the lowlands of Western Europe or an island kingdom in the North Sea but the lands of East Asia. "American companies are losing 'many millions' of dollars in potential business in China," claimed one observer, because "software has been widely pirated here." The US government charged that this piracy "required concerned efforts by Chinese engineers," and hence pointed to a "very serious decision made at a very high level in the Chinese ministries, research institutes and state-run corporations that have acquired US software."

THE SOFTWARE INDUSTRY RESPONDED TO the evidence of national piracy by strengthening its global defense infrastructure. The fortresses of the software distribution routes are not made of stone and steel but of security standards, copyright standards, trade agreements, and treaties to share the burden of policing the world's computers.

This defensive effort has been only marginally successful. Some of the biggest national markets outside the US, notably those of China and Russia, have seen only small reductions in piracy. The piracy rate in China has fallen from a high of 92 percent to 82 percent. The rate in Russia has dropped only from 87 percent to 80 percent. The best news from these markets is the fact that they're expanding so rapidly that the revenue from legitimate products has grown substantially. The Business Software Alliance indicates that in China, this revenue increased 88 percent in a single year during the early 2000s when the Chinese government started enforcing some copyright agreements.

Caribbean privateers and buccaneers were replaced by individual pirates, crews that mutinied against their captains and preyed upon the Spanish trade. Their ships were harder to eradicate because they found ample hiding places on isolated islands or in the small bays of the North American continent.

Their modern counterparts are the individual pirates who distribute software on peer-to-peer networks or offer it for sale in small stores (or at street corner food carts). In some regions, the small pirate distribution networks are far stronger and more effective than legitimate distribution channels.

"They are the only way you can keep your computer operating in some parts of the world," is how my friend Emily explained these networks. "The stuff you buy at the normal computer store comes with a disk that you load first. It prevents the annoying little registration thing from coming up."

Emily had just returned to the US after working for two years in central Asia. I was inclined to discount her claims, as she comes from the generation that learned about electronic music through the illegal file-sharing networks of the 1990s, the most visible aspect of piracy at the time. However, she quickly argued otherwise.

"It's a poor place," she said, "and so it is the remainder sale site for software from all over the world. If you buy movies, for example, they might come from the US, Australia, Europe, or Hong Kong."

"So why does that encourage piracy?" I asked.

"Each of those legal movies has a digital code saying where it's from.

"If you try to play it with legitimate software, the computer will eventually decide that you're in some specific part of the world, and it will prevent you from playing anything from another region.

"The only way to fix the problem is to use a pirated video player. You buy boot-legged DVD software for $1. When the pirates strip out the security, they also remove the code that sets the region. If you don't use that, you'll eventually have a computer that can only play films that were marketed for Micronesia."

If we follow the strategy that was used against the 17th-century Caribbean pirates, we would attempt to reduce piracy in distant markets by strengthening the distribution network, making it easier to buy software at a distance and easier to track the usage of software in remote places. Some authors suggest marking each copy of software so that it could be tracked through the network. Such technologies would "dissuade the pirate by increasing the likelihood of being caught."

At the same time, it seems unlikely that technology by itself will entirely prevent piracy. Emily likes to remind me that some of her pirated software uses the Interpol antipiracy screen as the background to the main menu.

"It's my favorite part," she says. "The digital Jolly Roger." It's the mark of the modern pirate stolen from antipiracy forces.

IN LOOKING FOR A UNIFIED solution to software piracy, some authors have suggested deploying an economic policy against stolen software. It's an obvious suggestion for an industry that has so thoroughly championed the market.

Most of the highest piracy rates are in countries that are poor, have no indigenous software industry, and can't easily enforce national copyright standards. In such countries, "focusing purely on enforcing intellectual property rights will have limited success," argued one pair of researchers. Legislative "and educational weapons may win a few battles, but the overall war against piracy cannot be won without addressing the current draconian pricing policies." They concluded that we can reduce the piracy rate in such countries only by making the price of legitimate software competitive with the price that pirates offer.

We probably won't eliminate software pirates in the near future, and we probably won't do it with a single strategy. We don't have the technical, financial, or political resources to do anything more than whittle away at the piracy rate. Furthermore, some legitimate firms have much to gain from illegitimate software. Piracy can keep a competitor out of the marketplace, increase the acceptance of certain ideas, and build a demand for related products.

Finally, the line between aggressive capitalism and organized crime can be thin and ill-defined at times. Piracy to one person can be a low-cost supply opportunity to another. Aggressive pricing can be a means of stopping a black market or a way to undercut a legitimate competitor. Accurate product tracking can strengthen a distribution network, or it can be an invasion of privacy.

Should the software industry succeed in reducing piracy, it will be able to claim that it has spread its business culture and ethics to every corner of the globe, an accomplishment that was denied the Spanish empire in the 17th century.

If we draw near to that point, we might find that we start to romanticize software pirates, just as we have romanticized the pirates of the Caribbean. Through the writings of Daniel Defoe, Lord Byron, and Robert Lewis Stephenson, we have come to view pirates as daring individuals who expressed their own individuality in the face of an oppressive colonial regime.

For the moment, we still tend to view software pirates as petty thieves, no matter how large an operation that they might run. However, if we come to feel that our lives are too much under the control of Redmond or Silicon Valley or some other technology capital, we might come to give our pirates a more heroic light and could discover, like the Spaniards of the 17th century, that the future better remembers us for our piracy than for our admirals of industry, for the digital Jolly Roger rather than for the flags of software corporations.

05
Where Are You From?
with Erin Dumbacher

"So how was Latvia?" I asked Erin when she returned from her year abroad.

"Estonia," she replied.

"Right," I said.

"The difference is important," she added.

Of course, she was right.

I admit that I was a little skeptical when Erin approached me with the idea of spending a year studying technology in the Baltics. I didn't think of the region as a promising center of innovation. Certainly, I knew that Finland identified itself as a major economic force in the cell phone industry and that Estonia had built a network infrastructure that had been thoroughly overwhelmed by a denial-of-service attack that may or may not have been instigated by its Russian neighbor.

Beyond these two things, I saw little of interest. However, the real issue was not the promise of the region, but the prospects for the individual.

Erin had designed that year to create a space for herself. She was going to spend some time making her first mark upon the field of technology. In many ways, it was the same kind of task her country of study had faced time and again.

For most of its existence, Estonia has been a small part of some larger empire. Its name derives from the words for "eastern land," which was applied to the region when it was a corner of the Swedish empire.

For almost 200 years, Estonia was part of the Russian empire. In the mid-20th century it was occupied by Germany and later became the northwestern edge of the Soviet Union. In the past decade, Estonia has been allied with the digital empire that is centered on San Jose.

In embracing technology, it has tried to establish a central position in the artificial geography of the Internet, a geography that identifies an organization by what it can do with data rather than where it is located.

> I, Erin, need to interrupt here. I'm the one who went to Estonia. David tends to remember stories the way he wants to think of them. It's not that he remembers them incorrectly; he simply puts his own ideas at the center and pushes everything else to the edges.
>
> I didn't go to Estonia only to study Skype. That would make as much sense as visiting New York City and spending the time walking through the original offices of Bell Laboratories.

(I think David did that once to see what the old laboratory structure on West Street would tell him about the researchers. I thought it odd.) I went to Estonia to see "E-stonia," the best example of a high-tech economy that has developed in a former Soviet state. Estonians make heavy use of the Web and boast of their e-government services—an online database makes possible everything from e-voting to obtaining e-prescriptions. Estonian friends mocked my American checkbook—none of them had ever seen such a thing. In Estonia, 98 percent of all bank transactions are handled electronically.

Skype is actually one segment of a competitive telecommunications sector in Estonia. In addition to the Skype-filled computer screens found in most homes and offices, the country has four mobile service providers, with broadband connections in two-thirds of the households, and wireless Internet available in most parts of the country.

Estonia's current president, Toomas Hendrik Iives, claims that the country's future "will be advanced best by investments... that reward doing and enterprise, innovation and creativity."

Born to Estonian parents who fled the Nazis first and then the Soviets, Ilves grew up in the shadow of the telecommunications industry in New Jersey. His country now has an information and telecommunications industry that is the largest in the Baltics, and his industry has deployed a broad range of services that include a resilient voice network and electronic voting technology that seems to be secure and popular.

Of course, this growing cyberinfrastructure has made Estonia particularly vulnerable to cyberattacks.

Two denial of service attacks in April and May 2007 overwhelmed government, media, and financial sites. These incidents demonstrated that no country is isolated in this age.

AFTER FIRST ATTEMPTING TO CLOSE the borders to halt traffic into the country, Estonian telecom managers discovered that they had no choice but to terminate all services for visitors and clients. They succeeded in reestablishing services only with the assistance of regional and international friends. Sweden supplied critical infrastructure experts. A firm in California offered platform services. Servers in Europe and the Mideast provided a coordinated response to the attacking bots.

In my effort to understand the Estonian IT landscape, I did visit the Skype offices. However, I have to remind David that the company's official headquarters are in Luxembourg, which is more or less the Delaware of the European Union. "Skype's leadership flies from Luxembourg to London to the Valley; their headquarters are everywhere, really," a Skype staffer told me.

Skype was founded in 2003 by five developers: three Estonians, a Swede, and a Dane. The team was first involved in taking Kazaa to market, which tried to exploit the Internet through peer-to-peer file sharing. The team left that business when the recording industry successfully argued that the service undermined copyright law, and brought their experience to Skype to make it a rare success in the era following the dot-com bust.

When we talked about writing an article related to my experiences in Estonia, David speculated that Estonian developers became interested in Voice over IP (VoIP) because they had lived with the old Soviet phone service, which was awful. Not only was the phone system regularly tapped, it had low-quality connections and very few phone sets. An entire apartment block might share a single telephone.

Admittedly, while the Soviet phone system was indeed bad, so were the phone systems in many other parts of the world at that time. None of them produced a company that capitalized on VoIP technology.

Before Erin goes much further, I need to make two comments. First, I don't disagree with her claim that I tell stories to make my own points. I simply want people to believe that I do it for good and benign purposes.

Second, I would argue that connecting VoIP to Kazaa and peer-to-peer file sharing misses an important aspect of its development—the step that took it from being an isolated technology to being a service that had to interact with large, powerful institutions. VoIP had its origins in the multimedia community that flourished in the 1980s. It was originally developed to help support the interactions of individuals working in different locations on a common task. "The primary focus in this stage was on audio and video conferencing over the Internet," explained one history of the technology.

By the early 1990s, researchers had identified VoIP as a valuable technology in its own right. Several firms developed software products that allowed two individuals to hold conversations using their PCs and the Internet. However, all of these systems worked in isolation. "Each product relied on a proprietary signaling protocol for call set up and tear down," continued the technological history, "which made it virtually impossible for two vendors' products to interoperate."

In 1995, the International Telecommunication Union began to develop a standard for a common set of protocols for VoIP that would allow the various commercial systems to communicate with one another. As this standard developed, the considerations included not only the problem of connecting two VoIP systems from different vendors but also the issue of connecting VoIP to the large switched telephone networks.

This VoIP standard proved to be a significant milestone in the development of VoIP, as it allowed the newer, smaller technology to interact with some of the largest technical institutions around the world. In most countries, the telephone company was a government entity, a highly regulated monopoly, or at the least a very large sector of the local economy.

By providing the means of connecting VoIP service to the local telephone grid, the standard might have solved a technical issue, but it also posed a substantial economic problem: the financing of local telephone grids.

Traditionally, phone companies used revenue from long-distance calls to subsidize the construction and operation of local nets. Local "facilities were used at both ends of every long-distance call," explained an analysis of telephone policy. "And the greatest part of the cost of the local network was fixed, not sensitive to the level of its traffic."

When the US divided the telephone monopoly into smaller units, regulators devised a regulatory and payment structure to support local networks. That plan unleashed a storm of political criticism. "After five years of nurturing the plan," reported a pair of researchers, "the government lost control of the public process altogether."

In the late 1990s, many of those working with VoIP acknowledged that bypassing "standard telephone charges was then regarded as one of the main economic drivers for VoIP." However, rather than immediately shifting large amounts of voice traffic to the Internet, voice quickly generated new traffic that the traditional phone network couldn't have easily accommodated—the traffic that supported business process outsourcing.

Just as firms began to implement the VoIP standard, they began to see that business process outsourcing could be a large industry that required massive amounts of telecommunications services. In just a few years, it had grown to become a $100 million dollar business.

Future growth depended upon the availability of inexpensive voice and data services. "Infrastructural facilities or lack of these have often been underlined as the most crucial in terms of work and the economy itself," explained a policy analyst from India. "This is all the more relevant for industries that depend fundamentally upon telecommunications generally and upon the telecommunications industry more specifically."

Did you see that? David was able to turn a discussion of technology innovations in Estonia into one of business processes and outsourcing to emerging markets. Let's get back to the main point. Although Estonia is a small country with a population of only 1.3 million, it has become a leader in e-government services as well as an active participant in the global information and communications technology business.

With its aspirations to be a leader in IT and telecommunications, Estonia somehow encourages turning instinctively to these technologies in times of crisis, great or small.

Last winter, I found myself grasping for my mobile phone when I spotted a pack of wolves grazing barely 50 meters from where I was standing. Until the moment I spied the wolves, I had been enjoying, or trying to enjoy, the process of learning how to cross-country ski on a cold, gray winter day in southern Estonia. My hosts were somewhere ahead, and my only companion was a six-year-old child who would only have been an appetizer for the wolves, should they decide to attack.

Quietly and with courage, I held up my phone. "Not to worry," I mimed to the child, "I have my mobile phone in hand."

Had the wolves turned on us, I suppose I could've made an emergency call to explain the situation to friends in Tallinn, family in America, or even a friend in Cameroon. "Wolves are attacking," I would have said. "I'll text you a photo; please send help." Somehow this was reassuring. We could have contacted someone. Perhaps that possibility is the most important thing in such a circumstance.

As Erin's experience indicates, the emergency call—the call that asks for help from someone who knows the region, has the skill to act, and is blessed by appropriate authority—is one example of the limitations of modern technology. In our current telephone systems, such calls are regularly sent around the world to be processed by someone located in a faraway place. For example, after the Haitian earthquake in 2010, when the country's infrastructure was barely operating, some emergency requests were processed by a company in California. Yet, the response to an emergency call usually needs to come from a source close to the caller's location.

The VoIP protocols can't always identify a caller's location, especially if the caller is tapping into the network over a wireless connection. Hence, Skype and several other services don't support emergency calls and can't guarantee a connection that can help you in case of a wolf attack.

Unless you get local help through other means, you've opted for a connection to the broader world in lieu of communal support.

When Erin was applying for a scholarship to conduct research in Estonia, she wrote an essay that began, "I'm one of those people with a complicated answer to the supposedly simple question, 'Where are you from?'"

Traditionally, we took our identity from the place where we were born and where our parents lived. For those of us who have become increasingly mobile, answering the question of where we're from has become more difficult as well. Now, where you're from might be the place you attended school. Or it might be the place where you bought your first cell phone and acquired an area code that would mark you for the rest of your days.

In spite of such mobility, many people have no choice when they answer that question. They live in a specific corner of an empire and are grateful that technology brings work and meaning to them. Their neighbors are those who will offer help when trouble comes. That trouble can be hackers from Russia, invading Swedes, or a family of wolves looking for a snack.

Exit
Everything is here
Wish you were beautiful

I never leave home, even when I am not there. I carry a little black rectangle that keeps me connected with my circle of friends and family. I pay bills, participate in business meetings, deal with city services, send pictures to relatives, and do a dozen other things all through the miracle of a little electronics and a lot of software. This existence is part of the mythical land of globalism, an emerald city where there is an infrastructure that supports the existence you know at home. Charles Babbage could tour Europe in 1819 because he both knew French and held letters of credit to the banking system that was emerging from the twin disruptions of the Revolution and Napoleon. We can follow in his footsteps if we have good telephone service and the appropriate PIN numbers to the organizational websites at home.

The bubble created by a good cell phone can be just as misleading as the world of international airports and luxury hotels. As long as you stay in either environment, you are never truly on your own.

Not that long ago, I was exploring the neighborhoods of Beijing. My wife was working, and I took the chance to see the landmarks that she had visited on prior trips. I found my way to the central square, after being carefully frisked by the guards who stood at the entrance, and decided that I needed to send a picture to a friend back home. I took a nice photo of Mao's portrait, addressed the e-mail and indicated that I wanted a copy sent to myself. I added the message "I'm standing in Tiananmen Square where there were protests in 1989" and punched the send button.

I had written an article on the use of computer networks during the China protests of 1989 and was slightly disappointed that I was not considered a dangerous person by the Chinese government. I had shown how a group of students in the United States had influenced the actions in Beijing and how they had adjusted their actions to make themselves a more effective organization. I know that the article had gotten a certain amount of attention from the Chinese community because I received e-mail from several of the participants. However, when I went to get a visa, I was never questioned about my contact with subversive organizations. Pay your money. Let them stamp your passport. Keep moving and let the next person talk with the clerk.

Nothing had happened at the visa office and nothing happened that humid morning in Tiananmen Square. I waited for my copy of the e-mail and nothing came. I walked around Mao's Tomb and nothing came. I talked with an electrical engineering student who seemed to be wandering the area and nothing came. I walked to the top of the old gate of the city and still there was nothing for me in the in box.

Deciding to try again, I resent the picture. This time the message read "I am in a place you know well." The copy of the e-mail reached my phone seconds after I released the original.

We can easily convince ourselves that national borders no longer matter. While I was looking at my e-mail, a group of students from an exclusive American university approached me and asked for directions back to their hotel. They had found an inexpensive airplane fare on an Internet site and had decided, with little prior planning, to take a vacation in China. They were more than a little disconcerted to find that many people did not speak English and that Beijing could be quite different from New York City. They, too, had been surprised to discover that their e-mail connections to the United States were monitored and censored.

Indeed, technological borders have a power that can exceed national divisions. Few are more potent than those visible lines that separate the parts of the United States that have strong wireless phone service with those that do not. Leave Route 25 in the intermountain basin, and you will see the datalink to your little black rectangle slow, falter and then vanish. At that point, you enter a new world, one where you cannot conduct business, call for help, or even identify yourself among friends. You will discover that the residents pay cash for transactions, listen to a device called a radio, and treat outsiders with a certain amount of caution.

The boundaries of the globalized age are shaped by a combination of political claims, economic liberalization, and technological investment. Yet, these boundaries do not affect all individuals equally. The same question that Thoreau asked of the telegraph can also be asked of the globalized Internet. If Tiananmen Square has nothing to say to Hoover Park, does it matter than they are linked by a high-speed digital connection? Do the two regions still reside behind the physical frontiers of the old nation-state? Is it our ideals that are global, and not we ourselves?

Chapter V:
Things Not Known

So if the Man cant sail to the Unknown
I guess the Unknown must sail to the Man.

Venus (1998)
Susan Lori Parks

Introduction
The Dogs that Came in From the Cold

Neither Harry nor Georgie is a perfect watchdog. Harry is the more effective of the two as he is both more cautious and more willing to pick a fight. He once concluded that my nephew was not to be trusted and bit his hand.

Nevertheless, Harry is proud, a weakness that apparently besets many a pure-bred dog. He will look at you and carefully assess whether you are the sort of person who deserves to pat so beautiful a dog as he. If you pass this test, he will walk quietly to your side and present his head to be scratched. Beggar, friend, murderer, thief—it makes no difference. As a trusted one, you will have a place in his circle.

Georgie gives little evidence of being a good guardian. She will run across the yard and leap into the arms of any visitor. All the world is her friend, and her friends are rewarded with nothing more severe than a nip on the nose. Yet I have seen her attack a neighbor's dog, one that has been her playmate at the local park. Apparently, she does not always trust her acquaintances.

Harry and Georgie are in the care of Danny, who works as a computer security professional for a local information technology firm. As I have come to know him, I have learned that Danny works on a different schedule from most of our neighbors. He can be home during the working week, running errands, watering the garden and playing with his boys. He has also spent evening after evening away from home while preparing for the deployment of some new system.

I have occasionally cared for his dogs when Danny has been working nights. On such occasions, Georgie is her delightful self, running from room to room to show how glad she is to see you. Harry will stand vigil by the door, occasionally emitting a muffled woof. He appears to be worrying about Danny and wondering if his human companion is doing something wrong.

Early in our friendship, I asked Danny to describe the nature of a security professional. He smiled and gave me the definition that I have since learned is common among his friends and compatriots.

"It is a hacker," he explained, "with a mortgage."

UNLIKE MOST PROFESSIONALS, DANNY DOES not belong to an established technical organization. "Think about it," he said. "It would be like belonging to the National Association of Horse Thieves." Nevertheless, he does attend Pundicon, a hacker's convention that helps keep the local security professionals aware of both the latest software developments and the latest threat to computer systems.

Pundicon is organized by a group of individuals who all seem to possess only a single name. There is one named Snug, another called Snout, a third goes by Bottom, and a fourth is Starveling. They dressed in a manner that was both informal and threatening. Dark images covered their tee shirts, and skulls were marked on more than a few boots.

Starveling, who apparently acquired that name as a 13-year-old when he was exploring computerized bulletin boards, occasionally uses the last name of Everyman.

"I have friends on all sides of this field," he explains. "White Hats and Black Hats and Gray." These terms are commonly used to describe the extent to which a hacker works within legal and social norms. My Black Hat friends think I have sold my soul to the devil," he continues. "My White Hat colleagues think I associate too much with individuals of dubious repute. My feeling is that we are all friends."

Other than the fact that Pundicon meets in a decidedly third-class hotel, it has much in common with other technical events. The meeting I attended had a plenary session with a speaker of great repute, a Fellow of the IEEE Computer Society. It also had breakout tracks and panel discussions. Though it embraces the trappings of a profession meeting, it does deviate from most conventions by promoting its own social mores.

As you walk the room, you feel that you are in the research lab of some nefarious organization that is hell-bent on destroying capitalism or liberal democracy or the entire pantheon of the international diplomatic system. Most of the sessions dealt with methods of exploiting the flaws of commercial software, and the exhibit hall included a game that tests the ability of attendees to identify software flaws.

To play the game, you purchase a memory stick from the information table and go from machine to machine in search of weaknesses that might be utilized to compromise a system. The winner gets a new high-powered gaming computer. The losers get a Pundiman, a fat little rubber man that carries a briefcase. Attendees are apparently allowed to hurl their Pundiman at any speaker they find boring.

The remaining exhibits were more conventional but also more disturbing. One person was showing how to intercept financial transactions from e-commerce sites. Another had a simple way of stealing domain names that uses a well-known public webpage. A third was showing how to reverse-engineer programs that use encrypted and obfuscated code.

The last session of this Pundicon meeting concerned ethical standards. Starveling, Snug, and a few others sat at the front of the room and tried, as others had before, to define a hacker, to identify the difference between hacking and security work, and, finally, to describe the ethics of their field.

The first subject was dismissed quickly when a speaker described hacking as a form of invention and hackers as the intellectual heirs of those lone inventors who labored for centuries in workshops and basements.

"The ordinary individual looks at computing technology and asks what it does," he explained. "You look at it and ask what you can do with it."

The audience generally accepted the notion that they were inventors, but they were not as willing to settle on any common criteria that separated security professionals from hackers or defined an ethical standard. The discussion quickly hit an awkward note and then soon moved out of control. The first speaker drew the wrath of the women in the audience by saying that he always identified himself as a hacker "because hackers are more attractive to girls." From that start, the temperature of the room rose as the participants realized that the distinction between the two job titles was somehow to be found in the motive of the worker and hence in the definition of the word "good."

A speaker of utilitarian bent drilled the room into uncomprehending silence as he attempted to connect the best accomplishments of security professionals to the work of foreign aid workers who were tending to displaced families in Burkina Faso. Another, who had apparently not learned the dangers of relativism, became the target of a volley of Pundimen when he attempted to find a good motive in the individual who had attacked Estonia's information infrastructure. His approach abruptly changed when one audience member complained, "Anything can be torqued any way. It can be used to help or to hurt." "By guileful fair words," says the bard, "may peace may be obtain'd."

Starveling used the momentary disruption to refocus the discussion. "How many of you," he asked, "do forensic work? How many of you look at the contents of memory to see if a program has violated a computer?"

Over the course of 10 or 15 seconds, most of the people in the room raised their hands. After looking at the group, Starveling then asked, "How many of you are licensed private investigators?"

At this point, most of the hands dropped. More than a few people looked puzzled. Starveling counted a half-dozen arms in the air and then said, "This is the number of people who can work next month. The state has a new law that forbids you from earning money by doing computer forensics unless you have a private investigator's certificate."

Already warmed for an argument, the crowd reacted in anger. Person after person took the microphone to denounce such regulations. They complained about government interference, expounded about professionals defending their own position in society, complained about organizations excluding the most qualified individuals from doing some task.

I could have offered the observation that their points were not new. The 19th-century sociologist Herbert Spencer (1820–1903) noted that professional classes often protect their position by promoting restrictive laws and educational requirements. However, I was not in the position to say anything, and in a rare moment of self-knowledge, I recognized that my comments were far too arrogant and contrary to be welcome.

The audience soon grew tired of arguing and departed for the conference's next stage, which involved drinking. However, before they left the room, a young woman made a point that was far more effective than the one I would have made.

"We have no one to make our case," she said. "We have no one to take our side and stand up for us."

This statement drew little attention, but it defined a central issue facing those who deal with computer security and outlined the key issue of professionalism.

Professions are defined by professional societies, organizations devoted to protecting and promoting certain knowledge or activities. Those societies codify the skills and education required to join the profession, and they identify the actions and behaviors appropriate within that profession.

When members of a society feel that a profession is in danger, they take action to protect it. Sometimes this work is done explicitly through rules and standards. Sometimes it is done implicitly. Usually, it is done in view of the major public social institutions.

FOR MOST OF THEIR EXISTENCE, the professional societies in the various fields of computing and computation have behaved like Danny's dog Georgie. They are glad to see you at the door, leap into your arms when you join, and lick your nose. However, they have rarely enforced an educational requirement on those who wish to call themselves computing professionals. If you can do the work, you are one of them. To get into Pundicon, you only need to show that you know how to exploit software. Most attendees, I learned, never attended college.

Shunning educational requirements, computing professional organizations have wielded their power by defining their discipline through publications and standards. They identify questions that are appropriate for study and define a class of answers that are acceptable as a means of expanding the field. Like Harry, they observe you closely to see if you do the sort of work they believe to be computer science. Rich or poor. Honest or not. Good or bad. If your work meets their standards, they will let you join the community through publication.

Professional ethics has become a central issue since professions began accepting a greater diversity of individuals. If the professionals all shared the same background, or education, or even socioeconomic class, then they often felt that had a common basis to trust each other. Once that common basis was gone, professionals felt that they needed a well-articulated statement of behavior.

Scientific societies, especially those associated with engineering, have found the task of defining ethical behavior hard. Members of such societies "are required to perform two roles," noted a pair of recent commentators on professional ethics. One role is "the responsible professional whose loyalty is to the standards of the profession, the other the responsible employee whose loyalty is to the organization." They also noted that government regulation further complicates these two roles, as such regulation places a third set of demands upon individuals.

The major computer societies have made valiant efforts to create ethical codes that are both meaningful and practical. The IEEE Computer Society's code of ethics includes the statement that the computer professional should "not put self-interest, the interest of an employer, the interest of a client, or the interest of the user ahead of the public's interest." It is a strong statement, one that demands the wisdom of Solomon to divide the interest of a client from the interest of the public.

The existing codes of ethics give us little guidance in dividing the role of the hacker from that of the security professional. They do give a little support to the individual who was trying to redeem his work by volunteering in Burkina Faso.

Software engineers shall "donate professional skills to good causes when opportunities arise," reads one code of ethics clause. However, not everyone has the opportunity to do such service, and, as many argued at Pundicon, most security professionals feel that their work is a service. "We do free R&D for the software vendors," claimed one.

"We hold the firms accountable," said another. "We do work that could never be done by government regulations," added a third. Such statements were met with general approval, but they also left unanswered the claims that have dogged hackers since they moved into public view.

The hacking community, for good or ill, is generally not perceived as inventors puttering in their workshops but as romantic outsiders, individuals who accomplish their ends by working on the edge of society.

Hackers do expose software vulnerabilities, but in doing so, they can put the public at risk. They have made vendors account for their actions, but they have also extorted unwarranted concessions from firms. They indeed serve as regulators, but as regulators they are accountable to no one but themselves.

Many aspects of human endeavor exist in that gray area between the darkness and the light and survive with little controversy. Hacking may occupy a special position because it touches not only on ethical issues but also on the very nature of computing itself. Modern computing is based on the idea of modifiable code and the widespread distribution of data and services.

The implications of an unauthorized modification of a program can be far greater than older forms of unsocial behavior. Train robbery and horse thievery, though profitable, usually touched only a limited community. In contrast, a self-replicating program can have global consequences. We "cannot simply align the world with the values and principles we adhered to prior to the advent of technological challenges," wrote the philosopher Helen Nissenbaum. Instead, we must grapple with the demands that "the presence and use of information technology have placed on values and moral principles."

OVER THE PAST TWO YEARS year or so, both Harry and Georgie have been serving as watchdog to Drew and Cooper, Danny's young sons. I believe that Harry is convinced that Cooper is a security risk, for he keeps a careful eye on the boy.

Perhaps he just wants to avoid having his tail pulled and his ears crunched, but he is watchful of the little one.

Georgie apparently sees the boys only as another set of playmates, and she gives little attention to them. She will lick their faces for a moment, especially if they have been eating, and then run off to greet some new friend. For both dogs, the day of reckoning is still a few years away.

Some day, either Drew or Cooper will approach the two, leashes in hand, face aglow, and ready for a great adventure. At that point, the two dogs will have to determine if the boy is something good or something bad. Someone to be trusted and obeyed or someone to be shunned and, if appropriate, disciplined. Disciplined by a pair of dogs who cannot claim that they define the standards of professional behavior.

01
Ethical Grocery Control

Even in its modern form, Jenkins' Grocery is a risky place for the uninitiated. The store seems entirely chaotic until you learn that old man Jenkins, who makes only rare appearances these days, organized the place around his personal theory of nutrition, a theory that identified the four basic food groups as sugar, fat, caffeine, and nicotine. The aisles twist and turn through the building like a perverse maze intended to separate husbands from wives and children from parents.

Yet the most disorienting aspect of Jenkins' is the ritual of the counter. At first, nothing about the checkout process seems amiss. You unload your purchases onto a counter topped by an aged piece of linoleum as one of the Jenkins boys places each item into a bag. When everything is safely bagged, the clerk, be it Martin, Colin, or Liam Jenkins, will tell you the total cost of the goods and then turn to enter the figure into the cash register. Prior to that moment, the transaction was processed entirely in the clerk's head.

The cash register is a new addition to the store. Until two or three years ago, the boys didn't even bother recording each sale. They would total the sales in their heads and stuff the cash into a box behind the counter. "We would have kept the cash box," confessed Martin, "if the district revenue office hadn't decided that we were not paying enough sales tax." Like many of the regulars, I believed that the cash register was actually acquired for another reason: to show that the store's income was legitimate.

Before the machine arrived, the Jenkins boys ran an active gambling operation. They would take bets on horses, ball games, and even sumo wrestling tournaments in Japan. Their casual chatter was spiced with claims of thousands won and lost. The store magazine rack was filled with copies of *The Racing Forum*. All of this vanished after the arrival of the cash register.

The new technology has not improved the grocery. Customers often face lines at the checkout counter where there once were none. Furthermore, the store is apparently under pressure from some higher authority to provide more detailed records of its transactions. "We may have to buy a scanner," one of the boys recently confided. The tone of his voice suggested that a device that could read product codes and determine prices was not going to be welcome in this store.

Martin complained that scanner would be the end of freedom, the introduction of the heavy hand of government into free market, the end of privacy. I countered his last claim by noting that the store had recently been featured in a *New York Times* front page story on gambling in the city.

"Right," he replied, "but they used a pseudonym, just like you promised for your essay."

I agreed and then turned our discussion to the processes that storekeepers use to keep control of their markets.

LONG BEFORE GROCERY STORES ADOPTED digital technology, they established systems of operation that gave the owners some control and influence over their customers. "The secret of chain store success seems to be the magic word, 'System!'" wrote one small-town merchant in 1916. Most of the elements of such systems were ideas that have long since become commonplace in the retail trade: buying goods cheaply and selling them dearly, rotating stock quickly, or moving customers through the store as expediently as possible. One of these early innovators was Clarence Saunders, who invented the basic floor plan of the modern supermarket.

Saunders' design forced customers to walk through a maze of shelves that began at the front door and ended at the exit. His store "was explicitly designed to process people past merchandise," explained historian James Beniger, "until they reached the last turnstile, complete with a counter and cash register—the only employee in the store." That single employee was a bottleneck.

Customers could race through the store and find themselves waiting in a long line at the checkout counter. Even with this drawback, grocery store owners were eager to adopt Saunders' design. By 1923, 1,200 stores operated in the US with Saunders' layout. With few exceptions, they all carried a brand name that was suggested by a farm animal twisting through a maze: Piggly Wiggly.

The "Saunders' bottleneck" soon became a defining element of the supermarket. "The fundamental point, which differentiates the supermarket from the variety store," wrote one economist, is that when a customer has "assembled her requirements from anywhere in the shop, she pays once only, at exit." To reduce the number of customers waiting to pay, store owners added additional registers at the exit. By the early 1960s, most professional grocers argued that a true supermarket had at least three registers.

IN THE FIRST PART OF the 1960s, the large grocery stores concluded that they could not expand capacity by merely adding clerks and cash registers at their exits. They determined that the problems of managing large stores needed a new technology that could price and track goods. "There is a real problem of control and prediction confronting the [industry]," wrote one observer, "if it is to improve operations and decrease the uncertainty risk inherent in change."

In addition to reducing the time it took to pay for purchases, the major grocery store operators wanted a system that would track inventory, reduce theft, and provide data to help them understand how their goods were purchased: how they were combined with other products and combinations when they left the shelves, what promotions encouraged sales. Running a grocery store was harder than it had been in the age of Clarence Saunders. Large stores stocked 10 times the number of items the original Piggly Wigglys carried, and their profit margin was one fourth of the margin of the stores from the 1920s.

The solution the grocers needed was not merely technological. If it had required nothing more than a new device, some lone inventor working in a garage or a group of engineers working in an industrial research laboratory would have solved the problem. The solution would be systemic, requiring both technical and operational specifications beyond the reach of any team of inventors. Such specifications would require compromises; hence, the grocers would have to write them.

The work that led to the grocery store scanning system began in 1966 at a meeting of the National Association of Food Chains, the trade organization of grocery stores. The group identified a technology that might be used to mark food items with a machine-readable code. This technology, which actually had its origin in the garage of a lone inventor, was used to track railroad cars. The first work on the railroad system had been done shortly after World War II, and its first deployment had been in 1961. The system was far from perfect—it regularly misread the code on the side of the cars. Still, the railroad industry was interested in using the system across the US.

The National Association of Food Chains wanted a system that would be universal and far more robust than the railroad system, which required printing the code on a specific type of material and drawing it past a fixed sensor at a certain speed. The members of the food chain association knew that they could not impose such requirements on the food processors or the staff in a grocery store.

The association prepared a technical specification for a machine readable Universal Product Code or UPC. They sent this specification to a select group of large technology companies. This specification dictated several key decisions in designing the code. The system would have to read codes on packaging material that was hard or soft, wrinkled or flat, convex or concave. It would have to accommodate clerks who slipped items quickly across the scanner as well as those who let the item dawdle in the light. Finally, it would have to acknowledge that the item could be held in any orientation—up or down, left or right.

Not long ago, while waiting impatiently in a lengthy queue at Jenkins' to purchase items from the fat and sugar food groups, I decided to try to decode the Universal Product Code on my purchase. I reasoned that it was some kind of binary code, and hence it couldn't be too hard to understand. However, the task proved more difficult than I had anticipated.

Twice I thought I understood the code, but a double check proved me wrong. Before I realized it, I was at the counter and Liam was taking the items from my hand. "That will be $11.37," he said as he turned to enter the number into the cash register.

During my brief attempt to decode the UPC, I assumed that the coding structure had to be fairly simple if it were indeed universal. A bit is a bit. Black is 1, white is 0. If you use a space for seven strips, you can represent 128 values, which is far more than you might need.

I had pored over the little bars hoping to see some combination of 0s and 1s that I could translate into something I understood. In the process, I missed two elements that the specification dictated. First, the code was not made up of seven black and white spaces—it consisted of four lines, two black and two white, of varying widths. These lines were easier to read than my idea of seven spaces, and it helped the system deal with the different speeds of the items moving across the sensor.

Next, I had falsely assumed that the bar code used a single method for representing numbers. In fact, the product code is divided into two halves, right and left, that use complementary means of representing numbers. (Technically, they also use odd parity on one side and even parity on the other.) This approach helps the system identify the product's orientation and correct any errors that might have been introduced in the operation. If you're going to try to break a bar code while standing in a line, you'll need to know these things.

SCANNING SYSTEMS WERE DELAYED BY the development of the UPC, the convention that would identify food items. The National Association of Food Chains required four years, from 1970 to 1973, to complete the standardized code. For a year, the system was tested by stores that volunteered to work with the new technology. The first commercial system was installed in 1974 at a Marsh supermarket in Troy, Ohio.

Two decades passed before scanning systems spread to most supermarkets in the US. During that time, people tended to focus on the technological wonders of the devices. A demonstration for US President George H.W. Bush in 1992 read the UPC from a damaged candy bar wrapper. Advertisements emphasized the convenience of the new system and the resulting short lines at the checkout counter. However, like the Piggly Wiggly system, the new scanners were intended to improve the grocer's position rather than to benefit the consumer.

Clarence Saunders designed his maze of shelves so that all shoppers would be forced to go past every item in his store before they reached the exit. The scanners were designed to make the customers surrender their shopping list to the grocer. "Scanner data, particularly in combination with other data on households," wrote a pair of commentators, "opens up the possibility of developing a new generation of models to measure response to a full range of marketing."

Stores would not only know what items you bought, they would know the combinations in which you bought them and the frequency with which you went shopping. "The situation can be likened to Galileo's invention of the telescope or Pasteur's use of the microscope," wrote one marketer. "Whenever a new, much more detailed look at the world is possible, there will follow a great flowering of measurement, theory, and practical applications. In the field of marketing, we have not been disappointed."

When old man Jenkins was a young grocer trying to earn enough to support a family, in that age when his store might have been considered new and modern, he might have known as much about his clientele as any of the modern chains. He knew who liked vegetables and who did not, who was expecting a baby or had a visiting relative, who could be trusted to pay a tab after payday, and who, if this was part of his business, could place a dollar on the third race at Los Alamitos. But the world is bigger now, and business is more complex. We apparently need to know more, and know it in more detail, than the path through Jenkins' Grocery.

The story of scanning systems cannot end here. Data, no matter how well processed, is not the same thing as knowledge.

NOT LONG AGO, A YOUNG man entered my office and stood over my desk. He was wearing a shirt with a label that read "Facilities Management" and was holding a laser scanner.

"May I ask what are you doing?" I said.

"Checking your furniture inventory," he replied, "to make sure that nothing is missing."

The university had recently announced that it was developing a property management system in the name of efficiency, which all of us assumed to mean standardization. At the time, I hoped that I would be overlooked in this initiative, as I occupied an office in a distant and decaying annex building. My furniture, which was far nicer than anything else in the building, had been scavenged from the medical school's trash pile. Physicians dispose of things that are considerably better than the new stuff that other schools buy. An oak chair. A double-sized bookcase. A modern desk with cherry finish. None of this was university standard.

The young man duly scanned all the bar codes on my furniture. With each beep from the device, I felt that I was being condemned by the facilities department and would return the next day to find my office stripped bare. All that would be left would be the genuine slate blackboard that hung on the wall and the collection of networking cables coiled in the corner.

When he was done, the young man looked at his little scanner for a moment with a puzzled face. I thought to myself, "Here we go. Tomorrow's headline will read 'Prof embezzles university furniture.'"

"This can't be right," he said.

"None of this furniture belongs in this room." He paused for a moment or two longer, looked at me, and apparently concluded that in the choice between reality and the system, reality would have to win. "Perhaps the scanner is wrong. I'll reset the database," he said. With that single keystroke, he demonstrated the reason that causes organizations to replace human judgment with technology. Without conferring with anyone else, he turned my furniture into university standard issue. I know that the Jenkins brothers wish that the government would do something similar for them. They felt that they had more control over their store when they could run tallies in their head and require their customers to trust the result.

02
Machines in the Garden

The view from my desk looks across a ragged collection of dandelions, smut-grass, and domesticated shrubbery that makes its pathetic claim to be a slice of a natural ecosystem in an urban environment. Small though it may be, this yard hosts a regular stream of animal visitors. Most are small mammals that claim a Norwegian ancestry to put some distance between themselves and the common rats that are their cousins, but a few are larger beasts that have tried to make their home amidst the human tenants: a blue heron, a brace of ducks, and an extended family of raccoons. Beyond the far edge of this landscape stands a row of six small houses.

When I first moved to the neighborhood, I concluded, without any evidence, that these buildings stood on the street that ran behind our house. Only after a year or maybe two had passed did I discover that these little homes are alley dwellings and are entirely contained within the block. They were built over a century ago to house the workers that kept the neighborhood clean: street sweepers, domestic maids, garbage pickers.

Garbage picking was a common occupation at the turn of the 20th century. Whole "families scavenged for a living," wrote historian Susan Strasser. "The biggest cities had neighborhoods full of streets with names like Bottle Alley or Ragpicker's Row." As in our neighborhood, the scavengers often lived in hidden enclaves amongst wealthier families. The two groups benefited from such close proximity: One set of families produced trash; the other disposed of the refuse while claiming anything of value. "Ignorance about trash was a luxury," Strasser wrote. "Most people were fundamentally oblivious to what happened to house-hold trash once it left their sight. It had been turned over to technicians as a prob-lem to be solved by refuse collection and disposal."

The computer and digital communication technology have allowed us to put some distance between ourselves and the dirtier parts of the modern economy. We no longer need to live near a garbage dump, a refuse transfer station, or even a recycling center. Yet, digital technologies are part of the industrialized economy, and one of the sad legacies of that economy is the mass production of garbage.

One measure of our modern wealth is the size of the garbage dumps that have arisen outside the cities, large and small. In many ways, computers have slowed the rise of those dumps by determining ways of using our resources more ef-ficiently. At the same time, they have increased the size of those dumps, as old computers, replaced by newer and faster offspring, move off the prime desktop space and slouch toward the world's landfills. Like so many industries that have had their place on this planet, the computer industry has a way to go before it is truly a green activity, before it leaves the Earth in better shape than it found it.

FOR A TIME, I WORKED with an environmental engineer named Jake. He and I were regular speakers on the technology and society circuit, where we told the youth of today that engineering was not a cold, mechanical activity but a noble vocation that expresses the ideals and aspirations of human beings.

Unlike me, Jake was both a competent engineer and a good storyteller who could explain how he had been able to improve the environment. He would visit factories and look at their manufacturing process, product operations, or waste disposal plans. He could quickly identify a weakness that ordinary mortals had missed. A leaking air hose. An extra quarter-mile traveled by delivery trucks. A reusable solvent dumped into a drain. When told of the problem, the factory management would fix the error, and the world was cleaner as a result. Profits were increased. Jobs were saved for future generations.

These talks benefited from the fact that Jake looked and acted the role of romantic hero. He was witty. He was good-looking. He rode a bicycle to work. By the end of his talk, he would have convinced every youth in the room that they were going to follow in his path. He even got them to march around the room singing a recruiting song that followed the tune of a 1950s television tune. "Engi-neer," began the chorus, "P-h-D. M-O-N-E-Y."

In private, Jake was far more sober. One evening, when we were relaxing over a glass of expensive designer water, he confessed to me that he had recently abandoned a book project. "I was going to write about the reengineering that we would need to make the economy truly sustainable," he said, "but I quit in a fit of depression. No one would be willing to accept the sacrifices required by a truly sustainable economy. No one would even be willing to read about them." After staring at the bubbles in his water for minute, he added, "There is simply no such thing as a green economy. There are only economies that are less brown. " Carbonated water can make a body morose at times.

THE COMPUTER INDUSTRY HAS MADE some improvements in three main areas that touch the natural environment: operations, manufacturing, and disposal. Of these three areas, the operational sector has perhaps made the most visible strides because it is the easiest one to analyze and quantify.

The biggest component of the operational impact is electricity, and electricity is measured in multiples of watts. The simplest way to reduce this impact is to reduce the number of watts the machine consumes. Stop the disk when it is not being used. Slow the processor when it is not doing useful work. Darken those displays that have nothing to show.

With a fairly straightforward analysis, we can reduce the electrical usage of a single computer. We find the problem a bit more difficult when we look at successive generations of computers. New models might actually use more electricity than their predecessors, but they might be more efficient because they can do more work.

However, we find it hard to quantify the concept of computing efficiency. "Green computing has no widely accepted metrics, so you must be careful to compare apples to apples when taking an architectural view," explained a recent overview of the issue.

The architectural view has stymied us for 60 years as we have struggled with the simpler problem of measuring a computer's overall speed. Do we report instructions per second? Operations per second? Throughput based on a fixed set of programs? If we use a fixed set of programs, how do we select those programs?

As we have been unable to answer these questions, we should not expect that we are any closer to finding a universal measure of efficiency. Do we use instructions per watt? Operations per watt? Watts required for a fixed benchmark?

In spite of the fact that we have no fixed answers to the problems of measuring energy efficiency, we have made some improvements to our large computers. The current generation of large scientific processors is 300 times more efficient, as measured by performance per watt, than its predecessors of 15 years ago. If these machines were run at the same speed as the older scientific machines, we would see a substantial savings in electricity. However, the new processors run considerably faster than the devices they replace. As a result, they actually consume roughly 30 times more electricity than the scientific computers of a generation ago.

"Today," reported a pair of experts, "several of the most powerful supercomputers on the TOP 500 list require up to 10 megawatts of peak power—enough to sustain a city of 40,000."

Of course, scientific supercomputers consume only a small amount of the electricity channeled to computers. The world holds only a couple hundred supercomputers, but it supports more than one billion laptops.

As we have done with the large machines, we have put these more common devices under the control of power-management systems. Viewed on a computer-by-computer basis, we have seen substantial power conservation over the past 20 years.

The second area where computing technology directly touches the environment is the factory, the place where chips are made and computers assembled. This is the world where Jake made a living by reducing waste, removing ineffi-

ciencies, and decreasing the use of toxic substances. The job of cleaning the factory floor is more complicated than the task of reducing electrical usage, but it
is still fairly amenable to the tools of engineering. We can isolate that job within
the walls of the fab, or the assembly facility, and focus our attention on a limited
number of issues, something that we cannot do on the third environmental issue
of the computing age, the disposal of unwanted equipment.

TRASH IS NOT UNIQUE TO the computer industry. It is merely one of the hall-
marks of mass production and mass consumption. "Most Americans produced
little trash before the 20th century," wrote Strasser. The majority of households
had ways of reusing much of what we now call garbage. Towns had scavenger
pigs that would eat unconsumed food, and families of scavengers who would
pick through garbage in search of usable food or materials. "Nothing is inherently trash," noted Strasser; "trash is created by sorting," by separating what is
desired from that which is not.

The industrial age has altered that sorting procedure. It has labeled as trash
many substances that once held value: rags, cooking grease, and packing materials. The computer age has further changed this procedure, reducing the time it
takes for something to be called refuse to the 18 months of Moore's law and adding to the garbage heap machines that are perfectly functional but can no longer
run the most recent software, read the most recent files, or connect to the most
recent network.

At the moment, we produce 40 million tons of high-technology refuse a year.
By some estimates, no more than 8 million of those tons are recycled. Traditionally, recycling is done at the edge of society. Garbage picking was done in the
alley, out of site of the houses on the main street. Composting piles are placed
far away from a home, often in the back corner of a lot. The modern recycling of
paper and metal occurs at the industrial fringe of cities.

COMPUTER RECYCLING USES THE TECHNOLOGIES of the globalized age. Modern transportation and high-speed communications make it possible to do such
work in Africa and southern China, far from computer stores, software labs, and
the shiny offices of computer companies. West Africa is the smaller of the two
recycling regions, but it still receives a massive amount of computer trash. One
environmental organization reports that the Lagos port in Nigeria receives 500
containers of used computer equipment a month. It is a "digital dump," reports
another group, "the place computers go to die."

The garbage pickers of our age sort through this material in search of working
machines that might be reused. They dissect the machines to extract the valu-

able elements: chips, copper cable, gold plating. Unlike the careful and immaculate process that built these machines, the recycling process is ugly, dirty, and hazardous. They break screens with hammers, burn boards with charcoal, and strip metal with solvents.

Several activist groups, trying to draw attention to the plight of workers at these recycling sites, describe these facilities in the bleakest of terms. "We've found excess heavy metals in the soil, as well as in plants and people who eat vegetables" grown in the contaminated soil, wrote one commentator.

The bulk of computer garbage is merely dumped in a heap. Every 18 months, a new generation of machines joins the pile. They are smaller, faster, and more efficient than their predecessors, but they are garbage nonetheless. These piles will be the lasting legacy of the information age. They will stand long after the plants in Silicon Valley and other technology centers have closed. They will be visible long after people have forgotten how to program in Java, configure a Unix system, or write columns about technology and society. Some day in the future, a distant generation will dig into these garbage heaps to understand our age. They will try to reconstruct our lives from smashed Game Boys, broken smart phones, and crushed laptops. "What did these things do?" they will ask. "How did they work?" "What were their owners like?"

I suppose that we should take as one of our Grand Challenges the task of making computing truly green, of putting into the Earth no more than we took out. It is not an easy task. Too much of what we do in the name of green computing merely moves the problem out of our sight and puts it in the hands of distant technicians with little incentive to dispose of the waste in a way that leaves the earth untouched by our technologies.

Jake lost hope of ever finding such a solution and abandoned his work in despair. Let us hope for someone of stronger mettle, who will pick through the refuse of environmental theories that we have created and find a strategy that will make computing truly green, or at least much less brown.

03
Open Sabotage

At least Sam wasn't a conspiracy theorist. Few experiences are more tedious than that overwhelming monologue by an individual who has stumbled across an evil truth that is invisible to all save him. No, Sam wasn't a conspiracy theorist. He believed that there was an open conflict in the technical community between the moneyed classes and the proletariat of working engineers. According to him, financiers, boards of directors, bankers, insurance executives, and accountants had no interest in the production of good technology or any benefits that technology might bring to ordinary citizens. They were concerned only with the value of their investments.

Sabotage was Sam's favorite word to describe the state of the technology industry. He used the word in the reverse of its common meaning. When he talked about sabotage, Sam wasn't referring to the acts of common workers undermining the operation of a production process. Instead, he was referring to the efforts of financial leaders to maximize their profits at the expense of optimal production, new development, or progressive innovation. The keepers of the vested interests were increasing the price of goods, clinging to inefficient technologies, and thwarting ideas that were good for the general public, such as open source. This last subject was often the topic that would get Sam talking about industrial sabotage.

When faced with speeches such as Sam's diatribes on sabotage, listeners have three strategies: they can become quiet and ride out the storm; they can argue in an effort to change the speaker's opinions; or they can attempt to break contact and find a new collaborator.

In dealing with Sam, the first strategy quickly revealed itself to be a failure. Without any resisting force, he could talk about the sabotage of open source software as long as there were hours in the day.

The second strategy was equally ineffectual in my hands. At one point, I noted that Sam's ideas about sabotage were similar to those of the economist Thorstein Veblen, who wrote about engineers and business in the years that followed World War I.

For a moment, Sam seemed interested in this connection. "What did he recommend?" he asked.

"Well," I said, "he argued that engineers should form an organization to take the control of production away from financial interests, an organization that he called "The Soviet of Engineers."

I should have known better than to use the word "soviet." I should have thought more carefully before I raised a historical example of a notoriously liberal economist, even though that economist was the uncle of a mathematician who greatly aided the development of the electronic computer.

My words were not a proper rebuttal. They were an effort to end an argument by employing the appearance of scholarship, and those words were repaid in kind. Sam showed himself distrustful of the word "soviet" and equally uncertain about the idea of engineers banding together. For the rest of the day, he railed about the ineffectiveness of all professional computer organizations including IFIPS, the ACM, CRA, and, of course, the IEEE Computer Society.

As have so many others in similar situations, I concluded that I could be more productive doing other work and moved to new tasks and new partners. However, I was in a position where I could do that easily. I had no boss, no assigned projects, no established goals. I didn't have to worry about the divided loyalties of the engineering profession, as so many engineers must. I didn't need to choose from among my own ideas, the ideas of my profession, and the ideas of my employer.

In spite of his railing at my ill-conceived remarks, Sam probably did believe in a unity of interests and goals among engineers and technical personnel. He was a strong advocate for ethics education and often claimed that the scientific method should lead engineers to common social ideas and common goals. At the same time, I think he knew that such idealism was challenged by the waves of malware that have infected our systems and remind us again of the truism that nothing is good or bad but thinking makes it so, that no system of thought lies beyond the motives of its originators.

RECENTLY, OUR UNDERSTANDING OF THE role of engineering skill in open sabotage has been challenged by the Stuxnet virus. Stuxnet is a program that infects a supervisory control and data acquisition (SCADA) system from the Siemens Corporation that is used to control industrial processes such as chemical plants, oil refineries, and nuclear power plants. While much about Stuxnet is unknown as of this writing, it appears to be a program that is targeted at Iran's Bushehr nuclear reactor, a project that has been the concern of countries in the Middle East and Europe, as well as the United States.

News reports have focused on Stuxnet's origins. They speculate that it was created by some secret service that wanted to impede the progress of the Iranian atomic program. Some suggest that it was a military effort launched by Iran's enemies.

Others have concluded that a group of criminal hackers developed the malware. There "were probably a number of participants in the Stuxnet development project who may have very different backgrounds," explained a well-circulated report. Some "of the code looks as if it originated with a 'regular' software developer with extensive knowledge of SCADA systems and/or Siemens control systems, rather than with the criminal gangs responsible for most malcode," the report noted.

Analysts have noted that some elements of Stuxnet appear to have been stolen, while others might have been borrowed from other malware programs. Even if this is the case, it seems likely that the code was developed by a team of engineers who followed standard software engineering procedures. They developed malware specifications, designed the system, coded the malware, and debugged the system on a realistic testbed. If they were as organized as they appear to be, members of the team were collecting malware assessment data from the news reports.

It is "feasible that what we're seeing here is the work of a more formally-constituted, multi-disciplinary 'tiger team,'" the Stuxnet report adds. "Such official but unpublicized collaborations," the authors conclude, "might be more common than we are actually aware."

Even if such tiger teams aren't that common or even if one wasn't used for Stuxnet, the idea of such teams forces us to confront the ultimate goals of engineering. Malware, like any technology that is used as a weapon, carries no absolute engineering values beyond the claims that it has been designed well and built according to specifications. What is a virus to one community is a savior to its neighbor. Nothing is good or bad, says the poet, but thinking makes it so.

Of course, engineers have had to contend with the military aspects of their creation as long as engineers have existed. After all, the term "civil engineer," which is now used to describe the builders of roads, bridges, and other civic projects, was originally coined in the 18th century to distinguish such professionals from military engineers, which was implied by the unadorned term "engineer."

We have even become used to the idea that weapons are created by large coordinated technical staffs. Such staffs appeared in the first world war and matured in the second. New weapons must be created "by teams of men with different skills and angles of approach," explained an historian of World War II engineering.

THE STUXNET CODE CARRIES SEVERAL elements that suggest to some that it is indeed a weapon from some country's military. Of course, we have enough experience with malware to know that misleading clues can easily be inserted in any code. If Stuxnet proves to be the agent of an established military, it will fit neatly into the past 60 years of warfare. Since the end of World War II, countries have regularly used technology to disrupt the productive processes of their enemies without creating a public act of war. It has been a way for one government to sabotage another government.

At the same time, we might ultimately discover that Stuxnet isn't the product of a government but the organized creation of a group with minimal resources and no territory to call its own. It might have come from a gang of organized criminals, a rival corporation, or a terrorist group. Over the past year, a pair of social scientists, Diego Gambetta and Stefen Hertog, have been arguing that engineering education, far from instilling a common sense of social value, actually encourages individuals to join terrorist organizations. The "number of militant engineers relative to the total population of engineers is miniscule," Gambetta and Hertog acknowledge, "yet engineers, relative to other graduates, are over-represented among violent Islamic radicals by three to four times the size we would expect."

Such ideas have produced the obvious responses from the engineering community, including a rather defensive statement from a former president of the National Academy of Engineering. We don't want to think ill about the education that has given us a career and an identity. Nor do we like to believe that the education that we received leads some people to do a bad thing. Yet we have lost some of the framework that allows us to see clearly what universal good might be.

Regularly, engineers are described as if they are actors working independently for the good of some universal society. While it might have been possible to make such a claim a century ago, today we find that most technical people are employed by institutions that are in competition. They are competing for market share, investment, the right to control a certain piece of territory, or the ability to govern a certain group of people. At that point, the good of society too quickly becomes the good of my employer. While nothing is inherently wrong with that state of affairs, we are doing little to erase the illusion of independent action and universal good and doing even less to help our students make wise judgments about questions that aren't easy to answer. "Is our organization doing good?" "Are our leaders making good decisions?" "Is our work being sabotaged?"

JUDGMENT, OF COURSE, COMES NOT from education but from difficult experience. During that brief period of my life when I was employed by a start-up firm, I found myself struggling to keep communication flowing across that barrier that separates technical personnel from business leaders. Somehow, I believed, a good choice of words and a clever illustration would allow both sides to better understand what the company was doing and what needed to be accomplished for the greater good.

At one point, after I addressed a group of venture and angel investors, one of the venture partners approached me and said, "You seem to have your head screwed on. Let me tell you something. There isn't a business here. In two years, you'll be wiped off the map with the next technology. Sell the business now. You've got enough assets to get $1 million or so. Don't worry about the technical staff. They aren't keeping up with new developments and they'll be happy wherever they go."

The decision to sell wasn't mine to make. If it were, I'm not sure I would have done so. I had spent much of the prior year working with the chief engineer and helping him explain to the company president the demands that he was facing. I liked the people and felt that I had helped each side trust the other. The engineers realized that they had a short time to get the service to market. The president recognized that the technical problems demanded more resources to complete the work. To recommend a sale of the company at that moment would have seemed like betrayal.

Yet the decision to do nothing seemed to sabotage the company. As time marched forward, the tensions increased. The chief engineer started to feel that the president was undermining the technical staff by establishing unrealistic deadlines. The president concluded that the chief engineer didn't understand the pressures on the company, especially after he found the engineer shoveling the company parking lot after a light snow.

"If we don't do it, we'll get a ticket from the city," the engineer claimed as the president ranted about credit lines and closing market windows.

The end came a week or two later. The bank called and terminated a loan. A short scramble suggested that nothing could be done. The few assets that had value were sold on the open market. Employees left without pay. Accusations circulated about blame and responsibility.

The chief engineer left the company convinced that this work had been sabotaged, certain that the president had been more interested in preserving his investment than in producing a good product. As is true in so many situations, I again had three choices: I could be quiet; I could argue another point of view; or I could leave. As I had little stake in the venture, only a debenture for a few worthless shares of founders stock, I made only a cursory effort to engage the chief engineer before departing.

THE RECENT REPORTS ABOUT STUXNET include claims from the Iranian government that it has arrested a number of people in connection with the case. We haven't received details about the arrests, at least none that can be verified by an independent agency. We can imagine that government may have arrested a foreign agent who planted the malware, or some loyal system programmers who thought that they had secured the site, or even a few from a local opposition party who may have had nothing to do with the reactor. In all cases, they were people who thought that they were doing their assignments properly and are now wondering how their work was sabotaged.

04
The Data of the Night

I always count. It's the data of the night. I'll be lying in the darkness, enjoying the gentle stir of a summer breeze, when I hear the first pop. It's never a loud sound, never an explosion or a blast as the movies suggest. You'd like to think that it comes from a cork flying from a bottle, a celebration of some event with at least a modicum of joy—but it doesn't. It's the pop of the pressure wave that follows a slug of lead out of the barrel of a gun.

One pop. Two. Then a pause. Three, four, and five in quick succession before a brief break. Numbers six through nine follow at regular intervals. Number 10 is a punctuation mark that prepares the neighborhood for the finality of number 11.

The final tally is almost always an odd number, which bothers me. It suggests that one bullet remains, anxious to be freed from its clip and begin its spiral flight toward its target. But there's nothing. Just silence. There are no screams. No screeching tires. No words shouted in anger. Just a quiet night that encourages your imagination to construct a story for the data. Tension between father and son. A deal gone bad. A suggestive gaze at a sister. A marriage torn by alcohol. A tough attitude encountering arrogant resistance.

The silence can hold for a minute, for two, for five. It tempts you to believe the data is fraudulent, that nothing happened, that you dreamed it all. It's a reassuring lie. We're simply not the kind of neighborhood where residents rush to the phone and call the police. Police bring questions that have bad answers, and bad answers bring new problems.

The quiet will first be broken by the helicopter. It will circle low over the trees, shining its light into windows and searching for a furtive soul. The police cars will follow, speeding from two or three corners of the city. The ambulance will be last, blaring its arrogant horn and muscling its way through intersections even if no life can be found to carry back to the hospital.

These nights have taught me that I'm a poor judge of distance. On some occasions, when I concluded that the gunfire was miles away, perhaps on the other side of the river, I've been surprised to see armed patrollers picking their way through the garages behind our house. At other times, when I was all but certain that the shots came from widow Douglass's home around the corner or from the yard of Harry and Georgie, my canine neighbors, I learned from the next day's news that the exchange occurred on a freeway that isn't even near our neighborhood.

FOR THE PAST DECADE, OUR beloved city has confronted the problems of nightly gunfire with a shot detection network, a web of sensors and computers that identifies a shot's location before the sounds have finished echoing off buildings and hills. The local police were quite proud of the system, one of the first deployed in the country, because it captured a detailed abstraction of all gunfire. "Every incident captured by the system," read the press release, "includes the precise location and direction of travel, ... the weapon caliber, the number of rounds fired, and the number of people involved."

Initially, the system was deployed only in the troublesome parts of town, the places where the familiar concoction of drugs, money, and sex encourage deadly violence as a casual form of conversation. In recent years, that network has expanded to cover most of the city, about 20 sensors per square mile. Occasionally, you can catch a glimpse of the deployment. A nondescript technician in blue coveralls will be mounting a small white box on the side of a building or the top of a utility pole while a patrolman in a car keeps watch at a safe distance. To the innocent eye, the worker is merely repairing some minor piece of urban infrastructure, but he or she is actually altering the topography as definitively as if a bulldozer were flattening hills and filling valleys.

Gunshot detection systems are a form of geographical information system, a technology that has expanded rapidly in the past two decades and has substantially altered how we deal with the physical landscape. Their origins go back to the electronic navigation systems of World War II, most notably the Loran system. Loran, a compaction of the phrase long-range navigation, utilized pairs of radio stations that would exchange synchronized pulses, little electronic shots that went out into the night. By timing these pulses, navigators could determine their relative position to those stations, allowing them to place their ship or plane on a hyperbolic curve that cut across the globe. By repeating this procedure with multiple pairs of stations, they could draw multiple curves and determine their location by identifying the intersection of those curves.

Computational problems were a bottleneck for the original Loran system. The system designers anticipated that they would provide navigators with a collection of charts that simplified the task of drawing curves and finding intersections. However, they were "not equipped with the computers and machines necessary for the task." By computers, they meant human beings, clerical staff trained in scientific calculation. To find enough human computers, the designers requested the assistance of the Mathematical Tables Project, a work relief project formed during the Depression to provide jobs for unemployed workers.

Workers in the Mathematical Tables Project labored in an old office building at the foot of Manhattan, far removed from the conflicts in Europe. Yet their work fundamentally altered the way the Allies viewed the European continent. "The most obvious use for such a system was to provide a nighttime aid to navigation," reported one of the lead designers, John Alvin Pierce (1907–1996). The

European Loran stations were ready for operation in the summer of 1944, but the commanders of the Allied forces decided to wait until the fall, when the long nights would allow for longer bombing runs to Germany. Loran guided the planes across the darkened land: Dortmund, Merseburg, Dresden, Essen. The "system was very useful for the last months of the European war," recalled Pierce. So "effective, in fact, that the Royal Air Force's Mosquito Force used it regularly for blind bombing of Berlin."

THE MODERN GUNFIRE DETECTORS UTILIZE a principle that inverts the operation of Loran. Like Loran, they locate events by finding the intersection of compound curves, but they switch the roles of transmission and reception. In Loran, the transmitters were fixed towers and the receivers were mobile ships and planes. For the gunshot detectors, the transmitters are mobile guns and the receivers are fixed microphones.

The receivers' fixed nature simplifies the calculations, even though we have long passed the day of having to rely on a staff of clerks equipped with Merchant adding machines to provide computational power. However, gunshot detectors require substantially more computations to protect our big cities at night than Loran required to lay them open to ruin.

The gunshot detectors begin with three megabytes of data, the digitized print of any sound that seems to be suspicious. They simplify the data into blocks of frequencies and amplitudes and compare these to patterns of known gunshots to sift the kernel of true danger from the chaff of fireworks, slamming doors, truck backfires, and angry watchdogs. Might it have come from a Glock, an AK-47, the M-16 of a gun-collecting Vietnam vet, or the old .22 that Wendell keeps under his bed?

The sonic data is accompanied by times. When did the sensor at 9th and D record the sound? The sensor in Hoover Park? The sensor on Michigan Avenue? With these times, a central system begins to trace the curves that constrain the guesses about the noise's location. Two sensors demand that it fall on one curve. Two more require a second curve. A third and a fourth follow. They intersect on a front porch, a bedroom, a sidewalk beside an occupied car. With the identification of the likely site of the incident, the system notifies a dispatcher to start the process that sends helicopters, police cars, and ambulances to the scene.

The makers of these systems generally promote their products as offering the benefits of efficiency, emphasizing claims that machines are cheap and people are expensive. With these detectors, it's possible to cover more ground with fewer officers. "Armed with an increased awareness and knowledge of what is transpiring within a specific area," claims one manufacturer, "responding agencies can proactively apply resources when and where they are most needed."

As valuable as such technology may be in the still of the night, it may be better used as a means of altering the landscape of trouble. Like all the artifacts of human settlement, gunfire has a geographic pattern that can be altered with time and resources.

The city of Detroit, Michigan, has deployed a broad phalanx of computing and police technology against one of America's more notorious patterns of gunfire, Devil's Night, the night of 30 October. Traditionally, Devil's Night was an evening of adolescent tricks and restlessness. Its origins are generally traced to Ireland and are connected to the restlessness of farm animals on the night before the fall slaughter. However, since the early 1980s, Detroit's version of the holiday has involved random gunfire and arson, with property destroyed and people killed.

In an effort to quell the problems of Devil's Night, the Detroit police have been tracking gunshots and gathering data on fires. "Over 4,000 incidences were mapped, and fire hot spot locations were identified and used to prioritize patrol deployment patterns," reported a team of researchers. The patrols disrupted the traditional gathering points of city youth and forced their celebrations in new, less harmful directions. After these changes, the "fire patterns were more random and not as concentrated," they claimed, "and the number of hot spots declined" from its high mark in the mid-1990s.

As with most technology, gunshot recognition systems raise issues of cause and effect. We find it difficult to claim, without reservation, that such systems actually reduce crime. During the same period in which Detroit's police tried to reduce the violence of Devil's Night, the city also experienced a decline in industrial output, a reduction of jobs, and the departure of residents.

Furthermore, gunshot detection systems are part of a larger shift in police technique that moves away from "traditional, rapid response-type approaches to policing toward community policing and problem-solving." Although these devices can be used to trigger rapid responses, they don't respond like community officers. They don't always provide enough information about the event and hence can make the response team vulnerable. They also occasionally are wrong. Reviews in the major police journals suggest that they correctly identify shots no more than 85 percent of the time.

The systems do a better job of building a record, of mapping the violence of the land. From them we know where shots are likely to be fired, the time of day they're likely to occur, and the people likely to be involved. They at least provide a framework for studying the underlying social issues. A conflict between father and son. A deal that shouldn't have happened. The sister who needed time to mature at her own pace.

However, the solutions this technology suggests are those of social geography. It points to areas where defenses should be built, where rival gangs should be separated, where gathering points should be restructured, where anger should be redirected. The manufacturers of gunshot detectors, as boastful as they are of their products, seem to grasp the limitations of their devices. One manufacturer, after arguing that its product would lead to a more efficient use of police, suggested that the detector would have its greatest impact in the annual budget meetings of the city. "In addition," according to the report, the police "are also armed with data to justify specific increases in assets and resources."

IN THE CALM OF MORNING, I'm usually treated to a more traditional approach to crime prevention. It's usually peaceful at that hour of the day. Rarely do we see any evidence of trouble from the prior night. I can hear the traffic in the distance; a yip from Georgie next door; the sounds of kids walking to school. Toward 7:00 a.m. or so, I often hear the counting of a steady rhythm.

"One, two, three, four, we study every fence and door."

Slowly, the voices grow louder, and soon a group of joggers dressed in olive drab appears.

"We meet our foe with ready feet
And make our fight out in the street.
There's not a house we haven't seen
We're here to serve, US Marines."

This squad has a long history in our neighborhood. It first arrived more than 200 years ago, when the threat of random gunshots came not from homeowners but an invading force of the British Army. After a few months of camping in a neighborhood park and a couple of spectacular nights of violence that would put Detroit to shame, the British moved to other areas, but the Marines remained.

In theory, the squad members are still expected to be ready to defend the neighborhood. They jog in the area to familiarize themselves with the local topography. They look for safe redoubts, good sniper posts, and solid defenses. In the process, I suspect that they also find sidewalks clogged with misplaced recycling bins, alleys filled with discarded children's toys, and routes blocked by illegally parked sport utility vehicles.

For the most part, this squad of Marines is involved in ceremonial duties. Presentations of the colors. Formal guards. Graveside services where fallen comrades are laid to rest. Even though they're not protecting our neighborhood from foreign troops or even from the caravans of tourist buses, I've been grateful for their presence. They proved useful in the fall of 2001 when they patrolled local streets in a time of national distress. There's something reassuring about people who are well-groomed, unfailingly polite, and carrying standard issue assault rifles.

On those nights when I listen to the sounds that suggest trouble at hand, I must admit that even the military patrols of 2001 were largely ceremonial. Our landscape of security is now shaped by digital systems that are far less obvious than a squad of jogging Marines or a patrolling police car. They index neighborhoods by times, calibers, and numbers of distant pops in the dark, adding to their records the data they can glean about the things that cause index fingers to apply vectors of force to the controlling lever of firearms. Records we'd rather not read and prefer not to keep. But they're part of the process by which we try to minimize the dangers of our neighborhoods, part of the records we use to make security decisions, part of the data of the night.

05
On the Fall of Sparrows

"Hey, David!" Frankie's voice was always loud enough to be heard across the full length of the park. I would usually find him under a clump of trees, sitting on a table, and watching people scurry for the subway on their way home after work. Whenever possible, I would stop to give him a little attention, as I doubted that he had much interaction with people during the day.

Our conversations would usually deal with the different projects in which he was engaged. A new movie. A basketball tournament. A television dance show. A go-go album. Frankie kept careful records of each of these activities in a battered notebook that he carried everywhere. I was never able to read his handwriting. Perhaps there was nothing to read. I could distinguish the pages in the book only by the pictures he identified as the friends who were helping with his projects.

Frankie's movie producer is a well-known star from the early 1960s, who died in some kind of tragedy a decade ago. At one point, I tried to explain to Frankie that this individual would not be able to help with his movie, but I received a sharp rebuke. Frankie considered the producer a close friend and would hear nothing ill spoken against him.

I'm never the best at identifying sports figures, but Frankie was convinced that one of the big NBA stars would be hosting the basketball tourney.

The president's daughters were going to appear on the dance show, although there was some question about whether the younger girl would have to go home early. For a singing partner, he had chosen the current first lady of France. I asked Frankie if this individual had mastered the rhythms of go-go, a genre that never seemed to spread far beyond our mutual city. Frankie assured me that he had seen her perform in a local club.

Occasionally, I would be crossing the park when Frankie was dining at the Moveable Feast, a charity that provides food for the homeless. He would be one of 15 or 20 individuals standing around an open van, eating spaghetti and steamed vegetables off a paper plate. Most nights, a volunteer named Liu will be moving through the crowd, calling each diner by name.

"How ya doing, Jeff?" "Frankie, good to see you." "Take another spoonful, Sarah. You need more than that."

Beyond Liu's greetings, small talk is not common at the Moveable Feast. Grace is rarely said. News of the day is seldom exchanged. As the guests focus on the food before them, Liu will quietly pull a clipboard from the van and record the evening's attendance. Eighteen in total. Jeff back after being absent for a week. Sarah looking a little pale. Anwar, new to the group. Elsie, carrying a new bedroll. It is the record of what the Moveable Feast does each night. It is the register to prove that the workers are being responsible for those entrusted to them.

The diners don't like to see the clipboard, don't like to be reminded that they are being watched and recorded. Jeff, in particular, fears that he is being controlled by the government, by secret radio, or by the executives of NBC, CBS, and ABC.

However, the evening record is not really about Jeff, Frankie, and Sarah. Liu's eyes may be upon the sparrows, that none may fall to earth without his knowledge, but his concerns have to go beyond the needs of any individual diner. How many homeless live in the city? How many do we feed each night? Where are the best places to send our van? How best can we shepherd our meager resources so that the most members of the flock can survive another day?

UNTIL RECENTLY, FEW PEOPLE WOULD have considered $81 billion to be a meager resource. Indeed, Liu and the other drivers for the Moveable Feast might suggest that they could feed most of the world's poor on such gleanings. Still, to the economists at the RAND Corporation, that $81 billion figure is the savings that the US might realize by establishing a national electronic medical records system.

"The US healthcare industry is arguably the world's largest, most inefficient information enterprise," wrote a team of RAND researchers. "It is widely believed that broad adoption of an electronic medical records system will lead to major healthcare savings, reduce medical errors, and improve health." In recent weeks, that belief moved into the realm of political debate in the US when the president called for new electronic medical records for veterans that would "contain their administrative and medical information—from the day they first enlist to the day they are laid to rest."

While the creation of such a system is an admirable activity, we are sophisticated enough with the ways of technology to know that no matter how successful it may be, it will encounter problems in all phases of design, development, and operation. Barring the sort of miracle that has rarely been seen on the face of this earth, it will cost more than anticipated, be delivered later than expected, and do less than promised. In many a cautionary tale, these three devils have conspired to squander organizational resources and thwart plenty of good systems.

However, even in the extreme, these problems—the issues of expense, schedule, and capability—are a minor part of the Information Age, the weights that drag on technology. The bigger challenge, the one that defies foresight, concerns the way these records will change medical practice. As we have learned, electronic systems are more than convenient modern-day versions of their paper-based predecessors. They change the flow of work, the habits of thought, the way we perceive our activities. In the case of healthcare, such changes could easily produce a system that is radically different from the one we know, especially when we note that many an expert has concluded that we are not likely to see any of the $81 billion savings unless there are "related changes to the healthcare system."

DEVELOPERS HAVE DESIGNED AND DEPLOYED many large information systems over the past 60 years. The system that might provide the most insight for the current work on medical records is that of the Social Security Administration. Deployed by the US in 1936 to provide retirement benefits to the country's oldest residents, this system strained the technology of its time. Within a year of its founding, the system had to register 1.8 million beneficiaries, collect a tax on the nation's payrolls, and begin writing monthly checks.

The Social Security Administration began with 750 employees and grew by a factor of 8 in a single year. The agency originally hoped to put all of its clerks in a single facility in downtown Washington, DC, but quickly discovered that the capital did not possess enough free office space or have enough unemployed office workers. As a temporary step, the agency opened a processing center in nearby Baltimore. Like many such decisions, the Baltimore facility soon became a permanent part of the system.

To collect and transmit information, the agency requested the assistance of the Post Office, as it had determined that it "would be advantageous and economical if a nationwide organization of an existing government agency might be utilized." To establish a database, the agency recorded information for each individual on a single 80-column punched card. It processed these cards with an IBM 403 accounting machine. "The development of mechanical devices," reported the director, "has made it far simpler to maintain records on this scale than it would have been 10 or 15 years ago."

From the start, the Social Security Administration anticipated that its information processing system would not only prepare checks for the beneficiaries but would also conduct research on poverty and public assistance. We "have been concerned with the larger problems of insecurity within our industrial system," explained one researcher. They looked at the impact of mill closings in New England and the economic activities of "groups not now included under the unemployment compensation and old-age insurance."

By modern standards, this research was simple and crude. The workers at the Social Security Administration were developing statistical methodology as the work progressed and quickly discovered that they did not have the intellectual tools they needed to capture a national picture of poverty. The first researchers did not even have a classification system that would describe all the jobs that could be found across the country.

Without such a system, their research was muddled at best. Did the farmer in Wyoming do the same tasks as the farmer in New York? More important, were they tied into the national economy in the same way? The agency required two years to devise a standard national classification scheme.

Beyond the research for public policy, the Social Security Administration planned that its data processing office would produce statistical studies that could be used to improve the work of the organization itself. Such work might include "methods of interstate cooperation under the social security program," suggested the administrator, or "classification schemes for account numbers." This kind of work was innovative for the time. The basic ideas of quality control were barely five years old. "Broadly speaking, there are three steps in a quality control process," explained Walter Shewhart, the founder of statistical quality control. These three steps were "the specification of what is wanted, the production of things to satisfy the specification, and the inspection of the things produced to see if they satisfy the specification."

By following the quality control process, the Social Security Administration identified not only problems with its systems but also issues that prevented the agency from operating on a truly national scope. By 1954, the administrators recognized that they needed to keep more than 80 columns of information on each worker if they were to handle all individuals equitably in the growing economy. However, they argued that they could not solve this problem by merely adding a second card. The "use of two cards would have made our operations more complex," explained an agency worker, "and would have increased costs."

With the recognition that the addition of a second punched card record would not improve its work, the Social Security Administration began the process of computerizing its data processing operations. It acquired a pair of IBM 705s and began to move its work from mechanical tabulators to electronic machines. In all, completing the task required six years, but when they were done, the workers realized that they had created a system that touched every aspect of economic life. Social Security numbers had become the common identifier for American citizens. Reports from Social Security data described the economic activity in the country. "It must be stressed that our electronic data process is not an adjunct to, but a part of, the total integrated record keeping system," explained one administrator. "It reaches into and affects almost every task and person in the Division as well as many others outside the Division and even outside the Government."

Like that original punched card system for the Social Security Administration, any comprehensive system of electronic medical records will stretch its reach beyond its original home and affect many other aspects of public and private life. Its influence will begin with the recognition that such a system will require procedures that encourage uniform, systematic operation across the vast collection of clinics, hospitals, and doctors' offices that exist in this country. Such procedures will be part of that last stage of the Shewhart cycle, the process that compares operational data to design specifications.

At first, the questions will be easy. Are all the offices getting the information they need? Is there any delay in transferring records? Is the information being understood? The scholarly literature is full of discussion of the ways of addressing these kinds of questions. There is a Uniform Medical Language System for recording and transmitting information, sets of security procedures for every conceivable situation, and means of connecting general record systems with systems for prescribing medication. In most of these discussions, the problem is difficult to separate from the content of records, especially when talk turns to issues of public health. Will the operators of an electronic medical records system be able to ignore evidence of a regional spread of a contagious disease? Or reports of a doctor who repeatedly prescribes unusual combinations of medicines? Or hospitals that have unusual failure rates? Once we are able to look at the detailed story of healthcare, will we be able to look away?

"It is not known what changes should or will take place after widespread [electronic medical record] adoption," claims a report from RAND. It is entirely possible that an electronic medical records system may bring no changes that are especially noticeable to patients. It is even plausible that such systems may leave medical costs unchanged, as several economists have taken aim at the assumptions that undergird the claim of $81 billion in savings. At the same time, it seems unlikely that physicians and clinics will pass through the transition unchanged. At the very least, they will all be able to rail at the failings of a common computer system.

The checklist of the Moveable Feast, Liu's record of the homeless in Washington, reaches across parks and boulevards, through alleys and past street corners. In recent months, it has also touched a little niche that stands about a block from my office.

A construction project left a small protected area that has become quite popular with the homeless. The area doesn't provide much of a space to eat, but it has become a regular stop for the Moveable Feast's van.

Frankie moved to this little shelter last fall, which put him closer to my office. A couple of times, I surprised coworkers by having a friendly conversation with him on the street. I think he was planning on starting a commercial business. He had more figures in his notebook and fewer pictures. But Frankie vanished shortly before Christmas. The poor are with us always, as the Good Book may tell us, but they do seem to have an unusual ability to move from place to place. I have no data to tell me where he went. Neither does Liu.

He notes that the number of diners has increased over the winter, but he hasn't seen Frankie at any of the stops. However, when Liu last saw Frankie, he seemed to be in good shape. It looked as if he had a warm coat and sturdy shoes.

The record is silent about Frankie's last known address or his opinion of the Moveable Feast. He is beyond our knowledge and would probably be beyond the knowledge of a system of electronic medical records, no matter how good it might become. This system, when it arrives, will have to prove a boon for the wealthiest of surgeons and the humblest of nurses; it will demand access to the most modern research hospitals and the street-side clinic that treats veterans like Frankie and his friends. It will have to be an eye watching the flights of greatness and the fall of sparrows, and it will have to treat all alike.

Exit
Honor Among Thieves

For years, I have refused to acknowledge that undergraduates are worthy of first names. First names suggest an intimacy with the adult world that these senior adolescents have not yet earned. They have not demonstrated the qualities that entitle them to a place in the community of educated men and women, so they deserve only the formal appellation of their family. Almstead. Dumbacher. Hooper. Eilts. Garlinghouse. Rasche. Only when they have accomplished something in their own right are they entitled to their own name.

"Major X" is one of the few students who have earned an exception to my general rule about names. Shortly after receiving her commission—she is an officer in the US Army—she joined an elite cybersecurity team. In this role, she is supposed to protect her identity, so decided that I could not refer to her by either her family name or her personal name. Major X she became, at least to me.

Over the years, Major X has helped me to understand the changing nature of cybersecurity. She has usually been quite responsive to my requests for information. Within a couple hours of receiving an e-mail message, she'll give me a call, chat a bit about her current assignment, answer my question, and ask about friends from her graduating class.

However, last summer, Major X vanished for a couple of months. As August changed to September, she sent me a quick note to say that she would call in a week. "On a job," she wrote. "Can't talk. Look at my photos on Facebook."

Major X is an inveterate photographer, though her pictures tend to be group shots of friends rather than images that tell a story. Over the past years, she has posted pictures of a beach volleyball game on some tropical island, a shopping spree in Harajuku, a day at one of the Disney theme parks, and an evening at the Grand Théâtre de Genève in which she is wearing a designer gown that has nothing in common with the clothes she favored as a student.

As I paged through the most recent set of photos, I resurrected a worrisome doubt that had haunted me for the past year or so. Did these photos represent real activities, I wondered, or did she post them to establish a false identity? After all, she has a career in computer intelligence and holds a high-level security clearance. Also, she is a cautious and reserved person. I have watched her move through a dinner party and leave no trail that suggested the nature of her job or the name of her employer. She has few reasons to expose her private life to the public or to suggest to outsiders how she thinks, how she strategizes, or even how she organizes her free time.

WHEN SHE FINALLY CALLED, I was curious to hear the story of her summer. "So, X," I asked, "how have you been?"

"Fine," she said, clearly giggling at my question. "I have been very fine."

As X normally appends the word "sir" to almost anything she says, I concluded that she was doing something unusual and decided to press a little harder. "What have you been doing this summer?"

At this point, the giggle became an open laugh. "You'll never guess," she said. "I gave a talk at DEF CON."

For a moment, I was at a loss for words. After all, DEF CON is not only the largest and most notorious of the computer hacker conventions, it is also held in the Nevada desert in the heat of summer. X would have gotten no stronger response from me if she had said that she just returned from a poker tournament hosted by the North Korean Secret Service.

"DEF CON?" I asked.

"Yes," she replied.

"And you were a presenter?" I continued.

"Yes," she said.

"And did they know that you were in the military?"

"Of course," X added.

"They didn't care that you weren't a hacker?" I tried.

"How do you know that I'm not, sir?" This last question was accompanied by another unsuppressed giggle, a giggle almost unbecoming to an officer. I believed that I knew the answer to the question, at least knew it as well as anyone could. After all, I had known Major X when she was merely sophomore X and was struggling through the lessons of algorithms and data structures. Yet, I had to admit that I probably harbor doubts about anyone connected to the hacker community just as we generally have doubts about anyone whose accomplishments are shielded by the public face of an organization.

AT BASE, DEF CON IS a conventional organization, a trade show and nothing more. It has talks, exhibits, breakout sessions, and social events. The attendees pay a hefty fee, wear a badge, and are given the opportunity to take a room from a special block reserved at the hotel. "If you want to meet smart people, learn about hacking, have fun with friends, hear some good talks, broaden your horizons and expand your knowledge," claims the conference webpage, "then DEF CON is where you should be." "Seriously," the page adds, "there is something for everyone to do."

The conference may claim something for everyone, at least everyone interested in computer security, yet it also sorts people into a hierarchy. The unwashed masses. The novices. The true believers. The inner circle. The leadership. Like most social organizations, it uses relatively simple means to divide people into classes. It gives badges to participants that distinguish the wearers as speakers, press, organizers, or exhibitors. It offers awards to identify the senior members of the society.

Consciously or unconsciously, the DEF CON participants support these distinctions with simple actions. They often favor a uniform dress of black slacks and tee shirts. They communicate with one another using a slang that can be disdainful of outsiders, that is both highly inventive and sufficiently offensive to prevent its use in a general audience publication.

Because the participants are involved with an activity that falls at the edge of polite society, they sometimes enforce social distinctions with brutal means. "Use the Internet at DEF CON at your own risk," counsels the conference material. "You will be sniffed. You have been warned." Those participants who do not know how to defend their computers from skilled intruders will find that their machines have been invaded and disabled. Beyond any physical and monetary damage, such an attack will bring a social stigma to the victim. The names of individuals who lose control of their machines are posted on a display in the hotel called the "Wall of Sheep."

I needed only a few minutes to confirm that X was indeed a speaker at DEF CON. "A Hacker's Guide to Government Cybersecurity Strategies," Major X, Super Secret Bureau of Hacking, US Army. It was one of the few talks that did not have a video record posted on the Web, which relieved me. While I would have enjoyed viewing a former student's accomplishments, I was fairly certain that she had embraced the social conventions of DEF CON, including the uniform dress code and hacker slang laced with military-strength obscenities. We don't want our children to grow up. We don't want to admit that they know evil. We want them to wear their dress uniform and end every statement with a dollop of military politeness.

DEF CON actually knew evil at its founding, but it too has passed from an innocent childhood into an uncertain maturity. "I started DEF CON to be a party for myself, friends, and the technology underground," reflected the founder, who is known by his nickname of Dark Tangent. "It is not meant to be an everlasting event or a summer camp for every kid who owns a computer."

When the conference was founded in 1993, hacking was still a new phenomenon. The first public events of hacking, Clifford Stoll's Cuckoo's Egg and Robert Morris's Internet Worm, were barely five years in the past. The technical community was unsure about how it should approach the problem of hacking.

"At present, there is no technological barrier that separates the explorer from the criminal," reported an industry panel. Furthermore, many were willing to defend the rights of those individuals who tried to gain access to systems. The "blame for breaches of security and infiltration of personal, private systems is sometimes placed on the owners of those systems for maintaining an attractive nuisance."

EVEN THOUGH THE PROFESSIONAL COMMUNITY had yet to develop a unified response to the issue of hacking, no one was willing to develop a graduate program for hacking or a professional society devoted to promoting the subject. The only way that hackers could build a body of knowledge was to use informal means: papers circulated among friends, electronic bulletin boards, and surreptitious electronic mailing lists. One group made a surprisingly bold effort on Bitnet. They created a visible listserv for hackers but required all potential members to hack their way onto the list.

While we have romanticized the private circulation of knowledge, we forget that knowledge dies without an organization to support it. Without a human organization that can sift information and raise the gold from the dust, knowledge will die, as rumor and innuendo overwhelm any truth that may be within our grasp. In the early 1990s, it was possible to collect a lot of information about computer hacking. However, much of it was not true. The birth of DEF CON was marked not only by a lack of information about hacking but also by tight economic times. The recession of 1990–1991 was one of the first periods in which technology workers were laid off from their jobs. As a result, many young programmers were looking for work.

"When I started [DEF CON] there were no real jobs for people our age in computer security," recalled Dark Tangent. Long-distance "phone calls were expensive. Unix was not free. The only people with good Internet access were universities and businesses, and PCs still cost quite a bit of cash."

Initially, DEF CON was a simple and informal activity, a place where people with common interests could meet and relax. As the years progressed, the conference grew, and as it grew, it acquired the trappings of a formal organization. "It requires more people to be involved in organizing the show," complained Dark Tangent, "more insurance to cover more damage, more planning, more Con events, and more volunteer staff to make things run more smoothly."

At one point in the early part of this century, Dark Tangent concluded, "DEF CON reached a point where it is too big for its own good." An organization may have a single parent, but it is sustained by a committee, even if that committee is known as "The Goons" rather than a more prosaic name, such as "The Planning and Budgeting Group."

If the Goons originally came from that 1993 generation of novice hackers, they soon learned the skills of mature leaders. The public information on DEF CON shows how its leaders reduced risks associated with the meeting, built an administrative structure to handle recurring activities, and started recruiting new leaders. "Don't spend all of DEF CON sitting on your laptop," proclaimed one webpage. "Get involved."

It is one thing to get involved in an organization that has socially acceptable goals, public officers, and financial records that have been audited by an accounting firm that is both solvent and free from criminal charges. It is quite another thing to be involved with a group that boasts of its connection to people of dubious intent, takes no advance registration, demands cash at the door, and seems to subscribe to a code of honor among thieves. Yet, against expectations, DEF CON is surprisingly open.

The website boasts a remarkable display of photographs of the event. Most are informal snapshots and are difficult to interpret out of context. Still, they contain a lot of information that could be used to identify participants. In a few cases, you can see someone trying to duck out of the photograph. In considerably more, you find people waving the photographer away or making an obscene gesture at the camera. You "need to be very careful when you take pictures of random people," warns the DEF CON information. "Often they get very upset about that and you may lose your camera or consciousness."

I looked through a couple hundred pictures to see if I could find any evidence of X. Even in those sessions that would have been of special interest to her, she was nowhere to be found. I had a brief scare when I thought I saw a familiar ponytail in a photo of a fairly bawdy and explicit conference social event, but a second photo showed that the woman was clearly not X. If she was at DEF CON, and I have to trust her word, she knew how to avoid the camera. Perhaps she didn't want to be identified with the hacker community. Perhaps she wanted that community to think that she didn't want to be photographed. Perhaps she was avoiding the camera because she really is a hacker.

After digesting the idea that X had spent a week at DEF CON, I asked her if she had learned anything.

"Not a lot," she replied. "Our unit knows most of the things that were being discussed this year. I did meet a number of interesting people."

"What did they do?" I returned.

"Tough to say," she replied. "I gathered that most of them did computer security for large companies, but we stayed away from such subjects. We only addressed each other by our handles."

"Handles?" I queried.

"Nicknames—Dead Man, Stretch, Stone in the Road, Bunbury."

"Bunbury?"

"To each his own, sir." she replied.

At this point, I switched subjects and asked what interesting problems she had found in her work. She responded by talking about the recent hacker attacks against systems in Asia. The press had concluded that these attacks were coming from North Korea. "North Korea has expanded its 'cyber combat' unit in charge of intelligence gathering through the Internet," claimed a source in Asia. "The General Staff of the North Korean People's Army has for years been running what it calls the 'technology reconnaissance team' which consists of about 100 hackers, mostly graduates of a leading military academy in Pyongyang."

"Do you think this is coming from Korea?" I asked.

"No," she said. "I don't think that they are that good."

"Where are they from?"

"That's the problem," she replied. "A lot of things that we see are coming from a single IP address in China. They're making no effort to disguise the origin."

"So either they are being brazen or someone is doing a good job of making you believe they are being brazen."

"Of course, sir" X replied, "And they could easily have been at DEF CON."

Chapter VI:
Spirit of the Future

> Do you know what I wanna do tomorrow?
> I hope it doesn't involve talking.

Wonder of the World (2003)
David Lindsay Abaire

Introduction
Value of Expertise

Of course the offer was flattering, but it seemed misguided or perhaps misinformed. The call came late in the morning. Was I David Alan Grier, the voice asked. I responded in the affirmative, though my voice revealed a little anxiety. The prior weeks had brought a series of calls for one Diane Grier, who was needed for some legal reason of great urgency. The voice at the other end of these calls never seemed satisfied when I stated that I was not this individual and knew no one of that name.

In this case, the caller said that he was organizing a conference in Silicon Valley and that he hoped I would be the keynote speaker. By itself, this idea seemed quite pleasing. Who among the chattering classes does not like to be invited to speak in front of a large and attentive audience? Still, I've learned that conference organizers may have one of many different motives for asking for a keynote speech, some of them not all that honorable. I asked why I might be a good person to address this group.

"You clearly are one of the leading experts in the field," explained the voice. "We've read your book *When Computers Were Human* and think that it really addresses some of the issues that we are facing."

Again, this was a most gracious compliment, but it didn't completely explain the motives behind the call. "*When Computers Were Human* is a book of history," I said, "It tells a story that ends just as the era of the electronic computer begins. Exactly what is the name of this field?"

"Crowdsourcing," came the reply.

Silence was the only honorable response at the time, though the hush of an open phone line can communicate only so many ideas at a given time. Finally, I summoned all the respect I could muster and said. "I've never heard of crowdsourcing. Are you sure that you have the right guy?"

My question led to a lengthy discussion that would have been fascinating even if it had not been supported by the promise of a keynote speech. In the course of about eight minutes, an old and esoteric story suddenly became relevant to a current activity. "We shed as we pick up, like travelers who must carry everything in their arms," said the playwright Tom Stoppard, "and what we let fall will be picked up by those behind."

In this case the story concerned the labor markets of the Works Project Administration (WPA), a relief organization that operated during the Great Depression. The WPA used these markets to find work for the unemployed. Such work generally required simple skills that would be possessed by any able person with a sixth grade education. Most commonly, WPA work involved construction or other manual labor. However, the WPA also used these markets to recruit laborers to process records and to do scientific calculation. The WPA's major computing office, the Mathematical Tables Project, was the central story of *When Computers Were Human*.

At the publication of *When Computers Were Human*, reviewers generally described the Mathematical Tables Project as a forgotten piece of ancient history, a tale that should make us all be grateful that we live in an era that has electronic machines that can do the dull and demanding work of calculating values of elliptic functions, balancing our checkbooks, or enforcing the rules of solitaire. The emotional power of the piece was enforced by the revelation that my maternal grandmother, Blanch O'Kane Gallup (BA Mathematics, 1921, University of Michigan) had been trained to do scientific calculation.

For roughly two years, I told and retold the story of the Mathematical Tables Project, which was the largest computing organization prior to the electronic computer. In these presentations, I quickly learned that I really had only one point that would sustain the interest of an audience, the idea that these were ordinary workers with ordinary skills. I explained that these workers tended to be unemployed store clerks and that most of them did not have more than 6 or 8 years of education. Furthermore, they worked with tools no more sophisticated than paper and pencil. Slide rules were not sufficiently precise, and adding machines were too expensive.

The market for historical stories of ordinary life is not large. With each talk or appearance, it becomes a little smaller. After an appearance on a national radio talk show, I realized that I had drained the well of interest for the Mathematical Tables Project. I shared the elevator with the host of the program that had preceded my presentation. "I heard you on the air," she said. "I thought it was interesting."

Interesting. Not useful, engaging or insightful. It was a tidbit to share at a dinner party and nothing more.

I had written *When Computers Were Human* to be part of the literature of scientific history. It sat uneasily in that literature, as it dealt with different classes of workers who contribute to the scientific endeavor. A large fraction of scientific history extols the virtues of geniuses and heroes. However, not all scientists are Einstein or Madam Curie. Not all of them lead a laboratory or direct a project. Modest workers have contributed to scientific knowledge, but they are rarely found in the stories of science.

Unbeknownst to me, *When Computers Were Human* also fit into a second body of literature, one that deals with workers, tasks, and management. Shortly after the publication of my book, that literature started to include works on employing large groups of workers in a common project. Perhaps the most prominent contribution to that literature was James Surowiecki's *The Wisdom of Crowds*, which was published a year before *When Computers Were Human*. At some point, a dedicated reader connected my book to Suroweicki. In a moment, the world shifted a bit. A historical anecdote became a useful lesson, an ancient idea became modern concept, and esoteric knowledge was converted into expertise.

EXPERTISE IS NOTORIOUSLY SHORT-LIVED AND is assigned value by a market that is often difficult to understand and impossible to predict. Such markets are always a bit anxious about expertise based on historical knowledge, as they emphasize the current worth of ideas and believe, rightly or wrongly, that we are not subject to the sins of our fathers. They believe that civilization has advanced beyond the failings of the past and that we will not repeat the errors of prior ages. We will not engage in vicious ideological warfare. We will not plunge the global economy into depression. We will not employ technology in ways that ruin our society, our health, our environment. We have learned those lessons. We are better than those who came before.

When Computers Were Human brought me into contact with an individual whose expertise had been a slow but steady climb in the market, Jean Bartik (1924–2011). Bartik was the last surviving member of the programming staff of the ENIAC computer in 1946, a group that was originally ignored by both the press and the scientific community. Its contributions were largely unreported for thirty years and came to the public attention originally through the rise of feminism and feminist history. This approach to history argued that the accomplishments of women were overlooked by narratives that favored male qualities.

Beginning in roughly 1986, the story of the ENIAC programmers became more and more prominent as feminist values became part of discussion of science and technology. They were often grouped with other women who contributed to the development of computing but were overlooked in the official histories. These women included Ada Lovelace (1815–1852) who worked with Charles Babbage, Grace Hopper (1906–1992) who was part of Howard Atkin's laboratory at Harvard, and Gertrude Blanch (1896–1996) of the Mathematical Tables Project. The ENIAC women gained more prominent roles at historical conferences, their stories were added to the ENIAC narrative, and they were the subject of documentary. For Jean Bartik, this attention culminated in the Pioneer Award from the IEEE.

When Bartik exited this world in the spring of 2011, I was asked to contribute to her obituary, as I had recently completed an oral history of her and had reviewed her memoirs. The writer and I spent a half hour on the phone discussing the basic problem of any news story. Why was life of Jean Bartik of value, and why did it deserve a prominent position in the national media? We both talked about the need to recognize the contributions of women to science and technology, but we both felt that such an approach had obvious limitations. The desire to record the contributions of women has identified a substantial number of female scientists, but few of them achieved the prominence of the ENIAC women.

At some point in our discussion, the two of us focused on the value of programming, the work done by the ENIAC women. In 1946, when these women were working on the ENIAC, computing research was focused on hardware. The leaders in the field were more interested in the problems of building computing machines than in running those machines. Forty years later, when the women were getting their first public attention, hardware was still an important topic of research, but it was losing its position to software. For roughly 20 years, software had been growing in importance and in 20 years more, it would be the dominant topic of research. The four decades that elevated software above hardware also gave Bartik and her peers the first measure of appreciation.

We are always tempted to believe that the market that values expertise, or contributions, or fame has turned to a stable state, that the future will evaluate the world as we see it. Yet we know that almost every American city contains a bronze monument to a long-deceased leader whose contributions are now forgotten if not judged embarrassing. The present need determines the value of our ideas, old or new. The reputation of Charles Babbage dwelt in semi-darkness until the field of computation needed a founder. Software has needed founders and so, apparently, has the field of crowdsourcing. When these fields have established themselves and no longer feel threatened by the novelty they have won, we will cast the founding expertise in bronze and move forward. Yet, even as a field of endeavor moves forward, it carries old ideas, ideas that it cannot always value and that the past could never recognize.

01
Someday You'll Understand

The incomprehension was clearly evident on the children's faces. They couldn't grasp what was happening to their parents. I was not in a position to intervene, and even if I had been, I could have offered nothing more than the reassurance that maturity and experience would bring enlightenment.

Across the street from where I stood was a pair of stores, the one on the left devoted to the shoes of a famous Italian designer, and the one on the right to the products of a sports car manufacturer of equal reputation. The latest fashions of Milan could be seen in one window, and the red gleam of speed was displayed in the other. As families approached these establishments, mothers would be pulled to one and fathers to the other. Forced to follow one parent or the other, the child inevitably found themselves in a business that sold products of no interest to them.

Some kids would cry. Some would pout. Others would find comfort in that universal children's game that involves running, screaming, and hiding in the aisles of a retail establishment.

If I had had the power, I would have explained to each child that this was the parting of the genders. Someday, they might like to know how their parents responded to the forces of designer shoes and high-powered sports cars and how such things caused men and women to think about the world in different terms.

I witnessed this activity because I had come to this place, to the city of Rome, to speak at an annual science festival. The festival helped adults understand the major issues of science and technology and encouraged children to become interested in such subjects. The festival's lobby was filled with a collection of computer-driven exhibits that attempted to unite the impossible goals of entertaining and educating those present.

Some of these exhibits were highly popular. Some were ignored. Some were delightful, others completely inscrutable. I could see why the train simulator drew long lines, and why the infectious disease model had no audience. I could also appreciate the fun in the digital arts station, but was mystified by the lack of interest in 3D photography.

I will admit that the delight I found in the photography demonstration came from the clever nature of the system that created the pictures rather than from the photographs themselves. The images weren't particularly compelling, but the system was a clever assemblage of devices that had been designed for other purposes. It consisted of 24 cell phones, a circular pen that could be used to exercise horses, a laptop, and several hundred cable ties.

The cell phones were connected to the top rail of the pen at intervals that corresponded to 15 degrees of the circle. Upon command, each phone would take a picture of whatever stood at the center of the enclosure and transmit the image to the laptop. A simple program on the laptop stored those images in a database and displayed them in rapid order, which gave the illusion of three dimensions.

Most kids walked by the photographic exhibit with barely a glance. From their perspective, a recent 3D movie was far more compelling and a home videogame was more intriguing. Perhaps they would be able to appreciate the value of the show only after they had struggled with the problems of creativity, when they had tackled an assignment to create something out of a bag of old cell phones, the old pony's pen, and Aunt Florence's obsolete laptop.

FOR MY TALK AT THE festival, I had been asked to explain the nature of invention and discovery that stood behind modern science and technology. In this effort, I am fairly certain I was only marginally successful. I am comfortable that I did better than the incomprehensible art exhibit, but acknowledge that I did not meet the standards set by the interactive map with the giant touch screen.

In my talk, I tried to convey the changing nature of discoveries and inventions. Yesterday's exciting find may not seem so novel tomorrow. The odd machine that was dismissed during its construction may prove to be an important new invention. The object that Clyde Tombaugh (1906–1997) identified as the planet Pluto (in 1930) is one discovery that has fallen from grace, while Babbage's analytic engine (1834), originally an object of ridicule, became the forerunner of the programmable computer.

Of course, neither Pluto nor the analytic engine has changed over the years. Tombaugh's object is still in orbit around the sun. Babbage's engine remains as it was in the 19th century. Yet, during the intervening years, we have changed the frameworks that we use to understand these two works. After Tombaugh's discovery, we slowly modified our understanding of planets in a way that excludes Pluto.

We now tend to view it as an object from the Kuiper Belt, a collection of small objects that orbits the sun at a distance and probably supplies the objects that become comets. We came to appreciate Babbage's machine as the foundation of our field only after Harvard researcher Howard Aiken began to understand the power of the computer program.

IN A VERY SHORT SPAN of time, we have altered the framework that we use to evaluate the invention of computing. Less than 25 years ago, we would have identified the power and flexibility of the modern computer as its major contributions to modern society. Today, those two properties would be considered far less important than the technology of digital communication.

One of the speakers at the science festival emphasized this change by arguing that the Internet should be awarded the Nobel Peace Prize because it was the most important technology in history. The audience roared its approval at this suggestion, and some individuals at the front of the room chanted, "Yes, yes!"

At the same time, at least one person standing near me didn't agree with that assessment. "Why should we give the Nobel Peace Prize to a technology that has made it easier for terrorists to work on a global scale and has radically reduced the cost of pornography?" he asked.

In fact, the speaker did not base his argument for the Nobel Prize in a technological framework that emphasized the engineering accomplishments or even on an economic framework that would consider the wealth that the Internet has created. Instead, he analyzed the network's value within the context of global development, with the frame that considers how poor countries are connected to the industrial economy. In particular, he based his case on the success of the One Laptop Per Child program.

As its name suggests, One Laptop Per Child attempts to give a small laptop computer to every child on the planet as a means of bringing the world's educational resources to countries and regions that lack strong school systems. "Information and communications technology is quickly changing the world," explained Muhammad Yunus (1940–), the recipient of the 2006 Nobel Peace Prize. The lives of the poor could be substantially changed "if this technology could be brought to them to meet their needs."

Yunus has been responsible for changing the framework used to finance business activities in poor countries. For most of the 20th century, most leaders felt that the best way to improve the economy was to give large loans directly to the governments of poor countries. Yunus inverted this idea by founding Grameen Bank, which gives small loans, as little as $5.00, to poor women. These loans pay for stock for a store, a few tools, a place to work.

"I was stunned by the result," explained Yunus in his Nobel lecture. "These small loans allowed the recipients to create profitable businesses. Further, the recipients repaid these sums, on time, every time." In spite of dire predictions from conventional banks, Grameen achieved a 99 percent repayment rate. It operates as a self-sufficient organization and has not taken money from a donor since 1995.

In its own way, the One Laptop Per Child program inverts the conventional approach to educational development by giving technology directly to children rather than to governments or educational systems. "The children become teachers," claimed the speaker at the science festival. Such an idea is easy to accept, as children the world over have successfully educated their elders to send text messages, compose e-mail, record television shows, and perform many other complicated tasks.

However, education involves much more than acquiring technical information or gaining elementary knowledge of reading, writing, and arithmetic. It involves the process of inventing ideas, placing them into a social or economic or scientific framework, and testing to see if those ideas are true. To help impart these sorts of intellectual skills, the One Laptop Per Child Program puts a library of 10 books on each machine, but such a library is more controversial than the machine itself. Books can shake the foundation of a society and overturn the cradle of youth. Words can offend. Characters can be unpleasant. Plots can be troublesome. A child cannot easily learn how a story fits into a cultural framework without the guidance of an experienced teacher or at least the help of an elder.

Furthermore, we know that education can threaten the stability of a country. The act of creating and testing ideas can lead to the conclusion that national institutions are broken and need to be fixed. In at least one country, the local military is managing the One Laptop Per Child Program. We hope that they are providing the wisdom of elders, the vision that helps children understand the stories of their culture, tells them honestly, "You will understand some day," and then takes the practical steps to ensure that they do.

SOMETIME AFTER MY ROMAN EXCURSION, I flew to the West Coast for a meeting. Once the plane cleared that magical 10,000-foot altitude, I took my laptop out of my briefcase and began to work on an article about software engineering. My neighbor to my right, seeing the subject of my paper, asked if I could explain a few things to him.

"I'll try," I responded, noting that he held a magazine devoted to commercial real estate development.

"What do you know about things like Facebook, smart phones, listservs, and Twitter?" he queried.

I looked at him for a moment and glanced a second time at his magazine. I concluded that he was roughly my peer and had simply missed many of the innovations of the Information Age. I started giving my standard explanation of social media, which proved to be grossly inappropriate for the actual question he intended to ask. While I was stressing the role of social media in giving commands and assessing actions in business, my seatmate laid his hand on my arm and said, "My daughters. How should I think about these things with regard to my daughters?"

I probably should have been humble enough to acknowledge my misunderstanding, but all I felt was a brief moment of gratitude that I had not started by describing the use of social media in the Islamic states of the Middle East.

"How old are they?" I asked.

"They're 12 and 14," he said. "The elder is a tomboy who will never wear a dress, and the younger is an aspiring fashion model who will wear nothing else."

"Have you let them use a computer or a cell phone?" was my reply.

"Not yet," he said. "We're just not sure what is out there."

"With good reason," I said. No longer the expert giving a speech, I directed the conversation to an age-old subject: how fathers can help their children develop into fully functioning adults; how they need to let go of a daughter's hand and let her walk forth into a wicked world.

We talked about how social media tools are establishing the way that the current generation communicates, and I noted that his daughters need to understand this technology as much as they need to know how to drive a car in traffic or use tools to maintain their home. At the same time, I acknowledged that digital communication had radically expanded the multiple ways for dishonest souls to engage in criminal deception.

"How do I know what to teach them," he asked, "when I barely know how to use this technology?"

"Let them teach you," was my reply. "A father's role is to validate, not to teach. Have them show you what they can do and bless them when they do it right." I don't think my seatmate was entirely satisfied with my advice. His face suggested that he was quite anxious about technology that he did not understand and would never master as well as his children. He was going to have to try to teach the lessons of life by sitting next to his daughters, watching them perform mysterious feats on the computer screen, and hearing them say "Don't worry, Daddy. You'll understand someday.

02
Satisfying the Public

Becky stood in the front of the hemispheric room where the corpse would have been placed. A long wooden table was all that remained to remind the audience that the auditorium had served, for nearly a century, as a laboratory for human anatomy classes.

The ring of seats at the front of the room would have been reserved for senior professors. The concentric circles of benches that climbed the room's steep ramp would have seated the students, future doctors all. Only the seats in the upper corners of the room might have been open to the general public. For a nominal fee, the curious and the confident could have watched as a learned scholar of anatomy peeled away the skin and exposed the inner structure of a recently executed felon for all to see.

Becky is neither a fresh corpse nor a bloodied professor of anatomy, as both have moved to more modern classrooms. She is a worker of miracles, a middle school teacher who can instill enthusiasm for science in the minds of 14-year-olds. Such creatures can be hard cases, as they are often only a few short steps away from becoming corpses themselves, a fact I know from a year-long term as a 14-year-old boy myself. Yet, the real miracle is not fitting the 14-year-old into science, as we so often try to do, but fitting science to the 14-year-old.

We live in an age of rising concern over scientific education and the next generation of scientists and engineers. As a consequence, we have established more opportunities for 14-year-olds to engage the scientific community. Becky has been more than ordinarily effective in exploiting those programs. Beginning with a fairly modest activity, she was able to establish connections with the European Physics laboratory CERN. She has taken her charges to visit CERN to talk with the scientists and even encouraged the students to think about questions and experiments of their own. The result of this effort has been a student-designed satellite.

The satellite, called LUCID (an acronym that combines the name of her school district with a description of the cosmic ray detector used in the project), is not conceptually different from the early American satellite, Vanguard I. Yet it illustrates the extent to which science has become a massive human endeavor that requires new ideas to fit into a complex, well-established structure. The LUCID project involves 10 schools in Becky's region of the UK, dozens of students and teachers, a special detector designed by a global laboratory, a space agency, and aeronautical engineers from the US and Europe.

The satellite itself is a CubeSat, a standard design that California Polytechnic and Stanford universities created to provide an inexpensive way to get experiments into space. "Due to the accelerated development schedule of most Cube-Sat projects," explained one of the early research teams, "students are exposed to seeing the end result of their work from concept to application. This valuable experience gives students a solid idea of the 'big picture,' or the complete mission cycle and the whole system of the spacecraft."

CubeSats have a standard design, 10 cm on a side, and standard systems. They also have a standard deployment mechanism, the Poly Picosatellite Orbital Deployer or P-POD. This is a tricky bit of engineering that terrestrial scientists often overlook. A giant spring was supposed to push the original Soviet Sputnik away from its booster. The Russian scientists were so proud of their design that they put a duplicate on display in the State Science Museum, although they failed to note that the original apparently did not work properly.

Finally, CubeSats also offer a systematic approach to assembling documents, export licenses, and formal approval. To most scientists, this step is usually a jumble of paperwork, an exercise in administrative trivia. However, it is really the step of fitting science to society. If we are building a machine in one country, fitting it to a rocket in a second, and launching it over the heads of the residents of a third, we owe the world a formal statement that work has been well done, or at least done to standards that we believe will minimize the chances that the rocket will fall on those trusting heads.

FOR ALL OF THEIR CLEVER innovations, CubeSats are a fairly conventional way to engage the public in the work of science. They are an educational tool, a means of teaching potential scientists about the means and methods of research. An equally common method of engaging the public has been to utilize the labor of individuals to gather or process large amounts of data. Even in the early 19th century, we can find reports of networks of individuals recording natural phenomena such as the group that gathered tidal data on the coast of England for William Whewell (1794–1866) or the weather observers who collected data for the US Navy in the 1850s.

For both of these groups, the work was hard and exacting. The weather observers, for example, had to be familiar with scientific instruments, collect data at four specified times during the day, complete a detailed form, and place that form in the mail so that it would reach the central weather office, located in the Smithsonian Institution in Washington.

Some individuals have argued that these large data collection efforts could also be educational, but most scientists have resisted this approach. They want to do good science and prefer to do as little training as possible. One of the largest sponsors of mass science in the 20th century, the Works Progress Administration, clearly stated that its job had nothing to do with education. Our work "is restricted, in general, to projects involving the collection, tabulation, or analysis of data," wrote administration director Harry Hopkins (1890–1946), and "our projects were evolved principally for the purpose of providing employment for needy persons with professional and technical training."

In our age, the tradition of WPA science has been developed and expanded in mass research that is supported by the BOINC (Berkeley Open Infrastructure for Network Computing) software system. The BOINC system lets individuals donate the work cycles of their home computer to a scientific project that needs large computing power. It is a form of grid computing, although a fairly simple example. A user downloads the basic BOINC software and chooses a project to support. The BOINC client then retrieves a computational task from the project's central server and does that task while the owner is not using the machine. It finally transmits the results to the central server for collation and organization.

An early version of BOINC was first deployed in 2005 for the SETI@Home project. SETI, the Search for ExtraTerrestrial Intelligence, looks for patterns in electromagnetic radiation that might have been caused by intelligent life. The methods of analysis are fairly straightforward, as they are drawn from the field of signal processing, but each method requires a substantial amount of computing, and each is applied to large datasets. The SETI researchers originally developed their own software but shifted to BOINC for all the reasons that we have for accepting standard software. It was simpler, easier to deploy, and more flexible.

SETI@Home was the first of many projects to use BOINC to handle scientific computation. The BOINC software now supports projects that fold proteins, sequence genes, test software, factor large integers, look for large primes, and search for the still elusive solvable Sudoku puzzle with only 16 preset numbers or clues. (Current research has found numerous solvable puzzles with 17 clues and one 16-clue puzzle that has two unique solutions. An anxious world of problem solvers awaits the results of this work.)

Each of these projects has created a community of supporters that follows the progress of research, volunteers more time when needed, wears the tee shirt, and defends its own. Even with this participation, BOINC projects have a boundary of expertise that is contained in the software. The volunteers are not actively involved in the research. The calculation is done in the background and is invisible to the user. While the volunteers are given credit for the computer cycles they donate to the work, they cannot connect their contributions to any specific result.

The workers on mass science are generally isolated from the final results by the traditions of scientific computation. As each task is run on at least two computers to check the result, no one can claim unique connections to any calculation. Further distancing the workers from the final conclusion is the complex nature of any scientific conclusion. Few of these conclusions are based on a single calculation. No one but Archimedes runs naked from the bath with a single insight into the scientific problem. While we would like to think that we could follow the progress of scientific work on our computers and cheer that a new discovery has been made, we know that cannot happen. Scientific discoveries are made by hypothesizing, analyzing, synthesizing, reasoning to a conclusion, and then verifying the results.

Our ability to follow the progress on our computers is not only linked to the drama of scientific discovery but also to our willingness to volunteer our computers for service in the search for knowledge. When a group of BOINC users gathers for a meeting, they often dwell on specific questions: "How can we get more people involved? How can we build a bigger BOINC grid system?" The question is often phrased in terms of persuasion or education. "How can we teach people that this effort is in their best interest?"

PEOPLE PROBABLY NEED TO BE taught that research is in their interests, just as researchers could better recognize that such research involves a form of economic decision-making. What do volunteers receive in return for downloading a strange piece of software and offering their computing cycles? They once received a cool screensaver but such things consume computing power and are no longer part of the system. Only some will be satisfied with the notion that their computer is doing work. More will be pleased to be part of a community that is dealing with grand questions. Certainly, there are those who will be satisfied with the tee shirt, especially if it has a really intriguing logo. Some would be pleased to receive actual cash for their computer time, but no one is particularly interested in building a structure that actually pays for work.

A common way of getting individuals to become involved with an activity is to give them a stake in the work, offering them an opportunity to make decisions about the tasks. Workers react favorably to situations that "contribute to their sense of importance and personal worth," reported the pioneering researcher in personnel management Rensis Lickert (1903–1981). Likewise, they "react unfavorably to experiences which are threatening and decrease or minimize their sense of dignity and personal worth." In the situations that employ systems such as BOINC, such a principle faces two objections, the first professional and the second managerial.

Professionally, we make a strong division between scientists and workers. We allow scientists the opportunity to make judgments about experiments and data but do not offer the same opportunities to nonprofessional workers. We claim that our judgments are based on scientific training and do not allow others to make those decisions until they have had that training.

Managerially, we find that expanding the ability of individuals to make decisions about the work can slow progress. "If any basic principle governs the decision-making process," wrote Herbert Simon (1916–2001), "it is that each decision should be located at a point where it will be of necessity approached as a question of efficiency rather than a question of adequacy." Because an organization of amateurs cannot guarantee decisions of efficiency, it seems that if we are to expand scientific projects that involve large numbers of ordinary citizens, we must be prepared to accept the consequences of unscientific judgments or inefficient strategies.

During the past couple of years, the scientific projects that involve help from the general public have begun to coalesce into a body of activities that has taken the name citizen science. They circulate newsletters, operate discussion groups, and occasionally hold conferences in university auditoriums that once served simultaneously as a research laboratory, an anatomy classroom, and entertainment for the public. Such a setting is appropriate, as this movement often attempts to recombine by means of the Internet the three elements of university activity: education, research, and service to the public. These three elements are now relegated to their own isolated locations: education in classrooms, research in laboratories, and public service on those dramatized shows about engineering problems that are now prevalent on the far reaches of basic cable television.

Citizen science may not be able to make major changes to scientific institutions, but it should be able to occupy some niche in scientific practice. As we have seen in other activities that attempt to coordinate the contributions of the general public with the Internet, these efforts have a way of disciplining work and overcoming gross inefficiencies associated with mass labor.

Mass labor, especially when it is a volunteer effort, can prove to be remarkably resistant to discipline. Volunteers are prone to follow their own inclinations no matter how much guidance a professional scientist might offer. One of the major citizen projects devoted to recording biodiversity claims to offer a global perspective on flora and fauna, but its volunteers have shown a remarkable propensity for collecting images from the world's wealthy shopping districts and resorts. Pictures of Yellowstone can be of great interest, but they are of little use when you hoped to see images of plants found in Yaoundé.

As Becky will tell you, every miracle worker knows that certain tasks will never engage a 14-year-old, no matter how important they may be. Sudoku is a puzzle for adults, and regardless of the importance of the search for the 16-clue puzzle, it is unlikely to win the attention of individuals who spend most of their time with computer games that offer fast cars, big guns, and ever-present danger. To engage such people in the dedicated work of research, you need a satellite and a rocket—although a corpse might do in a pinch. Above all, you need a miracle-worker who can give the public a stake in the science.

03
Pay Your Money and Take Your Chances

For years, I had a steady relationship with three Internet radio stations. They promoted interesting and engaging music that I enjoyed. One presented intellectually elitist classical music, another broadcasted disdainfully cool jazz from those crucial years of 1956 to 1963, and the third was devoted to completely incomprehensible avante garde pop. No matter which station I chose, I felt that I was working with people that I could trust, people who would provide me with the kind of music that I would use to shape my day.

Last spring all three stations began to falter. First, the classic station began its unstoppable drift toward short bland pieces by unknown composers. Next, the jazz station took the motto "Global Jazz for a Global Age" and demonstrated an unfortunate preference for songs that were hardly global and barely jazz. Their playlist slipped into that mushy world of major keys and slippery saxophones that provides more distraction than enjoyment. Finally, in a desperate effort to retain the youth of today as its listeners, the pop station embraced repetitious dance music. Each song had to fit into a tight little box that allowed no more than seven minutes of music, five recognizable words, two chord changes, and one inflexible drum beat.

Seeing no hope for improvement, I first went in search of other Internet radio stations. Finding little of interest, I took the advice of a friend and subscribed to Pandora, a music streaming service. "It will give you just the radio station that you would like," my friend said. "It will give you a new relationship with music."

My first experience with the music streaming service was delightful. Pandora lets you build an Internet radio station by combining one or more music streams. You create a stream by giving the software a target song that you know and like. The software will then feed music into that stream by identifying songs that are similar to the one you have selected. It uses a pretty straightforward algorithm with an ordinary distance metric. Within 10 minutes, I had identified a couple of target songs and had a new Internet radio station that I found pleasant enough.

I spent the morning listening to my new music source. Over lunch, I took another look at the database and made a discovery that led to trouble. Much to my delight, I found an esoteric art band from my youth, a record that had not been heard in decades. I selected my favorite tune from the record, added it to my collection, and waited for the streaming system to give me what I wanted.

It took less than an hour for my delight to sour into frustration and my pride of discovery to collapse into embarrassment. Once more, I learned that esoteric knowledge should never be mistaken for good taste. My favorite song had aged badly. To my adult ears, it was nothing more than a silly and shallow ballad that appealed only to teenage boys who believed the promises of fantasy literature.

Furthermore, it proved to be a complete singularity. It had no natural neighbors in Pandora. As a result, it became a regular fixture of my playlist. Every 15 to 18 minutes, Pandora would repeat the song as if it was determined to show me how pathetic my musical taste really was.

The problem was easy to fix, but its memory remained. I deleted the song and reset the stream, but this change resulted in only a slight improvement. As I listened to the stream, I began to realize that most of the songs were familiar derivatives of the original target songs and offered little new.

Less "than 3% of active music titles accounted for over 80% of sales," the streaming service had noted. The bulk of the day's music came from that unprofitable 97 percent of the music catalog, and most of it demonstrated an obvious lack of commercial and artistic value.

I DECIDED TO ABANDON THE service, dismissing it as a fad that would vanish from the cyber airwaves in a month or two. However, as I returned to my work and started playing a familiar MP3 file to fill the quiet of my office, I realized that I had made a mistake in identifying Pandora as a new form of the radio station. Radio stations create community through their broadcasts. "Carried from house to house to ship from sail to train," wrote the playwright Bertolt Brecht (1898–1956) about his infatuation with radio. "Last thing at night and the first in the morning." As he laid down to sleep he asked, "Promise me not to go silent all of a sudden."

In contrast, Pandora offers no community. It's a tool for exploring a set of objects in the vast reaches of musical space, "an effective means of browsing and discovering new music" that we will like, according to the Pandora literature. In the words of computer scientist Douglas Engelbart (1925–), it is technology that augments our intellect. "By augmenting human intellect," he wrote, "we mean increasing the capability of a man to approach a complex problem situation, to gain comprehension to suit his particular needs, and to derive solutions to problems."

Once I realized that Pandora was not a means for recreating the communities of my formerly favorite radio stations, I recognized the complex problem I was trying to solve. I enjoyed hearing new music, but I was unwilling to invest large amounts of time and money to search for that music. I had limited time to attend concerts by unfamiliar artists and had no patience for pawing through alphabetical lists of songs, even when those songs had been categorized by genre and style. Pandora gave me a tool to find interesting music, but it required me to change my relationship to music critics.

Years ago, I accepted the sarcastic dismissal of music criticism that had been articulated by the guitarist Frank Zappa (1940–1993). He argued that critics were "people who can't write, interviewing people who can't talk for people who can't read." With Pandora, I found that I could ignore the literary failures of music journalists and still profit from their experiences. I could harness their judgments as input to Pandora and use that tool to identify interesting artists in genres that I didn't know.

Over a couple of weeks, I developed a strategy that fed recommendations from music critics into Pandora. I often found the original recommendations overwrought—merely novel for the sake of novelty. However, in Pandora, several of them led me to interesting discoveries. I found a Mexican guitarist with stunning technique, a British hip-hop duo that were surprisingly skilled with words, and a mixed-voice choir that made my heart melt.

As I began to understand how I might use Pandora, I was reminded of my first encounter with Engelbart's ideas for graphical interfaces, ideas that included computer mice, icons, and other concepts now so familiar to us. That encounter involved a system that had been written by a couple of computer technicians to represent the work they had to do. The technicians had developed little icons for the objects that they handled: the punched cards, swappable disk drives, and other elements of the old third-generation mainframes. They used the mouse to move these objects through the tasks of a typical day: read a deck of cards, punch a deck, mount a disk, start a job. They even went so far as to duplicate the failures of the physical objects: a dropped deck of cards, a dented plate on a hard drive. It was a system that didn't look through the complexity of the problem at hand and see a better solution. It looked backward, not forward.

Of course, the task of looking forward, even with the aid of a new technology, is remarkably difficult. We often don't see the problem clearly or even define its fundamental elements. Pandora is an example of a music information retrieval system. At base, these systems are merely databases that allow individuals to make queries to retrieve objects. The old jukebox is actually a crude example of such a system. It took a nickel and retrieved a song in response to a two-symbol code.

Modern music retrieval systems utilize fairly well known structures and algorithms for storing and organizing data. They are divided into two broad classes of systems. The first uses some form of music notation to organize its information. The second uses a transformed version of audio data as the basis of search and organization. While some, like Pandora, search descriptions of the songs, the most interesting search the music itself. Most can be designed to return perfect matches or near matches. Some of the more impressive systems will take an ill-hummed melody and still return a match from their databases.

All of these systems require a means of categorizing and organizing music; otherwise, they would be forced to check each item in a search of their database. Historically, musicians have never used anything more than a crude set of categories to organize music. Ludwig von Köchel (1800–1877) set the basic standard in 1862 when he created a catalog of the music composed by Wolfgang Amadeus Mozart (1756–1791). Köchel listed the pieces chronologically but kept a little metadata in the form of the key signature and the type (sonata, symphony, and so forth). His listing contained one hint of things to come: a few opening notes that he called the incipit. Readers were supposed to hum the incipit to help them recognize the piece.

Köchel's approach changed little during the 19th and early 20th centuries, though it was occasionally modified for certain kinds of music. Hymns and folk-songs, for example, were often categorized by syllable counts. This allowed singers to use old tunes with new words.

THE FIRST EFFORTS TO FIND formal methods for categorizing music came in the first decades of the 20th century, when musicologists moved beyond the standard catalogs of the European composers and started to collect folk music. In the US, pioneering musicologist John Lomax (1867–1948) assembled the first of these collections. In 1911, Lomax reported that he had collected well over 100 "cowboy songs" from the American Southwest. "Of some of the songs," he explained, "I have from five to 20 slightly varying versions." However, he had no formal means of describing the nature of these variations.

As an example of the scale of the challenge, Lomax cited a single song that had expanded as it had passed from voice to voice. "I know of one person who claims to be able to sing 143 stanzas of it," he noted. The creators of these songs had time in a way that Lomax did not. They were isolated in the vast land of the west, far from cities, books, and magazines. "It was perfectly natural for them to seek diversion in song."

Writing 60 years later, Lomax's granddaughter suggested that the great diversity of folk music might forever prevent it from being archived in a simple, unified way. "The classification problem suggested here is by no means a new one," she wrote, "and can be simply stated: Is a song a function of its lexical content or its social usage?" Was a song best categorized as lullaby because it was sung to drowsy babies or as a ballad because of its structure? "Of course, as far as the act of archiving goes, it doesn't really matter," she added, "You pay your money and you take your choice."

Musicologists were slow to embrace the methods of formal language theory and complexity analysis that started to develop in the late 1950s. One of the early applications of this theory to music came from the computer science community in a 1984 article by Don Knuth. Using the methods commonly applied to algorithm analysis, Knuth argued that a forgettable 1970s disco song was representative of the simplest class of music: those songs that could be expanded to any arbitrary length with only a finite amount of material. This effort is best understood as a means of illustrating the techniques of computer science than as a serious piece of musicology. However, it is better understood as a paper that uses music to illustrate an issue in computer science.

AS A GROUP, MUSICOLOGISTS WERE unsure of the value of such analyses, as they did not seem to answer the questions they considered. Formal grammars "are only really interesting when they can be used to drive a model of human performance on a task that involves understanding," argued one musicologist. "What task of musical understanding could use these rules?" He could offer no answer to the question.

Sometimes we understand how technology can augment our abilities only after a crisis shows us the value of a new approach to a problem. Music information retrieval systems became a subject of serious study only with the Great Napster Crisis of 1999–2001, the two-year period in which a simple, peer-to-peer music retrieval system opened the canon of Western popular music without regard to the rights of authors or performers.

Prior to 1999, neither the music literature nor the technical literature showed much interest in music information retrieval systems. You could find an occasional overview article in the general magazines in the field and a couple of discussions of familiar algorithms and how they can be adapted to music information systems, but you found no consistent thread, no body of knowledge in which one idea builds upon the next.

Music information retrieval systems proved to be one of those topics that didn't fit well into an existing technical field. To most researchers, it was nothing more than a clever example of some form of technology. It became a serious field of study only when a group of scholars identified such systems as tools that could simplify their work. Those scholars were not computer scientists or even musicologists; they were researchers involved in the National Science Foundation Digital Library Initiative.

It was "a short happy tale," reported two individuals who helped to establish the field of music information retrieval systems. During those years that Napster began circulating music on the Internet, researchers in the field established a conference, began publishing technical articles, and developed a set of categories that described their work. This effort established a place for music information retrieval systems, though that place is not quite part of library science nor an aspect of computer science and is certainly not a branch of musicology. It is a body of knowledge that allows researchers to pay their money and take their chances. To sort through the work of others to find what they want.

04
The Value of a Good Name

I can usually spot when it is about to happen, but this time held a surprise. The guard at the front desk asked to see identification so that he could give me a visitor's badge. I had come to be part of a meeting on the future of technology. Such meetings are profoundly rational experiences that tend to reinforce the preconceptions that people bring to the table.

The guard took my District driver's license and looked at it carefully. He then looked at me and then returned to the license. I could feel a question coming, but it was not the one I expected.

"Mr. Grier," she said.

"Yes," I responded.

"By chance are you related to Roosevelt Grier?" she asked.

I almost laughed at that point. Roosevelt Grier was a professional football player from the late 1960s and the example that my father had used to teach us that our family included a broader range of people than we might have expected. Roosevelt Grier is an African American, and I trace my ancestry to Ireland and Scotland. The Griers were a small landless tribe of the Scots and hence spent a good part of history looking for a place to live. There are not that many of us, so you can usually find a familial connection.

"Yes," I said. "He is something like a fifth cousin."

"I knew him as a kid," she responded. "I went to Sunday School with him. Is he still a minister?"

"To the best of my knowledge," I answered. "I've never had personal contact with him, but I think I know where he fits into the family tree."

I often get questions about family connections, but they are usually much more personal. Whenever I see the subject line "Are you David Alan Grier?" I take a deep breath before proceeding. Yes, I'm David Alan Grier and have been so all my life. However, if you have to ask that question, then you probably want to talk with someone else.

The last time I received such an e-mail, the correspondence was actually intended for me, but the sender wanted to talk to someone who no longer exists. A researcher in Asia had found some papers that I wrote during graduate school and wanted more information. He hoped that I had written more papers on the same subject—that I could share the data set from my experiments and the program that I originally used for the research.

I explained that I appreciated his interest in my research, but that I had pursued that work a long time ago and much had changed in the intervening years. Hence, I was now doing different work. My correspondent acknowledged the note, but didn't seem to get the point of my reply. "Was I not David Alan Grier?" he asked. If that was not so, why couldn't I share my program?

MOST COMMONLY, WHEN PEOPLE SEND e-mails asking if I'm David Alan Grier they're trying to reach the Broadway actor who shares my identity, name for name, letter for letter. In these cases, I indeed have to explain that I'm not that person, even though I have much in common with him. Beyond our names, we share the same hometown and the same birth year. Our fathers worked across the street from each other, and, for a time, his website sold my books. One of my students has performed with him, and the child of one of his colleagues enrolled at my college. For most of our adult lives, the two of us have been involved in a collision of identities.

Before the rise of the Internet, David and I would have been able to resolve the confusion over our names only if we had belonged to a common community. The Social Register, for example, might have noted that I belonged to the branch of the Pennsylvania Griers who emigrated to the West or that he came from a particularly distinguished line of the Ohio Griers.

In the modern age, we put our personal information on a social networking site and hope that the search engines can somehow distinguish us. As a result, we learn that the world is wide, that the variety of names is smaller than we would like, and that modern technology is just as likely to confuse individuals as it is to separate them. "Be grateful that your homonym is a famous actor," wrote one friend. "I share a name with a little girl who still likes Hello Kitty and can't use e-mail without adult supervision."

Indeed, I enjoy knowing that someone shares a bit of my identity, that he experienced some of the same events that I've seen in my life, with a different point of view. At the same time, the other David Alan Grier has been a constant reminder that we no longer have complete control over our identities. We've lost part of that control to identity theft, to the threat of losing the names and numbers and protocols that we use to command our assets. We've also lost some of the control over how we shape and develop our identities—how we describe ourselves, interact with institutions, and accumulate our history. We once did these activities in the presence of neighbors and families and friends, but we increasingly do them in the company of institutions that have a financial interest in our good names.

The first discussions about identities begin at the birth of a new child and involve a relatively small number of people. The new parents look into their baby's tight little face and ask if it resembles that of a Nate or a Miles, an Anna or an Ella. They weigh the choices that would honor the different branches of the family and consider the consequences of drawing a name from the current offerings of popular culture.

Behind this decision lurks the hand of the baby industrial complex. Once the identity is decided and registered with the state, the marketing arm of that complex begins to promote its products to the new child—the diapers, formula, clothes, toys, medical regimes, educational programs, and other goods that mark the seven ages of childhood.

No matter how carefully that name is chosen, it forms only one part of our identity, a part that proves to be remarkably fluid. In the United States, we use a system that assigns names in order to place an individual within one generation of a family and makes no effort to ensure an identity's uniqueness. It's primarily a task given to local government. Currently, 6,000 units of government, including "every county in Texas and every township in Maine, issue birth certificates," noted a recent report on the topic. "The relationship between you and the piece of paper recording that someone with your name was born on your birth date in your hometown is very thin indeed."

The American naming system also allows certain modifications to our original identity, especially if they occur at key moments in life. When my father left his home for college, an act that marked his embrace of the wandering history of the Griers, he dropped the name on his birth certificate, "Tommy," and took a more formal name without bothering to consult any legal authority.

Our names are part of our descriptive identity, which is one aspect of all the elements that distinguish us. In addition to our names, the descriptive identity includes all labels that place us within a community. Increasingly, the most prominent part of the descriptive identity has been the e-mail address, a label that we share not only with friends and family but also with an Internet service. Once we've decided how we want to be addressed on the Internet, we negotiate with our server to see if such a name is available or to determine if it will offer us a reasonable alternative.

Like our names, our e-mail addresses can be readily changed, but in making that change, we must always involve our Internet service. My nephew recently decided to abandon the Internet identity he had used for the past six years, Spike. Zombie. He chose that label as he was passing through the dark tunnel that arches over the male years of 15 and 16. However, he discovered that his e-mail service didn't make it easy to change his name. After several attempts, he decided to just abandon it and start his adult life with a new account and e-mail service.

"There are no good statistics on e-mail addresses," notes a recent study of the industry. However, anyone who has worked in a college and witnessed the flood of freshman arriving each fall can attest to the number of addresses abandoned from sheer embarrassment—characters from the Harry Potter series, rainbows and unicorns, cartoon heroes and fairy tale princesses. All of them vanish as their owners take another step into adulthood.

BY THEMSELVES, DESCRIPTIVE IDENTITIES WOULD be of little interest, except for the fact that they're often connected with the second form of identity, called the instrumental identity. Instrumental identities are the words and numbers that allow us to interact with institutions. These identities include account numbers, driver's license numbers, student identification numbers, and stage names. Such identities have value to the institutions and individuals. My name, or I should say, my homonym's name, is protected by the Actor's Equity Association, which maintains a registry of names and prevents performers from using "a name professionally which is the same as, or resembles so closely as to tend to be confused with, the name of an existing enrolled member."

A colleague of mine has long advocated a national identity registry for the United States. "It will simplify all the problems with the Internet and banks," he claims. His proposed registry would follow the Korean naming convention. "Everyone would have a three-part name. The first word would identify the family, the second the generation, the third the individual."

I have to remind him that a large segment of Americans have considered instrumental identities to be private matters and have fought any effort to establish a national framework for such identities. When the government introduced Social Security numbers in 1935, many objected to the program on the grounds that it would establish a national identification system. "In European countries, people carry police cards and are subject to police surveillance," argued one opponent. He felt "that that kind of surveillance" was part of the Social Security Administration's plans. As proof of his assertion, he asked, "Why has it arranged for millions of cards to be carried by every American worker?"

The proponents of Social Security argued that a single registry brought tangible benefits to American citizens and in the process identified the battle line between privacy and security, convenience, and control that has been fought ever since. "An employee is expected to keep his original account number throughout his working life, regardless of changes in locality or occupation," explained the original literature of the Social Security program. In an effort to mollify critics, it said that Social Security cards would be marked "Not to be used for Identification" even though this phrase would be mocked as patently untrue. By the end of the 20th century, Social Security numbers were commonly used as bank numbers, driver's license numbers, and student identification numbers.

In 1998, the US Congress began to discuss the problems of instrumental identity, prodded not by concerns over government surveillance but by reports of theft, fraud, and the actions of private corporations. "Proposed bank mega-mergers and the emergence of financial services conglomerates will result in immense databases of customer information," reported the Department of the Treasury. Consumers "are becoming increasingly anxious about how their personal information is being handled by the different companies with which they do business and about their lack of control over its dissemination." From this discussion, Congress decided to limit the use of Social Security numbers and, in the process, encouraged private industry to start utilizing a third form of identity, authorial identity.

AUTHORIAL IDENTITY IS THE IDENTITY of our life story, the identity of our acts and accomplishments. Last winter, I had a surprising demonstration of the power of such identity when I was contacted by my credit card company. After the operator asked me to identify my name, birthday, hometown, primary school, and grandmother's birth name, she explained that she had detected some problems.

"Your credit card has been compromised," she said. "We've cancelled it as of this moment and will issue you a new one. It will arrive in two to four business days. Do you have enough cash to get you through the next couple of days?"

I thanked her for her concern and said that I was in good shape, even though I was traveling. Before I ended the call, I asked her, "How did you know it was compromised?"

She worked at her computer for a few moments and then said, "Your credit card was last used to purchase $47.53 of gasoline in Muncey, Indiana, but you've never driven a car in the state of Indiana."

Her last comment surprised me and forced me to reflect for a moment. I had certainly visited Indiana, but I couldn't recall ever driving in the state. "Hello?" she said after a moment. "Are you still there?"

"Yes, I am," I said. "The credit card company knows that I've never driven in Indiana?"

"Yes," she said without a moment's hesitation. "Apparently, we do."

I had long accepted the idea that the financial industry might know every transaction I ever made, every bad check I ever wrote, and every consumer preference I ever held. However, the notion that it would know the details of my life down to the states in which I had never used a car was both troubling and consoling. It troubled my thought because it suggested a level of surveillance far more detailed than anything conjured by the opponents of Social Security in 1935. It gave the balm of consolation because it suggested that someone was observing my most detailed actions and, after some fashion, was caring for me. This database had become a neighbor in a small town—a relative in a tight family.

IN MY FILES, I HAVE a document that once belonged to an ancestor that may be common to the other David Alan Grier and me. It's a last will and testament, dating from the 17th century and signed with an X. There was no need for a full signature, no need for a number, no need for a six-digit PIN, because the individual who marked the document lived in a community of a couple dozen families and was known by all. The other residents could recite his history, his habits, his desires, and his authorial identity. If someone questioned the document, plenty of people in the community could attest to its validity and identify the signer.

In an arc that has stretched over three and a half centuries, we've moved from small towns to global communities, from identities that were once held by common stories to complex descriptions that are held in giant databases. Though industrialization once promised the anonymity of urban life, it has returned us to the point where our identity is defined by a story, albeit a story owned by a commercial enterprise rather than a collection of neighbors. We're not an account. We aren't a number. We aren't a name, even if that name is David Alan Grier.

05
Working the Crowd

At times, especially following a major crisis in the nuclear industry or an attack on the global cyberinfrastructure, our office becomes a little media market. Reporters contact us seeking a comment that's provocative, insightful, or counterintuitive, depending upon their tastes. In exchange, they offer a brief moment of fame, a boost to the ego with a personal appearance on *Great Day Pocatello!* or a quote in an obituary for someone who might once have been famous.

My colleagues and I generally try to approach these transactions rationally, attempting to provide informative answers for educational and policy purposes. However, when the choice is difficult, especially when we're facing deadlines or working on other tasks, we throw the request onto the trading floor and ask if this question is truly worth our time and effort.

Occasionally, we find ourselves extremely busy when questions about science and technology are kept in the public by current events. One spring began with a crisis at a Japanese nuclear reactor, moved to a problem at a cloud computing site and ended with a public auction of the NASA space shuttles. The NASA auction generated an unusual demand for comments by scholars of science policy even though it was merely an effort by the space agency to put its accomplishments on display at the expense of others. It is a process that they have used before and, unless the program has reached its concluding note, they will use in the future.

At the bargain price of $28 million plus change, the old shuttle orbiters generated far more demand than the supply on hand. In all, 29 organizations responded to NASA's request for information in the hopes of securing one of the relics. When the announcement was made that the shuttles would be placed in Washington DC, New York, Florida, and California, 25 of these groups were disappointed, and more than a few of them were willing to express their feelings in an effort to change the decision. For example, organizations in Texas and Ohio provoked their congressional delegations to denounce the "blatant politics" behind the decisions and claim that "NASA ignored the intent of Congress and the interests of taxpayers."

The public evidence suggests that NASA, a giant engineering organization with a well-formed understanding of national politics, approached this decision in a rational, engineered manner. Not only is NASA inclined to trust numerical approaches, its representatives understand that quantification can be used to deflect criticism. "The appeal of numbers," wrote the philosopher Ted Porter, "is especially compelling to bureaucratic officials who lack the mandate of a popular election or divine right." He argued that a decision made by numbers "has at least the appearance of being fair and impersonal."

NASA actually has a 15-page policy document defining space artifacts and describing how they may be loaned to various types of organizations for "public affairs, industrial outreach, and education programs." Hence, it requested a fair amount of information from the organizations that were interested in acquiring a shuttle orbiter.

Much of this information was already in numeric form that directly related to the requesting organization's wealth and popularity. These statistics included attendance figures for the past five years, the budget for the same period, endowments, the local region's population, and the number of hits on the organization's public webpages. Other information could easily be quantified using social science techniques, such as the additional assets that the organization could use or its experience with "artifacts of national significance." Even the most subjective question, which asked how the organization would use the shuttle "to inspire the American public and students in particular," also required the description of a concrete procedure that could be used to "assess, evaluate, and measure these objectives."

With proposals providing quantifiable information, the NASA board could have easily slipped into a familiar procedure. This would have involved creating a matrix with 29 rows—one for each museum—and some appropriate number of columns. The board would have converted much of the information into a five-, seven-, or nine-point scale with the low value representing a poor contribution, the middle value being neutral, and the high value expressing a substantial asset. A quick summation of figures would have identified the proposals with the highest numeric score. Then the board could have determined if this result could be presented to the public as a final judgment.

Such an approach, though rationally disciplined, is less connected to the scientific method than it might appear. It's actually part of a market process, in which the parties lay all of their assets on the table and ask if they have sufficient wealth to complete a trade.

Markets include not only quantification but valuation, the act of ranking the importance of goods, services, and ideas. Valuation is often far from scientific. It "is vague and arbitrary," wrote the economist Jean-Baptiste Say (1757–1832), "when there is no assurance that it will be generally acquiesced in by others." It can also be quite dynamic, as the desires and aspirations of those in the market change.

The world of computation has had an awkward relationship with markets. For computable answers, we rely on logic, mathematics, and probability. In his 1854 master work, *An Investigation of the Laws of Thought*, George Boole (1815–1864) argued that the "mathematical sciences occupy a fundamental place in human knowledge, and that no system of mental culture can be complete or fundamental, which altogether neglects them." We use these tools to participate in, model, and predict the opportunities in markets, but we rarely allow markets to give us an answer to our computational questions beyond the current value of the products we create.

In the past four or five years, markets have begun to creep into computational processes as a way of answering difficult questions, questions that deal with the efficient use of resources. One of the more intriguing forms of computation that employs markets has come to be known as crowdsourcing.

Crowdsourcing is generally understood to be a way of using the Internet to employ large numbers of dispersed workers. As an example of a crowdsourcing application, an employer can post a task on a website and invite workers to undertake all or part of it. Sometimes the task requires substantial skill and training, such as a programming assignment or resolving a legal problem. In other cases, it requires only basic human perception, such as the ability to identify faces in a photograph and judge the emotion such faces are expressing.

In general, crowdsourcing is an industry that's attempting to use human beings and machines in large production systems. These systems prove to be useful and efficient when each element does the work it can do best: machines carry out repetitive tasks while people make judgments, handle pattern recognition, and synthesize ideas. Perhaps the most familiar version of crowdsourcing is Wikipedia, which relies on tens of thousands of volunteers to construct an online encyclopedia. Another common example is Amazon's Mechanical Turk, which offers human intelligence tasks or HITs.

At this point, the list of firms interested in this field is long and growing rapidly. It includes companies that handle customer relations, create metadata for photographs and other nontextual items, and gather data on product placement and consumption.

All crowdsourcing applications have four basic elements: a division of labor, computing and communications technology, a crowd of human workers, and a labor market. Sometimes, the market is used merely to recruit workers to the project. In Wikipedia, for example, the market is implicit in the basic wiki interface. Workers bring to that market the material they've written on specific subjects. The transaction is completed when the work is accepted for publication. The worker is compensated by the privilege of having the work posted online, at least temporarily.

In other cases, the labor market is used to extract ideas from the workers as a whole. Recently, I was talking with Rob, the owner of a firm that offers crowdsourced translation services. At base, his organization allows companies to put documents that they wish to have translated on the Web and pays workers to translate them. His system has a few additional tools that enhance the quality of the work. It provides an initial mechanical translation, offers style rules, and saves translated text for possible reuse. It also allows the employer to gather useful information from the labor market. "The value depends on who's using the final translations," Rob said. "You get the greatest value when you're translating documents to be used in the field."

Rob has two types of clients: one type gathers information, the other disperses it. In the first case, the organization draws its translators from those who gather the information.

The second kind of client is a class of firms that sell large, complicated products that come with lots of documentation. Traditionally, the firm would create all of its documents in English and then pay for the translation of a few key documents, such as an overview of the system or an index of key documents. Paying to have all of the documents translated into all possible languages would likely create a lot of text that would remain unused.

In Rob's system, the translators are drawn from the people who actually work with the product. Generally, they're bilingual customers who are supplementing their income. They're presented with all the base language documents and are allowed to choose the documents they want to translate. According to the theory of markets, the crowd will choose to translate the documents that are of most value to them and, by extension, to those who are supporting, maintaining, and extending the product.

Of course, this market theory of translations has drawbacks that counter the potential advantages. All markets tend to have a notoriously narrow vision. Participants value those things that will help them today rather than something that might be useful next year, such as that rare document containing information that will only be needed in the case of a massive failure. While the defenders of market-based decisions will support these choices by arguing that the market makes the most efficient choices, not one of them desires to face an acute crisis with a procedure manual that needs to be translated from another tongue so that it can be used properly.

So, like all markets, we modify the rules of crowd labor markets to protect ourselves against risk. Some of these modifications can be handled through the pricing mechanism of the market itself. If the organization needs to have certain documents translated first, it can offer premium prices for that work.

However, the standard market mechanisms won't solve all the weaknesses of the labor markets in crowdsourcing. Critics have noted that the dispersed labor pool in crowdsourcing leaves plenty of opportunities for workers to make mistakes, cheat, plagiarize, and even get paid for vacuous submissions. Most companies engaged in crowdsourcing use a complex set of rules for their labor markets to minimize potential problems. "Each piece of data is independently checked by multiple crowd workers," explains the leader of one company. His organization also rates each worker by seeding the market with tasks for which it already knows the result. "Ineffective workers are filtered out," he adds.

Of course, free markets are never truly free. In many spheres of modern life, we've structured markets to minimize both risks and transaction costs: supermarkets, online auctions, even the little media mart that forms in our office whenever science and technology are in the news. The reporters who come to us know that we're unlikely to feed them a quote that supplies wrong or embarrassing information. They've restricted their crowd of workers to a mere handful of policy wonks, a handful that they believe will provide them with a good product.

Exit
The Evolving Present

"When we bought the house, there was a wall here," said Jenn, as she pointed to a gentle wave in the plaster, "and these floorboards were covered with blue linoleum."

The broad planks, recently covered in a glossy varnish that left the nicks and scars for all to see, suggested the story of the neighborhood where Jenn and Don lived.

When Don's ancestors arrived in the area some eight generations ago, the town had been a small community, a day's ride from a large port city. For a time it had been an important intellectual center, where a local minister began his rise to national prominence by railing against the evils of slavery. The Industrial Age had brought wealth to the town, but the railroad had carted that wealth to distant suburbs, and the automobile had evacuated those last citizens who had any means to depart.

For three decades, the area had been a depressed wasteland until the generation of Jenn and Donn saw the desirable aspects of the area: walkable shopping district, quaint homes, and a central location. The new residents encouraged those subtle changes that mark a revitalized area: artistic restaurants, purveyors of designer coffee, and a high-speed data service.

Like so many characters in this column, Jenn and Don are former students who have graciously donated their evolving life stories to science. In making this contribution, both have been assured that their contributions will increase the stock of knowledge, make the country safer, and the world "perfect in all respects," as Charles Darwin (1809–1882) liked to say.

Although Jenn laughed when I suggested that her life might be a model for others, she was pleased nonetheless. It was a strong, knowing laugh. She has persevered long enough in the information technology business to know that no one can predict how a career, a product, or an organization will evolve. Some 15 years ago, Jenn entered the unforgiving ecology of technology entrepreneurship with humble needs and great expectations. Like most, she began as a programmer and spent a few years learning her trade. Her first big opportunity came with a company that managed a big piece of the American government's infrastructure. She became a system designer and soon had people working for her. "It was a great job," she said, "and a forward-thinking organization. We produced some great work because we had quality assurance people engaged in every part of the project. The skills I learned there have been important to my career."

For a time, Jenn thought she had the perfect job, but in a moment the world shuddered on its axis and she felt a cold wind blow from the north. The company failed to renew a major contract and had to shed employees. Jenn and Don packed up their belongings and went in search of a new niche.

Jenn's next company was a temporary stop, a well-protected garden. "The firm was maintaining a legacy product," she recalled, "and was something of a closed shop. Those who had attended the right school were part of the inner circle, the rest were not." It gave her a place to regroup but no opportunity to advance. Two senior officers not only possessed the accepted academic credentials, they were also married to each other.

When presented with the opportunity to join a new startup, Jenn jumped at the chance. "Seventh employee," she bragged. "Two years after that, we had a hundred."

The founders had a clever idea for a system that would help companies manage their assets. The company had a product ready for release when the technology bubble burst in 2001. The employees worked hard, struggling to build a customer base as the economy pushed competitors into their small business environment.

The firm took aggressive steps to defend its place, releasing employees and sending production to southern India. Jenn took equally firm actions to protect her place. Step by step, she moved to jobs in marketing, sales, and training. "They needed it, and I was good at it," she recalled.

The end came when another company made a bid to buy the firm.

"All they wanted was the customer list," Jenn said ruefully. She was wondering where she might move next when one of those customers called her and asked if she wanted to be a production engineer for them. "With that offer," she added, "my computer career ended." She was ready to put that part of her life aside and begin something new. Evolutionary change "and natural selection arising from the competition of tribe with tribe," wrote Charles Darwin in *The Descent of Man*, has "sufficed to raise man to his present high position in the organic scale."

THE BUSINESS COMMUNITY, ESPECIALLY THE part involved with high technology, has long embraced the notion that progress is an evolutionary process that comes with markets, competition, and the survival of the fittest. "It is to competition," wrote industrialist Andrew Carnegie (1835–1919), "that we owe our wonderful material development, which brings improved conditions in its train."

In the world of the computer, we have applied the idea of evolutionary change to almost every aspect of the field. We have created family trees of computer languages and genealogies of processors that begin in original paradise with the ENIAC and spin through multiple generations until they arrive at the modern age.

In computer products, we have all but institutionalized evolution. In particular, software products begin with the germ of an idea, advance to a beta release, and are released as version 1.0. In their ascending lifespan, they are upgraded to 1.1, rearchitected as 2.0, advanced to level 5.0 so that they do not appear to lag behind a competitor, and retired with a final identifier such as version 7.46 that marks the final stage of their development.

Good ideas evolve. Bad ones drop along the way. Some, not strong enough to survive in the general market of ideas, might be fortunate enough to find niche ecologies where they serve a limited purpose. Some software engineers have taken the metaphor of evolution so seriously that they view programs as evolving organisms. "Large-scale, widely used programs such as operating systems are never complete," wrote one pair of scholars. "They undergo a continuing evolutionary cycle of maintenance, augmentation, and restructuring to keep pace with evolving usage and implementation technologies."

The software evolution metaphor offers a certain amount of insight into the nature of program development. It has provided computer scientists with a basic set of principles that suggest how large systems grow and change. These principles claim that all programs are in a state of constant change, a change influenced by the forces of market feedback mechanisms. The feedback generally pushes programs to increase in size and complexity, even though each new generation tends to preserve the familiar traits of prior versions.

Following in the footsteps of the pioneers of evolutionary biology, modern researchers have wrestled with the notion that software evolution might not be progressive, that it might not produce continually improving generations of products. "The quality of [evolving] systems will appear to be declining," noted one early team of researchers, "unless they are rigorously maintained and adapted to operational environment changes."

Charles Darwin would have understood the source of such sentiments. "He found himself in an unresolvable bind," observed one natural historian. "He recognized that his basic theory of evolutionary mechanism—natural selection—makes no statement about progress." Natural competition might not always select traits that are best for an organism's long-term survival. In such cases, a promising species could be pushed to extinction. To one of his close colleagues Darwin confessed, "After long reflection, I cannot avoid the conviction that no innate tendency to progressive development exists."

IN SPITE OF THE PARALLELS between the concepts of software evolution and Darwin's theories of biological change, these two theories describe quite different processes. Programs, after all, are not living beings that reproduce themselves and change as they try to survive from generation to generation. They are artifacts, the products of human organizations. They accumulate the products of concentrated labor, growing and changing in the process. As artifacts, software tells us the story of the organizations that produced it, the way that a collection of pottery shards tells us how a lost community grew and evolved.

Most software products follow a common arc that starts with a single point of origin, a Rift Valley, where the record begins. For example, if we trace the evolutionary path of a simple product such as the Web browser, we would begin in Geneva, Switzerland with a program called World Wide Web, which was developed by Tim Berners-Lee in 1990. This program has antecedents in the operating system that controlled Berners-Lee's computer. That transition, which moved a block of code from one application to another, can also be treated as a moment of evolution, the kind of radical jump postulated by biologist Stephen Jay Gould. However, the browser of Mr. Berners-Lee provides a more convenient starting point.

For a brief period, the World Wide Web program was the only browser, and it existed only in a single environment. However, within six months, it was ported to other machines and began to engage the attention of new programmers. These programmers worked to add new features, correct shortcomings, or, at times, create new browsers from scratch. By the mid-1990s, the software market was filled with a dozen different Web browsers, including Arena, Cello, Mosaic, Samba, Midas, Viola, and Erwise. Some were supported by a single individual. Some were backed by a strong company with substantial capital. Most fell between these two extremes.

As the market grew, the browsers evolved. Those backed by stronger organizations expanded their position in the market by adding features and adopting the best ideas. Those supported by weak organizations fell by the wayside. A few examples, such as the text-based Lynx browser, found niche environments that allowed them to flourish for a season. For Lynx, the niche was a little ecosystem of slow computers and low-bandwidth network connections.

With the expanding market came competition, and with competition came mortality. Those designs that were inferior to their peers or supported by weaker organizations died before their time. Radical designs fail. Successful products split into new versions. Such is the common pattern of evolution. Among the current population of surviving browsers, we can trace two or perhaps three distinct lines of development back to Berners-Lee's original program.

The evolutionary model does not allow for the spontaneous creation of life. New products come from old. The leaders of new organizations gain their expertise from service in existing companies. Of course, the world is filled with individuals who try to disprove this observation, and a few succeed.

Though the browser ecosystem seems stable, it resides on a sensitive fault line that delineates human judgment from logical computation, global connections and personal sphere. Yet this ecosystem has witnessed surprising additions to the species that may be found there. Each new addition has contributed new ways of coordinating labor, of balancing the local and the global, of engaging people and machines. It will likely see new developments until it is no longer a valuable means of coordinating production, until it becomes a fossilized remains of an old industrial age.

The neighborhood of Jenn and Don is one of those ancient fossils of industrial production. The area is centered on an old river mill that once spun cotton lint into thread, wove thread into cloth, and exchanged cloth for the golden coin of young fashion designers. The fashion remains, as the building now serves as a home to a half dozen little innovative companies, but the gold is long gone, claimed first by companies that were located 800 miles to the south and now by firms that stand 12 time zones to the west. The mill is still connected with fashion, as it is a retail outlet for designer clothing, but it no longer generates the wealth it once did, and it no longer coordinates the economic and social activity of the area.

The neighborhood no longer organizes its day around the mill shifts. Most of the local workers are employed in the urban center nine miles to the east, or in new suburbs that lie to the west or, like Don, on computer servers that reside in California, or Scotland, or on some unclaimed island in the Pacific Ocean. Those who work in the old mill do not live in the neighborhood, as the wages of a waiter or a clerk or a security guard will not cover the costs of local housing.

The tools of computation may be more flexible than the physical structure of a 19th-century water mill, but we know that they, too, get frozen in place. We use certain protocols, file formats, command sets merely because they were established by some computer system three or four or five decades old. These are the fossils from the evolution of the information age. They may not be as quaint or as sympathetic as the old industrial towns of New England, but, like those towns, they occupy the landscape of our time. Perhaps they just represent points where development pauses. Perhaps they are the mark where evolution stops.

Epilogue:
Uncharted Territory

It's like you punched me in the face
and then asked me to do a math problem

Lungs (2011)
Duncan McMillan

I was sitting near the back of the room at the Pratt Institute with hunched shoulders and bowed head, a position that in an earlier age would have communicated that I was lost in my own thoughts. In our time, it meant that I was answering e-mail on my cell phone.

In processing my messages, I meant no disrespect to Todd, who was the main speaker for the gathering of librarians. However, I felt that I knew much of what he was going to say, as I've been following his work for more than a year. Todd has been developing a system that can manage complicated workflows for large numbers of workers. He has only recently started working on this problem, having spent the prior 10 years with various IT companies.

Although he gets into more technical detail than others might include in such a forum, Todd gives a good talk. His reassuring voice tells the audience that they shouldn't underestimate themselves, suggesting that they'll get the point if they simply listen carefully. Because I didn't expect to hear much new information until the end of his presentation, I felt that I could do a little work while he described how we now conceive and organize tasks.

Sitting down the row from me was a young woman who was doing a far better job of handling multiple tasks than I. By all appearances, she was using her cell phone to communicate via text messages and perhaps even tweeting a summary of the talk to a distant audience.

As Todd got into the central part of his presentation, my neighbor started to slow her work. Then she put her phone on the chair next to her and began fidgeting. At first, I thought she might have had an unfortunate exchange with one of her electronic correspondents. But she became more agitated as Todd drew to the end of his slides, suggesting that perhaps his comments had distressed her.

The woman's hand was the first one in the air when questions were requested. When she had the opportunity to take the floor, she fired a string of questions suggesting that Todd's presentation had somehow challenged her view of the world. She said that she didn't understand how it's possible to find a consistent workforce, day after day. How can employees learn the system if they regularly switch jobs? How is it possible to guarantee that the work will be done correctly?

Todd responded to her questions with both grace and charm. However, her challenge clearly found sympathy in the audience. Todd's ideas were new to them. As trained librarians, they didn't quite know how to fit these ideas into their view of the world. They knew that that world was changing, and they wanted to be part of the innovation that came with these changes. Ultimately, innovation always involves fundamental challenges to the way we think.

Emotional reactions to innovations are nothing unusual. "As the births of living creatures at first are ill-shapen," wrote Francis Bacon in 1597, "so are all innovations." They might bring great utility to the world, but they're troubling, he noted, "by their inconformity." Because they don't fit into the current world view, innovations stir public emotions when they appear.

I first experienced the emotional disruptions that innovation causes when I was in my teens and just learning to program. Someone who had seen my code and perhaps wanted to help me break a few bad habits had given me a copy of Edsger Dijkstra's classic letter, "Go To Statement Considered Harmful."

Although the target of my anger might not have been clear to me, by the time I reached the end of Dijkstra's letter, I was quite upset. I might have been revolting against Dijkstra's ideas, or I might have been upset to find that anyone felt I would benefit from reading the letter. Either way, I wasn't pleased and was ready to side with Dijkstra's critics. "I was taken aback by Dijkstra's attack on the go to statement," wrote John Rice of Purdue University, "which is an obviously useful and desirable statement. I reject the implication that the 'quality' of a program is directly correlated with a minimal use of the go to and similar statements." Rice argued that Dijkstra had offended the programming community and that, from his point of view, it was "not clear to me that there is a real motivation for the attack."

As with many teenage programmers, I was ill-disciplined and liked to freely transfer control around a block of code with no attempt at structure or order. I felt that my approach was more flexible and that I was smart enough to handle such complexities. My self-confidence quickly collapsed and my anger dissipated when I learned that Dijkstra's letter was a decade old, that his ideas had triumphed, and that I was on the losing side of history.

In my voyage through the world of computing technology, I've been fascinated by the tension between the logical and the emotional, the computational and the human.

Even those who are deeply engaged with the logic of machine development, programming, and system design find that the emotions that accompany innovations in this field can sorely test their rational principles. Sometimes, these emotions can energize our endeavors and encourage us to pursue more advanced ideas. Sometimes they make us timid, as they suggest that we're walking on uncertain ground. Sometimes they evoke anger when they challenge our secure view of the world.

Perhaps no challenge to the emotions is greater than the one that philosopher Bertrand Russell faced when he was working on one of the founding documents of our field, the *Principia Mathematica*, in which he strove to base mathematics on a firm foundation of logic.

Midway through the work, Russell encountered the contradiction that now bears his name. This contradiction can be expressed in the claim that you should never join a club that would be willing to take you as a member, but it's better summarized by a piece of paper that asserts two different claims. The first is a sentence that states, "The sentence below this one is false." Immediately below it is the assertion, "The sentence above this is true."

"There was something wrong," Russell noted, "as such contradictions are unavoidable on ordinary premises." He originally assumed that the problem would be relatively easy to fix but soon concluded "that it would be a big job."

Russell continued working and completed an outline of his book without addressing the contradiction. After finishing the outline, still frustrated by the contradiction, Russell faced an emotional crisis that he could only describe in the blandest terms. "I went out bicycling one afternoon," he explained, "and realized that I no longer loved my wife."

Russell's behavior is hardly a typical example, even in the field of logic. He confessed that he had become so consumed with his work on the contradiction that he "had no idea until this moment that my love for her was even lessening." The consequences from this realization initiated one of the more contentious periods in a life that was heavily marked by contention.

In the computing fields, we're often quick to claim that we achieve our results by logic and that they aren't touched by any other emotion beyond a love for the truth. Workers in the field occasionally have paid a high emotional price for their accomplishments, but they've also received strong rewards.

Granted, we can find plenty of contributors who expanded our stock of knowledge by careful, rational work, but we also can find those who found a key idea in a momentary spark of inspiration as well as others who were hounded by doubts they couldn't shake. These innovators include Tim Berners-Lee, who drew guidance for the World Wide Web from a thumb-indexed encyclopedia that he had cherished in his youth; Edmund Berkeley, the author of the seminal book Giant Brains, who believed despite all evidence to the contrary that the computer would reorganize society along rational lines; and John Backus, whose 50-year career is remembered for a single contribution that he created in his first years of employment.

Of all the moments of doubt and frustration that have marked the story of computing, none has produced more emotion than the one concept that is central to our field: the invention of the stored memory program. We know the groups who claim to have invented the program. We know the emotions that the rival claimants express toward each other. Nevertheless, we lack the documentation to make a rational conclusion that would identify a single inventor of the program.

For nearly 40 years, we've had standards for how we should train and educate the individuals who desire to become part of our field. We have opinions about how we should develop mathematical skill, programming skill, and even design skill. However, we do nothing to describe the kinds of emotions that computer professionals should express or the kind of character they should exemplify.

The only real discussion of character is found in biographies, but we have very few biographies of computing people. Although we have seen a recent biography of Steve Jobs, we have no complete story of John von Neumann, only a sketch of Seymour Cray, and just a few paragraphs on Edsger Dijkstra, one of the great software pioneers.

The Library of Congress lists only 16 biographies of computing engineers. The list gets longer when we add biographies of business leaders, electrical engineers, and other contributors to the field. However, most of these volumes tell about accomplishments. Few probe how these leaders thought, how they made decisions, or what shaped their character.

Of all the factors that have influenced the computing era, the emotional response to rapid change may ultimately prove to be more important than the rational forces of logic. The computing fields have driven forward at a relentless pace that has mocked the standard speed of innovation, which was historically set by the length of the human life. The historian I. Bernard Cohen noted that the rapid change of any technical field is in conflict with the span of the human career. "Every scientist has a vast interest in the preservation of the status quo to the extent that he does not want the skills and expert knowledge which he has acquired at great cost in time and learning energy to become obsolete," Cohen observed.

Yet we force mature computer scientists to cope with multiple changes in concepts and theories in the course of an ordinary career. Some of these changes are cyclical. I've been pleased to see that some of the ideas that inspired my choice of career return to current practice as if they were freshly discovered. Some are evolutionary. Some are innovative and truly demand that we think in new ways.

I recently had a discussion with a friend who had made a major shift in a career that was already quite successful. "How did you decide to change fields?" I asked.

"My students convinced me it was a good idea," he replied. "They kept arriving at my door with interesting problems, and eventually I decided to make the change."

Although change might be the hallmark of our character, that change also can stir up an emotional storm we don't always see. Over the years, I've been praised for accomplishments that weren't completely mine, critiqued for ideas that were common to the field, and—once—punched in the chest for proposing an idea that offended a senior researcher.

In the end, we've created a rich field that has touched almost every aspect of human endeavor. Historically, the standard internalist view of science and technology emphasizes how ideas develop and marginalizes the human element. The invention is more important than the inventor. Yet it's the inventor who brings the new idea to the world, makes it understandable, and explains how it might be used.

TODD TOOK QUESTIONS WELL AFTER the hour appointed to end his presentation. The audience grasped that there was something in his approach that would ultimately change their lives in profound ways, and they wanted to know as much about that change as Todd could describe.

I waited in that now-familiar e-mail posture as Todd finished answering the questions. Afterwards, he agreed to walk with me to my next appointment so that we could discuss his plans for the next couple of weeks as we moved through the neighborhood. He was pleased with his presentation, excited about his plans, and a little anxious about the tasks he needed to complete.

That sense of accomplishment and anticipation generated by our conversation was shattered moments after Todd left me at the supposed site of my next meeting. I have never completely understood the algorithm for assigning street numbers in New York City; hence I was three-quarters of a mile from my destination.

So, with limited time, I pulled a bit of technology out of my pocket and again peered into the small screen. Using the problem-solving skills I have honed over a career, I located the proper address, estimated my arrival time, sent an e-mail asking for accommodation, and marched into the darkness of the evening to begin a new adventure in the land we believe to be the known world.

Acknowledgements

T his book owes much to three good friends. The first is Scott Hamilton, the late managing editor of *Computer* magazine, who saw the promise in my writing and gave me the opportunity to write a column for six years. The second, his colleague Judi Prow, was my able editor for that period. She tolerated my obscure references, poetic turns of phrase, and bland irony that occasionally misfired. Without her firm hand, this project would not have been as rich. My humble thanks to both.

The third is Doug Caldwell, Doug the Rocket Scientist, who came into my life when he decided to marry one of my best friends. His lively conversation on technology and engineering and science were a cherished part of my visits to California. With each trip, we started our discussions and immediately veered into new territory. They shaped every essay in this book. For his friendship, I am deeply grateful.

I also need to thank the Editors in Chief of *Computer*, Carl Chang and Ron Vetter, for their support as well as numerous staff and editorial members including

Jenny Stout, Monette Velasco, Brandi Ortega, Brian Brannon, Evan Butterfield, Neville Holmes, and a list that would encompass much of the wonderful editorial group at the Computer Society.

Then, of course, are those who volunteered their stories to this project. They include Kari Kae Almstead, Anna and Ella Cain, Tamara Carleton, Sean Cheung, Christian Conn, Emily Danyluk, Philip Ducharme, Pascale Dumit, Melanie Emmen, Kelly Filiak, Danny Gottovi, Melissa Hooper, Nate and Miles Jones, Kathryn Nash, Pere Garlinghouse, Peter Grier, Amy Grier, David Alan Grier, Harry and Georgie, Joseph Konrad, Freddie Mac, Hank Paulson, August Rausche, Michael Spector, Paul Sternal, Major X.

Many read all or part of this manuscript, including Liz Harder, Michael Young, Erin Dumbacher. Thank you all for your comments.

I need to thank Caitlan Dowling and Gaurav Dhiman for their help in preparing the manuscript. Jamila Reddy for her help with the illustrations as well as her team of Caitlan Dowling, Claudia Paige Dana, Sara Eshleman, Evan Faber, Caitlin House, Rohan Kocharekar, Eleanor Leader, Eddie Ledford, and Danielle Mohlman. My thanks need to extend to the Studio Theatre and Adrien-Alice Hansel.

Kate Guillemette gets special thanks as the editor of this volume.

And finally, I needed to thank an ever growing list of friends, students, colleagues, Computer Society members and readers, who offered me their stories and didn't complain when I wrote them my own way.

Notes

Preface: Of Our Time

Page xii   "Living as we do in the closing year"
 Edward Bellamy, *Looking Backward*, Boston: Ticknor, 1888, p. iii.
Page xiii   "individuals most effectually promote the general progress"
 Charles Lyell, *Principles of Geology*, London: John Murray, 1830, p. 3.

Chapter I: The Land Around Us

The Forces of Localization
Page 3   Society for the Promotion of Goodness
 They know who they are.
Page 3   community networks
 Matt Barranca, "Unlicensed Wireless Broadband Profiles," Spectrum Policy Program, New America Foundation, April 2004; Antonios Alexiou,

Christos Bouras, and Dimitrios Primpas, "Design aspects of open munici-pal broadband networks," *Proceedings of the 1st International Conference on Access*, 2006, ACM International Conference Proceeding Series, vol. 267, no. 20.

Page 4 Wireless Leiden

R.D.J. Kramer, A. Lopez, and A.M.J. Koonen, "Municipal broadband access networks in the Netherlands," *Proceedings of the 1st International Confer-ence on Access Networks* (AccessNets 06), ACM, Sep. 2006.

Page 4 "We're just taking money from hardworking families and giving it to people who can afford [smart phones] and laptops"

Anthony Sciarra, "Municipal Broadband: The Rush to Legislate," *Albany Law Journal of Science and Technology*, 233, vol. 17, 2007.

Page 4 "This is a major step toward achieving our vision of The Entire City Connected"

Greg Goldman quoted in Joni Morse, "Philly to Earthlink: Wi-Fi Network Works," *Wireless Week*, May 24, 2007.

Welcome to the Family

Page 8 "This strategy has been used successfully in many industries, in-cluding computer hardware."

Mark A. Ardis and David A. Cuka, "Defining families—commonality analy-sis," *Proceedings of the 21st International Conference on Software Engineering* (ICSE 99), May 1999.

Page 8 "Development of a product family adds complexity to the require-ments capture and analysis process"

Juha Kuusela and Juha Savolainen, "Requirements engineering for product families," *Proceedings of the 22nd International Conference on Software Engi-neering* (ICSE 00), ACM, June 2000.

Page 9 "took his design"

Herman Goldstine, *The Computer from Pascal to von Neumann*, Princeton University Press, 1972, p. 256.

Page 9 "This error [that it is part of the IAS family] has been repeated so frequently in the literature"

N. Metroplois and J. Worlton, "A Triplogy of Errors in the History of Com-puting," *IEEE Annals of the History of Computing*, vol. 2, no. 1, Jan. 1980.

Page 9 "compatibility constraint on the design of each of the seven ma-chines we envisioned in the family"

Brooks quoted ibid.

Page 10 "The following ground rules should be imposed on the groups working on the logical structure of the proposed processors"
Final Report of the SPREAD Task Group, Dec. 28, 1961.

Page 10 "The impact of any new family on current IBM systems…"
Ibid.

Page 11 "if we avoid some of the effects of fragmentation…"
Reza Kamali, Lillian Cassel, and Richard LeBlanc, *Proceedings of the 5th Conference on Information Technology Education* (CITC5 04), ACM, Oct. 2004.

Edward Elgar's Facebook

Page 13 "due and credible publicity"
Thorstein Veblen, *The Higher Learning in America,* New York: Sagamore Press, 1918, p. 98.

Page 14 "overwhelmed any other tune that might be used to accompany an American graduation."
Luther Noss, "Music Comes to Yale," *American Music,* vol. 3, no. 3, Autumn 1985, pp. 337–346.

Page 15 "invisible colleges."
Derek de Solla Price, *Little Science, Big Science,* New York: Columbia University Press, 1963, p. 119.

Page 15 "Not only do such groups form the natural units…"
Ibid.

Page 15 "This is not just good-neighborliness"
Ibid.

Page 15 "custom-built information system to replace their own capriciously functioning system."
Ibid.

Page 15 "not one which was tightly knit or closed to external influences"
Diana Crane, "Social Structure in a Group of Scientists: A Test of the 'Invisible College' Hypothesis," *American Sociological Review,* vol. 34, no. 3, June 1969, pp. 335–352.

Page 15 "Social links have been greatly facilitated by the drastic advances in communications"
Fred Katz, "Social Participation and Social Structure," *Social Forces,* vol. 45, no. 2, Dec. 1966, pp. 199–210.

Page 16 "proves useful will depend not only on how viable the hypotheses turn out to be"
Ibid.

Spirit of Combination
Page 20   "The word 'encyclopedia' signifies 'chain of knowledge'"
Denis Diderot, "Encyclopedia," in *L'Encyclopedie*, 1751. See http://hdl.handle.net/2027/spo.did2222.0000.004.
Page 20   "we should not die without having rendered a service to the human race"
Ibid.
Page 20   "Opinions grow old and disappear like words"
Ibid.
Page 22   "a column of wide-ranging topics and hopelessly obscure references."
The column is the DC Decoder in the *Christian Science Monitor*.
Page 22   "its meaning is unclear to the computer, because it is not represented in a machine processable"
Max Volkel et al., *Proceedings of the International World Wide Web Convergence Committee*, ACM Electronic Library, 2006.
Page 23   "popular song"
"Ants Go Marching," Dave Matthews Band.

Mental Discipline
Page 26   the "idea of mental discipline contained inherent weaknesses as a conception"
Laurence Veysey, *The Emergence of the American University*, Chicago: University of Chicago Press, p. 55.
Page 27   "Black boxes litter the societies of high modernity"
Donald MacKenzie, "Opening the Black Boxes of Global Finance," *Review of International Political Economy*, vol. 12, 2005, pp. 555–576.
Page 27   "engineering problems were typically solved in an empirical fashion"
Emil Cauer, Wolfgang Mathis, and Rainer Pauli, "Life and Work of Wilhelm Cauer (1900–1945)," *Proc. MTNS2000*, Perpignan, France, June 19–23, 2000.
Page 27   "All known wave filters"
W. Cauer, "New Theory And Design Of Wave Filters," *Physics*, vol. 2, no. 4, Apr. 1932, pp. 242–268.
Page 28   "dividing the work"
Charles Babbage, *On the Economy of Machinery and Manufacture*, London: Charles Knight, 1832.
Page 28   "isolates those functions that are more or less self-contained"
W. Morven Gentleman, "Off the Shelf Black Boxes for Programming," *IEEE Transactions on Education*, vol. 12, no. 1, Mar. 1969, pp. 43–50.

Page 28   "grandmother had"
See Preface, *When Computers Were Human*, Princeton University Press, 2005.

Migration to the Middle
Page 33   "The major reason for the change"
Daniel Bell, "The World and the United States in 2013," *Daedalus*, vol. 116, no. 3, Futures (Summer 1987), pp. 1–31.
Page 34   "Computer science as an academic discipline"
Nathan Ensmenger, *The Computer Boys Take Over*," MIT Press, 2010, p. 229.

Newspaper Joe
Page 37   "received a handout"
John Fawcett and Elizabeth Rambeau, "A Hobo Memoir, 1936," *Indiana Magazine of History*, vol. 90, no. 4, Dec. 1994, pp. 346–364.

Chapter II: Of What We Speak

Managing the Audience
Page 42   "Stagehands are still needed, but the computer adds a layer of control…"
Jesse McKinley, "Act II: Enter the Computers," *New York Times*, Oct. 17, 2002, p. G1.
Page 43   "Every day the writers rewrote their scenes"
Simon Louvish, *Monkey Business*, New York: MacMillan, 2000, p. 306.
Page 43   "A stage director would take a stop watch"
Ibid. p. 214.
Page 44   "Hush, I think I just heard a line from the script."
Ibid. p. 176.

The Age of Accountability
Page 47   "I myself am a trained test driver…"
Testimony of Akio Toyoda to Congress, Feb. 23, 2010.
Page 49   "General Motors has become an essay in federalism…"
Peter Drucker, *Concept of the Corporation*, London: Heinneman, 1947, p. 47.
Page 49   "enables all units of the company to produce more efficiently…"
Ibid. p. 228.
Page 49   "Where it should have moved long before of its own volition…"
David Halberstam, *The Reckoning*, New York: Morrow, 1986, p. 436.
Page 50   "comply with US air pollution and fuel efficiency standards…"
See David Alan Grier, "Controlling the Conversation," *Computer*, vol. 40, no. 9, September 2007, pp. 8–10.

Page 50   "While software modularity is commonplace in software engineering"
Razan Racu et al., "Automotive Software Integration," *Proceedings of the Design Automation Conference 2007*, 2007, pp. 545–550.
Page 51   "Mature reaction on component changes"
Harald Heinecke, "Automotive System Design—Challenges and Potential," *Proceedings of the Design, Automation and Test in Europe Conference and Exhibition* (DATE 05), 2005.

The Problem of Design
Page 54   "According to the story, Kahn constructed…"
Don Clark, "Motorola, Kahn Team Up Again, On Digital Photos," *Wall Street Journal (Eastern Edition)*, Feb. 7, 2000, p. 1.
Page 54   "inner nature of the machine…"
Herbert Simon, *The Science of the Artificial*, MIT Press, 2996, p. 7.
Page 55   "world's most expensive loveseat"
Richard Russell, "The Cray-1 Computer System," *CACM*, vol. 21, no. 1, 1978, pp. 63–72.
Page 55   "the Connection Machine could easily have been mapped…"
Tamiko Thiel, "The Design of the Connection Machine," *Design Issues*, vol. 10, no. 1, Spring 1994, pp. 5–18.
Page 55   "convince viewers of the machine's uniqueness"
Ibid.
Page 55   "thousands of visitors waited for hours in lines up to a mile in length for the opportunity to experience the Futurama"
Roland Marchang, "Designers go to the fair II: Normal Bel Gedes, The General Motors Futurama and the visit to the factory transformed," *Design Issues*, vol. 8, no. 2, Spring 1992, pp. 23–40.
Page 56   "It gave poor Howard Aiken an awful pain…"
Oral Interview of Grace Murray Hopper with Uta Merzbach, Jan. 7, 1969, Smithsonian Archives Center.
Page 56   "stripped away the walnut panels and heavy curtains"
John Harwood, "The White Room: Eliot Noyes and the Logic of Information," *Grey Room* no. 12, 2003, pp. 5–31.
Page 56   "If you get at the heart of the matter"
Ibid.
Page 56   *"2001: A Space Odyssey…"*
Ibid.

The Dictator and His Web Design

Page 60   "Great and Dear Leader"

Now out of power, though not through assassination. More sophisticated website, but not really much improved.

Page 62   "websites were often designed, built and managed by a single individual through sheer force of will"

Louis Rosenfeld and Peter Moreville, *Information Architecture for the World Wide Web*, Sebastopol, CA: O'Reilly, 1998.

Page 62   "should work toward a universal linked information system"

Ibid.

Page 62   "When I first started doing Web work back in 1994…"

Jesse Reisman, "Web Site Design: Less is More," *IT Professional*, vol. 1, no. 5, Sep./Oct. 1999, pp. 63–64.

Page 62   "If this is just you…"

Louis Rosenfeld and Peter Moreville, *Information Architecture for the World Wide Web*, Sebastopol, CA: O'Reilly, 1998.

Page 63   "The recommended practices and requirements set forth in this [standard]…"

ISO/IEC 23026:2006, *Software Engineering—Recommended Practice for the Internet—Web Site Engineering, Web Site Management, and Web Site Life Cycle*, ISO/IEC, 2006.

Bad Alignment

Page 66   "Always Be Closing."

Tom Sant, *The Giants of Sales*, New York: AMACOM, 2006, p. 38.

Page 67   "We like to believe that there is law and order in the world"

Walter Shewhart, *Economic Quality of Quality of Manufactured Product*, New York: Van Nostrand, 1931, p. 121.

Page 67   "All Nature is but Art, unknown to thee"

Alexander Pope, "EPISTLE I: ARGUMENT OF THE NATURE AND STATE OF MAN WITH RESPECT TO THE UNIVERSE," *The Complete Poetical Works of Alexander Pope*, ed. George Gilfillan, Edinburgh: W. P. Nimmo, 1868, Project Gutenberg.

Page 68   "standardized operating methods, plant facilities and equipment"

Quoted in Paul Miranti, "Corporate Learning and Traffic Management at the Bell System," *Business History Review*, vol. 76, no. 4, Winter 2002, pp. 733–765.

Page 69   "Wickenden created an extraordinarily detailed plan for his committee."
   Charles F. Scott, "The Investigation of Engineering Education," *The Journal of Higher Education*, vol. 1, no. 2, 1930, pp. 91–97.

Investing in Ignorance
Page 72   "learning how to pick the olives from a flood of martinis being pumped through a fire hose."
   Dennis Fowler, "The Next Internet," *NetWorker*, vol. 3, no. 3, 1999, pp. 20–28.
Page 73   "perhaps the most basic of all aspects of information processing"
   Robert J. Marzano and John S. Kendall, *The New Taxonomy of Educational Objectives*, Thousand Oaks, CA: Corwin Press, 2007, pp. 45–55.
Page 74   "A recent study estimates that [such markets] may account for 20 percent of the volume of equity trades in the US..."
   Kuzman Ganchev, Yuriy Nevmyyvaka, Michael Kearns, and Jennifer Wortman Vaughan, "Censored Exploration and the Dark Pool Problem," *Communications of the ACM*, vol. 53, no. 5, May 2010, pp. 99–107.
Page 74   "to make more money on the transaction than the rules of the blind market would allow."
   Ibid.

On Top of the News
Page 78   "effects go both ways: the audience also affects the communicator."
   Ithiel de Sola Pool and Irwin Shulman, "Newsmen's Fantasies, Audiences, and Newswriting," *The Public Opinion Quarterly*, vol. 23, no. 2, Summer 1959, pp. 145–158.
Page 78   "Publishers saw themselves as guardians of age-old editorial standards"
   Elizabeth MacIver Neiva, "Chain Building: The Consolidation of the American Newspaper Industry," *The Business History Review*, vol. 70, no. 1, pp. 1–42.
Page 79   We merely collect and tabulate the figures with entire impartiality and present them for what they are worth"
   Literary Digest, Oct. 16, 1920, p. 1.
Page 79   "Literally thousands of people are employed in the colossal task of printing, addressing, stamping, distributing, and tabulation"
   Literary Digest, vol. 48, no. 11, Sep. 15, 1928.
Page 80   "If you do not sell prior to death to put your estate in order"
   John F. Wolfe quoted in Elizabeth MacIver Neiva, "Chain Building: The Consolidation of the American Newspaper Industry," *The Business History Review*, vol. 70, no. 1, pp. 1–42.

Page 80　"During the 20-year period in which small papers adopted this technology, the number of family-owned newspapers dropped from 1,300 to 700."
Ibid.
Page 81　"We didn't want to be a storefront in someone else's shopping mall"
William Webb, "Washington Post debuts its Digital Ink online service," *Editor & Publisher*, vol. 128, no. 30, July 29, 1995, pp. 25–26.
Page 81　"By spring, the *Washington Post* had determined that the service was unlikely to attract more than 11,000 subscribers and started to replace it with a conventional Internet webpage."
Mark Jenkins, "The Washington Post recovers from a digital false start," *Brandweek*, vol. 37, no. 30, July 22, 1996, pp. N14–16.

Chapter III: The Exercise of Power

Doug the Rocket Scientist
Page 83　"Doug the Rocket Scientist"
When I originally wrote these stories, I identified this character as "Derek the Rocket Scientist," as I felt that I needed to obscure the identities of my characters when I wrote about them in the pages of *Computer*. At this point, I feel it appropriate to use the proper names of Doug Caldwell and Chery Glaser.

The Society for the Promotion of Goodness
Page 89　"The Society for the Promotion of Goodness"
Originally published as "Politics in Play."
Page 92　"Baltimore, Denver, Duluth..."
Julius Weinberger, Theodore Smith, and George Rodwin, "The Selection of Standards for Commercial Radio Television," *Proceedings of the Institute of Radio Engineers*, vol. 17, no. 9, 1929, pp. 1584–1594.
Page 88　New York has "no tie-in with either New Jersey or Long Island..."
Ibid.
Page 93　"Reconfigure the flow of electricity to minimize..."
M.G. Lauby and W.P. Malcolm, "Intelligent Systems Applications to Power Systems," *International Conference on Power Systems* (ISAP 07), 2007, pp. 1–6.

Celestial Navigation
Page 95　"Celestial Navigation"
Originally published as "Derek the Rocket Scientist."

Page 98   "Bathurst takeoff height"
   Taken from a letter from Charles Lindbergh to Anne Morrow Lindbergh,
      Apr. 28, 1942. It is published in Anne Morrow Lindbergh, *War Within and
      Without,* Mariner Books, 1995, p. 262.

The Rev. Swaminathan's Ashram and Software Society
Page 101   "The Rev. Swaminathan…"
   Originally published as "The Theosophist's Bathroom."
Page 102   "unite firmly a body of men of all nations in brotherly love…"
   Helena P. Blavatsky to William Q. Judge, Apr. 3, 1888, *Five Messages from H. P.
      Blavatsky to the American Theosophists,* Los Angeles: The Theosophy Com-
      pany, 1922, p. 4.
Page 103   "inclined more and more to a communist philosophy…"
   Jawaharlal Nehru, *Autobiography,* Mumbai: Allied, 1962, p. 362.
Page 103   "Dried cattle dung… contributes as much to total energy consump-
      tion as does electricity…"
   W.L. Cisler, A.E. Bush, and H. Tauber, *IEEE Transactions on Power Apparatus
      and Systems,* vol. 85, no. 8, Aug. 1966, pp. 864–878.

This Is the Way We Would Build a Barn
Page 107   "This Is the Way We Would Build a Barn"
   Originally published as "Raising Barns."
Page 108   "haphazardly thrown together by inexperienced amateurs…"
   Warren Roberts, "German American Log Buildings of Dubois County, Indi-
      ana," *Winterthur Portfolio,* vol. 21, no. 4, Winter 1986, pp. 265–274.
Page 108   "Modern barns should replace those of ancestors when necessary…"
   R.A. Moore, ed., *Seventh Annual Report of the Wisconsin Agricultural Experi-
      ment Association,* Madison, Wisconsin: Wisconsin Agricultural Experi-
      mental Association, 1909, p. 122.
Page 109   "Software production today appears in the scale of industrializa-
      tion somewhere below the more backward construction industries…"
   M.D. McIlroy quoted in "Software Engineering," *Report on a conference spon-
      sored by the NATO Science Committee, Garmisch, Germany 7–11 October,
      1968,* ed. Peter Naur and Brian Randell, Jan. 1969, p. 10.
Page 109   "Production of large software has become a scare item for management"
   E.E. David quoted in Naur and Randell, op. cit., p. 68.
Page 109   "60 senior programmers met in Garmisch, Germany"
   See Mike Mahoney, "Finding a History for Software Engineering," *IEEE An-
      nals of the History of Computing,* vol. 26, no. 1, 2004, pp. 8–19.

Page 109 "Is it possible to have software engineers in the numbers in which we need them"
  Alan Perlis quoted in Naur and Randell, op. cit., p. 125.
Page 109 "That to my mind is truly engineering"
  A.G. Fraser quoted in in Naur and Randell, op. cit., p. 128.
Page 109 "We have a Dutch proverb, 'One learns from experience'"
  Edsger Dijkstra quoted in Naur and Randell, op. cit., p. 128.
Page 110 "learn as much as possible"
  Ibid.
Page 110 "because then they will talk together frequently"
  J.N. Buxton quoted in Naur and Randell, op. cit., p. 91.
Page 110 "this structure is reflected in the structure of the organization making the product"
  Edsger Dijkstra quoted in Naur and Randell, op. cit., p. 89.

Attention to Detail
Page 113 "Attention to Detail"
  Originally published as "Dumb Grids and Smart Markets."
Page 113 "Using digital sensors, computing modeling..."
  James McGreevey, *New York Times*, Aug. 24, 2003, p. NJ11.
Page 114 "The characteristics of an individual are therefore of interest only in that they form a contribution to the characteristics of the group..."
  P. Schiller, "The Application Of Statistical Methods To Electricity Supply Problems," *Journal of the Institute of Electrical Engineers Pt II.*, vol. 95, no. 44, 1948, pp. 161–174.
Page 114 "we can sell these small customers at a profit..."
  Samuel Insull, "The Relation of Central Station Generation to Railway Electrification," Annual Convention of the American Institute of Electrical Engineers, Boston, MA, June 26–27, 1912, *Transactions of the American Institute of Electrical Engineers*, vol. 31, no. 1, 1912, pp. 231–282.
Page 115 "idle capacity of today's electric power grid"
  Gary Locke and Patrick D. Gallagher, *NIST Framework and Roadmap for Smart Grid Interoperability Standards*, Release 1.0, NIST Special Publication 1108, Office of the National Coordinator for Smart Grid Interoperability, 2010, p. 73.
Page 115 "It is becoming increasingly difficult to site new conventional overhead transmission lines..."
  "GRID 2030," A National Vision For Electricity's Second 100 Years, United States Department of Energy Office of Electric Transmission and Distribution, July 2003.

Page 116   "The Smart Grid will ultimately require hundreds of standards, specifications, and requirements"
NIST Publication 1101, op. cit.

Page 116   "Cyber security must address not only deliberate attacks, such as from disgruntled employees, industrial espionage, and terrorists"
DOE Publication, op. cit.

Page 117   "an impressive array of statistical data"
Thomas Hughes, "The Electrification of America: The System Builders," *Technology and Culture*, vol. 20, no. 1, 1979, pp. 124–161.

Page 117   "There is no greater problem in the industrial world today..."
Samuel Insull, op. cit., p. 265.

Chapter IV: The Global Life

Managing at a Distance
Page 128   "whatever communication they could manage"
James Beninger, *The Control Revolution*, Harvard University Press, 1986, p. 136.

Page 128   "language of quantification is a technology of distance"
Theodore Porter, *Trust in Numbers*, Princeton University Press, 1995, p. ix.

Page 129   "It may be admitted that office work is difficult to measure"
William Henry Leffingwell, *A Textbook of Office Management*, New York: McGraw Hill, 1932, p. 355.

Page 129   "Control involves a very extensive knowledge of numerous details"
Ibid.

Page 129   The Gilbreths, "sort of a school for scientific management"
Frank B. Gilbreth Jr. and Ernestine Gilbreth, *Cheaper By the Dozen*, New York: Random House, 1948, p. 2.

Drinking with the Dinosaurs
Page 132   "That time of year"
William Shakespeare, Sonnet 73.

Page 133   "The notion that learning from failure is desirable is difficult to dispute"
Mark Cannon and Amy Edmondson, "Confronting Failure: Antecedents and Consequences about Failure in Organizational Work Groups," *Journal of Organizational Behavior*, vol. 22, no. 2, Mar. 2001, pp. 161–177.

Page 133   "For the want of a nail"
Benjamin Franklin, "Poor Richard's Almanack, June 1758," *The Complete Poor Richard Almanacks*, facsimile ed., vol. 2, 1970, pp. 375, 377.

Page 134   "Objectives are missed and schedule and cost targets overrun with distressing regularity"

George Glaser, "Managing Projects in the Computer Industry," *Computer*, vol. 17, no. 10, Oct. 1984, pp. 45–53.

Page 135   "Projects that depend on technological breakthroughs for their success present special management problems"

George Glaser, "Managing Projects in the Computer Industry," *Computer*, vol. 17, no. 10, Oct. 1984, pp. 45–53.

Page 135   "Despite the importance of learning from failure, it is more common in exhortation than in practice"

Cannon and Edmondson, op. cit.

Open Borders

Page 139   The roots of this idea "are most deeply entwined…"

R.J. Creasy, "The Origin of the IBM 370 Time Sharing System," *IBM Journal of Research and Development*, vol. 25, no. 5, Sep. 1981, pp. 483–490.

Page 140   "We did not know if the system would be of practical use to us…"

Melinda Varian, "VM and the VM Community: Past, Present, and Future," SHARE 89, Sessions 9059-9061, Aug. 1997.

Page 140   "the VM advocates kept the product alive"

Creasy, op. cit.

Page 141   "I predicted that the computer would…"

Russell Kirsch, e-mail to author, Jan. 9, 2009.

The Digital Jolly Roger

Page 144   "80 percent of software"

Software & Information Industry Anti-Piracy 2007 Year in Review; Business Software Association, "Fourth Annual Software Piracy Study," 2007.

Page 144   "Software piracy, like the classic Caribbean piracy"

See Business Software Association, "Fourth Annual Software Piracy Study," 2007, p. 1; Carlos Marichal and Matilde Souto Mantecon, "Silver and Situados: New Spain and the Financing of the Spanish Empire in the Caribbean in the Eighteenth Century," *The Hispanic American Historical Review*, vol. 74, no. 4, 1994, pp. 587–613.

Page 144   "characterized by a kind of anarchic morality"

Calvin Mooers, "Preventing Software Piracy," *Computer*, vol. 10, no. 3, Mar. 1977, pp. 29–30.

Page 144   "The problems start when people cannot"

Mark Johnson, "Software piracy: stopping it before it stops you," *Proceedings of the 16th Annual ACM SIGUCCS* (SIGUCCS 88), Oct. 1988, pp. 295–298.

Page 144   "not only individuals; among them, in fact, are a few of our largest
and most highly respected corporations."
   Mooers, op. cit.

Page 145   "They formed a seafaring republic"
   Jennifer Marx, *Pirates and Privateers of the Caribbean*, Malabar, Florida:
Krieger, 1992, p. 128.

Page 145   "required concerned efforts by Chinese engineers"
   Daniel Southerland, "Piracy of US Software in China is Big Problem, Commerce Officials Warn," *Washington Post*, Jan. 14, 1989, p. D10.

Page 146   "piracy rate in China has fallen from a high of 92 percent to 82 percent"
   Business Software Association, op. cit.

Page 147   "dissuade the pirate by increasing the likelihood of being caught."
   Bertrand Anckaert, Bjorn De Sutter, and Koen De Bosschere, "Software piracy prevention through diversity," *Proceedings of the 4th ACM Workshop on Digital Rights Management* (DRM 04), Oct. 2004, pp. 63–71.

Page 147   Legislative "and educational weapons may win a few battles…"
   Ram D. Gopal and G. Lawrence Sanders, "Global software piracy: you can't get blood out of a turnip," *Communications of the ACM*, vol. 43, no. 9, Sep. 2000, pp. 83–89.

Where Are You From?

Page 151   "The Primary Focus in this stage…"
   Hong Liu and Petros Mouchtaris, "Voice over IP Signaling: H 323 and Beyond," *IEEE Communications Magazine*, Oct. 2000, pp. 142–148.

Page 151   "Each product relied on a proprietary signaling protocol"
   Liu and Mouchtaris, op. cit.

Page 152   "As this standard developed…"
   Liu and Mouchtaris, op. cit.

Page 152   Local "facilities were used at both ends…"
   Richard Vietor and Dekkers Davidson, "Economics and Politics of Deregulation: The Issue of Telephone Access Charges," *Journal of Policy Analysis and Management*, vol. 5, no. 1, Autumn 1985, pp. 3–22.

Page 152   "After five years of nurturing the plan"
   Ibid.

Page 152   Bypassing "standard telephone charges…"
   Liu and Mouchtaris, op. cit.

Page 152   "Infrastructural facilities or lack of these have often been underlined"
   Advait Aundhkar et al., "Nature of Teleworking in Key Sectors: Case Studies of Financial, Media and Software Sectors in Mumbai," *Economic and Political Weekly*, vol. 35, no. 26, Jun. 24–30, 2000, pp. 2277+.

Page 153   "after the Haitian earthquake…"
Vaughn Hester et al., "Scalable crisis relief," *1st Annual Symposium on Computing for Development* (ACM DEV 10), Dec. 17–18, 2010.

Chapter V: Things Not Known

The Dogs that Came in From the Cold
Page 161   "required to perform two roles"
Toni Makkai and Valerie Braithwaite, *Law & Social Inquiry*, vol. 18, no. 1, Winter 1993, pp. 33–59.
Page 161   "not put self-interest, the interest of an employer, the interest of a client, or the interest of the user ahead of the public's interest"
Don Gotterbarn et al., "Software Engineering Code of Ethics, Version 3.0," *Computer*, Oct. 1977, pp. 87–92.
Page 162   "cannot simply align the world with the values and principles we adhered to prior to the advent of technological challenges"
Helen Nissenbaum, "How Computer Systems Embody Values," *Computer*, Mar. 2001, pp. 120–122.

Ethical Grocery Control
Page 166   "The secret of chain store success seems to be the magic word, 'system!'"
Rolla Drake quoted in T.F. Bradshaw, "Superior Methods Created the Early Chain Store," *Bulletin of the Business Historical Society*, vol. 17, no. 2, 1943, pp. 35–44.
Page 166   "until they reached the last turnstile, complete with a counter and cash register"
James Beniger, *The Control Revolution*, Cambridge, MA: Harvard University Press, 1986, p. 334.
Page 166   "assembled her requirements from anywhere in the shop"
W.G. McClelland, "Economics of the Supermarket," *The Economic Journal*, vol. 72, no. 285, 1962, pp. 154–170.
Page 166   "a true supermarket had at least three registers"
F.J. Charvat, *Supermarketing*, New York: MacMillan, 1961, p 7.
Page 166   "There is a real problem of control and prediction"
Donald Stout, "Research and Control in a Modern Supermarket," *The Journal of Industrial Economics*, vol. 3, no. 1, 1954, pp. 60–71.
Page 167   "one fourth of the margin of the stores from the 1920s"
George Mehren, "The Changing Structure of the Food Market," *Journal of Farm Economics*, vol. 39, no. 2, 1957, pp. 339–353.

Page 167   "it would have to acknowledge that the item could be held in any orientation."
  D. Savir and G.J. Lauerer, "The characteristics and decidability of the Universal Product Code Symbol," *IBM Systems Journal*, no. 1, 1975, pp. 16–34.
Page 168   "you'll need to know these things"
  Ibid.
Page 168   "The first commercial system was installed in 1974"
  Sharon Levin, Stanford Levin, and John Meisel, "Intermarket Differences in the Early Diffusion of an Innovation," *Southern Economic Journal*, vol. 51, no. 3, 1985, pp. 672–680.
Page 168   "Two decades passed before scanning systems spread"
  See Larry Hamm and Gerald Grinnell, "Evolving Relationships between Food Manufacturers and Retailers," *American Journal of Agricultural Economics*, vol. 65, no. 5, 1983, pp. 1065–1072.
Page 169   "Scanner data, particularly in combination with other data on households"
  Steve Baron and Andrew Lock, "The Challenges of Scanner Data," *Journal of the Operational Research Society*, vol. 45, 1995, pp. 50–61.
Page 169   "Whenever a new, much more detailed look at the world is possible"
  John Little, "Operations Research In Industry," *Operations Research*, vol. 39, 1991, pp. 531–542.

Machines in the Garden
Page 171   Whole "families scavenged for a living"
  Susan Strasser, *Waste and Want*, New York: Metropolitan Books, 1999, p. 271.
Page 171   "Ignorance about trash was a luxury"
  Ibid.
Page 173   "Green computing has no widely accepted metrics…"
  Joseph Williams and Lewis Curtis, "Green: The New Computing Coat of Arms?" *IT Professional*, vol. 10, no. 1, Jan./Feb. 2008, pp. 12–16.
Page 173   "consume roughly 30 times more electricity"
  Wu-chun Feng and K.W. Cameron, "The Green500 List: Encouraging Sustainable Supercomputing," *Computer*, vol. 40, no. 12, Dec. 2007, pp. 50–55.
Page 173   "several of the most powerful supercomputers… require up to 10 megawatts…"
  Ibid.
Page 174   "the Lagos port in Nigeria receives 500 containers of used computer equipment a month…"
  Sam Olukova, "Nigeria: an E-Waste Dump, Lagos Imperils People," Bassel Action Network, www.ban.org.

Page 174   "The Place Computers Go to Die."
  Ibid.
Page 174   reusing the discarded chips
  J.Y. Oliver, R. Amirtharajah, V. Akella, R. Geyer, and F.T. Chong, "Life Cycle Aware Computing: Reusing Silicon Technology," *Computer,* vol. 40, no. 12, Dec. 2007, pp. 56–61.
Page 175   reducing the flow of material to these sites
  Jan Krikke, "Recycling e-Waste: The Sky is the Limit," *IT Professional,* Jan./Feb. 2008, p. 50–55.

Open Sabotage
Page 179   "New weapons must be created…"
  Aleksandr Matrosov, Eugene Rodionov, David Harley, and Juraj Malcho, "Stuxnet Under the Microscope," ES/ET Technical Report, 2010.
Page 180   The "number of militant engineers relative to the total population of engineers is miniscule…"
  David Berrey, "Engineering Terror," *New York Times Magazine,* Oct. 2, 2010.

The Data of the Night
Page 184   "includes the precise location and direction of travel…"
  SureShot press release, Sep. 1, 2009.
Page 184   "not equipped with the computers and machines necessary for the task"
  Melville Eastman to Julius Furer, July 2, 1942, ONR Records, RG 77, NARA.
Page 185   The "system was very useful for the last months of the European war"
  J.A. Peirce, "In Introduction to Loran," *Proceedings of the IRE and Waves and Electronics,* May 1946, pp. 216–234.
Page 185   "Armed with an increased awareness and knowledge of what is transpiring within a specific area"
  SureShot promotional material, Sep. 1, 2009.
Page 186   the "fire patterns were more random and not as concentrated"
  Corry Watkins, "Technological approaches to controlling random gunfire," *Policing,* vol. 25, no. 2, 2002, pp. 345–370.
Page 186   "traditional, rapid response-type approaches to policing toward community policing and problem-solving"
  Ibid.
Page 186   "they correctly identify shots no more than 85 percent of the time"
  Ibid.
Page 187   "are also armed with data to justify specific increases in assets and resources"
  SureShot promotional material, Sept 1, 2009.

On the Fall of Sparrows

Page 190   "It is widely believed that broad adoption of an electronic medical records system…"
Richard Hilestad et al., "Can Electronic Medical Record Systems Transform Health Care? Potential Health Benefits, Savings, And Costs," *Health Affairs*, vol. 24, no. 5, 2005, pp. 1103–1117.

Page 190   "contain their administrative and medical information…"
Remarks of President Obama, Apr. 9, 2009.

Page 191   "related changes to the healthcare system"
Ibid.

Page 191   "would be advantageous and economical if a nationwide organization"
First Annual Report of the Social Security Administration, 1935–36, p. 22.

Page 191   "The development of mechanical devices has made it far simpler to maintain records…"
Second Annual Report of the Social Security Administration, 1936–37, p. 24.

Page 191   "have been concerned with the larger problems of insecurity within our industrial system"
First Annual Report, op. cit., p. 22.

Page 191   "groups not now included under the unemployment compensation"
Ibid., p. 75.

Page 192   "The agency required two years to devise a standard national classification scheme."
Third Annual Report of the Social Security Administration, 1937–38, p. 136.

Page 192   "methods of interstate cooperation under the social security program"
First Annual Report, op. cit., p. 60.

Page 192   "the specification of what is wanted, the production of things to satisfy the specification, and the inspection of the things produced…"
Walter Shewhart and W. Edwards Deming, *Statistical Method from the Viewpoint of Quality Control*, 1936, pp. 1, 44, 45.

Page 192   "use of two cards would have made our operations more complex"
Report to Mr. Cole, Apr. 2, 1963, NARA, RG XXX, p. 2.

Page 192   "It reaches into and affects almost every task and person…"
Ibid.

Honor Among Thieves

Page 198   "At present, there is no technological barrier that separates the explorer from the criminal"
John Lee et al., "Positive Alternatives: A Report on an ACM Panel on Hacking," *Communications of the ACM*, vol. 29, no. 4, 1986, pp. 297–98.

Page 200   "The General Staff of the North Korean People's Army"
Kim So-hyan, "North Korea bolsters cyber combat unit," *Korea Herald*, May 6, 2009.

Chapter VI: Spirit of the Future

Value of Expertise
Page 202   *When Computers Were Human*
When Computers Were Human, Princeton, NJ: Princeton University Press, 2005.
Page 202   "We shed as we pick up, like travelers…"
Tom Stoppard, *Arcadia*, London: Faber and Faber, 1993.
Page 203   *The Wisdom of Crowds*
Surowiecki, New York: Random House, 2004.
Page 204   Oral History and Pioneer Award for Jean Bartik
See the IEEE History Center: www.ieee.org/history_center.

Someday You'll Understand
Page 209   "If this technology could be brought to them to meet their needs"
Muhammad Yunus, Nobel Speech, http://nobelprize.org/nobel_prizes/peace/laureates/2006/yunus-lecture-en.html.

Satisfying the Public
Page 214   "and the whole system of the spacecraft"
Ryan Nugent, Riki Munakata, Alexander Chin, Roland Coelho, and Jordi Puig-Suari, "The CubeSat: The Picosatellite Standard for Research and Education," http://www.cubesat.org/index.php/documents/papers.
Page 215   "were evolved principally for the purpose of providing employment for needy persons"
Harry Hopkins, Letter of Transmittal, Index of Research Projects, vol. 1, Works Progress Administration, Washington, DC, 1938.
Page 216   "contribute to their sense of importance and personal worth"
Resnsis Likert, *New Patterns of Management*, New York: McGraw Hill, 1961, p. 102.
Page 217   "it will be of necessity approached as a question of efficiency"
Herbert Simon, Administrative Behavior, New York: Free Press, 1946, p. 215.

Pay Your Money and Take Your Chances

Page 219   favorite song

I will only confess that it derives from the community of musicians that surrounded Robert Fripp.

Page 220   Brecht "Radio Poem"

"Auf den kleinen Radioapparat," *Poems, 1913–1956*, eds. John Willett and Ralph Manheim, with Eric Fried, London: Methuen, 1976, p. 351.

Page 220   Less "than 3% of active music titles accounted for over 80% of sales"

US Patent 7,003,515 B1, Feb. 21, 2006.

Page 220   "an effective means of browsing and discovering new music"

Ibid.

Page 220   "we mean increasing the capability of a man to approach a complex problem situation"

Douglas Engelbart, *Augmenting Human Intellect: A Conceptual Framework*, Stanford Research Institute, Oct. 1962.

Page 221   "people who can't write, interviewing people who can't talk"

Linda Botts, *Loose Talk*, New York: Quick Fox/Rolling Stone Press, 1980.

Page 221   Most can be designed to return perfect matches or near matches.

R. Typke, F. Wiering, and R. Veltkamp, "A Survey of Information Retrieval Systems," *Proceedings of the 6th International Conference on Music Information Retrieval* (ISMIR 05), 2005.

Page 223   those songs that could be expanded to any arbitrary length with only a finite amount of material

Don Knuth, "The Complexity of Songs," *Communications of the ACM*, vol. 24, no. 4, 1984. The song is "That's the way (I Like It)" by H.W. Casey and Richard Finch, 1975.

Page 222   "I have from five to 20 slightly varying versions."

John Lomax, "Cowboy Songs of the Mexican Border," *The Swanee Review*, vol. 19, no. 1 1911, pp. 1–18.

Page 222   "challenge, Lomax cited a single song that had expanded as it had passed from voice to voice. 'I know of one person who claims to be able to sing 143 stanzas of it'"

Ibid.

Page 223   "What task of musical understanding could use these rules?"

Mark Steedman, "A Generative Grammar for Jazz Chord Sequences," *Music Perception*, vol. 2, no. 1 , Fall 1984, pp. 52–77.

Page 222   "You pay your money and you take your choice."

Bess Lomax Hawes, "Folksongs and Function: Some Thoughts on the American Lullaby," *Journal of American Folklore*, vol. 87, no. 344, 1974, pp. 140–148.

The Value of a Good Name

Page 227   "The relationship between you and the piece of paper…"
Mark Kleiman, "The False ID Problem," *Journal of Policy Analysis and Management*, vol. 21, no. 2, Spring 2002, pp. 283–286.

Page 228   "a name professionally which is the same as…"
Screen Actors Guild Membership Rules and Regulations, Mar. 2010.

Page 228   "Why has it arranged for millions of cards to be carried by every American Worker?"
John Hamilton quoted in "Hamilton Predicts Tags for Workers," *New York Times*, Nov. 1, 1936, p. N5.

Page 228   "An employee is expected to keep his original account number throughout his working life"
Annual Report of the Social Security Administration, Fiscal Year ended June 30, 1936, p. 23.

Page 229   "Proposed bank mega-mergers…"
Consumer Electronic Payments Task Force, "The Report of the Consumer Electronic Payments Task Force," American Banking Association, Apr. 1998.

Working the Crowd

Page 231   "NASA ignored the intent of Congress and the interests of taxpayers."
Statement of Senator Sherod Brown, Apr. 12, 2011, www.thewrightflyer.com/2011/04/brown-statement-on-nasa-shuttle-announcement/.

Page 231   "The appeal of numbers"
Ted Porter, *Trust in Numbers*, Princeton University Press, 1996, p. 8.

Page 232   "public affairs, industrial outreach, and education programs"
NPR 4310.1, Identification and Disposition of NASA Artifacts (Revalidated w/Change 2 1/31/06), http://nodis3.gsfc.nasa.gov/.

Page 232   "artifacts of national significance."
"NASA Follow-up Request for Information on Space Shuttle Orbiter Placement," 417639main_2010 Follow-up RFI on Orbiter Placement_a.pdf

Page 232   "mathematical sciences occupy a fundamental place…"
George Boole, *An investigation of the laws of Thought*, London: McMillan, 1854, Project Gutenberg, p. 327.

Page 232   Valuation "is vague and arbitrary"
Jean-Baptiste Say, *Treatise on Political Economy* II.I.4, www.econlib.org/library/Say/sayT.html.

The Evolving Present

Page 238   "And natural selection arising from the, competition of tribe with tribe"

Charles Darwin, *The Descent of Man,* Project Gutenberg.

Page 238   "that we owe our wonderful material development, which brings improved conditions in its train."

Andrew Carnegie, "Wealth," *North American Review,* vol. 148, no. 391, June 1889, pp. 653–665.

Page 239   "They undergo a continuing evolutionary cycle of maintenance…"

M. Lehman and F. Parr, "Program evolution and its impact on software engineering," *Proceedings of the 2nd International Conference on Software Engineering* (ICSE 76), IEEE Computer Society Press, Oct. 1976.

Page 239   "The feedback generally pushes programs to increase in size and complexity…"

M.M. Lehman and J.F. Ramil, "Towards a theory of software evolution—and its practical impact," *Proceedings, Symposium on International Principles of Software Evolution,* Nov. 1–2, 2000, pp. 2–11.

Page 239   "The quality of [evolving] systems will appear to be declining"

M.M. Lehman, J.F. Ramil, P.D. Wernick, D.E. Perry, and W.M. Turski, "Metrics and laws of software evolution—the nineties view," *Proceedings of the 4th International Software Metrics Symposium,* Nov. 5–7, 1997, pp. 20–32.

Page 239   "He recognized that his basic theory of evolutionary mechanism—natural selection—makes no statement about progress…"

Stephen Jay Gould, *Wonderful Life,* New York: W.W. Norton, 1989, p. 257.

Page 239   "After long reflection, I cannot avoid the conviction that no innate tendency to progressive development exists."

Darwin to Alpheus Hyatt, Dec. 4, 1872, quoted in Gould above.

Epilogue: Uncharted Territory

Page 244   "As the births of living creatures at first are ill-shapen," wrote Francis Bacon in 1597

Francis Bacon, "Essay XXIV," *The Essays or Counsels of Francis Bacon,* London: J.M. Dent, 1625, p. 102.

Page 244   "Go To Statement Considered Harmful"

Edsger Dijkstra, *Communications of the ACM,* vol. 11, no. 3, Mar. 1968, pp. 147–48.

Page 244   "I was taken aback by Dijkstra's attack…"

John Rice, Letter to the Editor, *Communications of the ACM,* vol. 11, no. 8, Aug. 1968, p. 538.

Page 245   "There was something wrong"
   Bertrand Russell, *Autobiography*, London: George Allen and Unwin, 1975, p. 150.
Page 247   "Every scientist has a vast interest…"
   I. Bernard Cohen, *Revolutions in Science*, Cambridge, MA: Belknap Press of
   Harvard University Press, 1985, p. 17.

Index

A

aggregate demand 113, 114
Aiken, Howard 56, 208, 256
American Telephone and Telegraph (AT&T) 68–70
automobile 47, 50, 51, 79, 101, 102, 105, 117, 184, 185, 188, 207, 211, 229, 230, 237

B

Babbage, Charles 28, 155, 204, 205, 208, 254
Bell, Alexander Graham 54
Berners-Lee, Tim 62, 138, 240, 246
black box 27, 28, 73
Blanch, Gertrude 204